MEMORIES OF MANY MEN

And of Some Women:

BEING

PERSONAL RECOLLECTIONS

OF

EMPERORS, KINGS, QUEENS, PRINCES, PRESIDENTS, STATESMEN, AUTHORS, AND ARTISTS, AT HOME AND ABROAD, DURING THE LAST THIRTY YEARS.

BY MAUNSELL B. FIELD.

NEW YORK:
HARPER & BROTHERS, PUBLISHERS,
FRANKLIN SQUARE.
1874.

Entered according to Act of Congress, in the year 1873, by
HARPER & BROTHERS,
In the Office of the Librarian of Congress, at Washington.

TO

JOHN ADAMS DIX,

THE ENLIGHTENED STATESMAN, THE DEVOTED PATRIOT,
THE GALLANT SOLDIER, THE ELEGANT SCHOLAR,
THE CHRISTIAN GENTLEMAN, AND
THE HONEST MAN,

THIS LITTLE BOOK,

ALBEIT UNWORTHY OF SO EMINENT A PATRON,

Is Most Respectfully Dedicated

BY

THE AUTHOR.

PREFACE.

I MAKE no pretensions to have written any thing in this little book which rises to the dignity of even minor history. I know that it is all liable to be treated with disdainful scorn by the serious and dignified muse whose recording pen traces the solemn and heroic records of the world's march through time, and the immortal achievements of the great. And yet it seems to me that the random, hap-hazard recollections of men and things herein set down can hardly fail to entertain and amuse, although they may not instruct the curious reader. If my anecdotes are sometimes trivial, most of them, at least, concern persons famous, some in civil, and some in military life. If their perusal should not add any thing to the real knowledge which you already possess of those to whom they relate, they may, nevertheless, succeed in presenting to you in bolder relief some of the peculiarities which distinguished them.

I have made no attempt to be otherwise than desultory. I have wandered on through the garden of memory, dreamily and almost at random, plucking here and there, it might be flowers, and it might be weeds, as they presented themselves to my hand; and I venture to offer them, unsymmetrically arranged and loosely tied together, for your acceptance. Some of them you may find worthy to be pressed and preserved with your own collections; and others you may drop by the wayside, as having neither fragrance nor beauty. In either event, I shall be content.

How many of those about whom I have written have passed away! WEBSTER, and ADAMS, and VAN BUREN, and PIERCE, and MARCY, and SCOTT, and SOULÉ, and LINCOLN, and SEWARD, and STANTON, and FESSENDEN, and GREELEY, and CHASE, are all gone! The martyr President was carried through the land in a triumphal march to a now neglected and crumbling tomb! But yesterday I followed the remains of the great Chief Justice to their temporary resting-place in the beautiful Georgetown Cemetery. IRVING, and THACKERAY, and DICKENS, and HAWTHORNE, and COOPER, and JAMES, and WILLIS, and POE, have passed before us to the silent land. The EMPEROR NAPOLEON III. no longer wields a sceptre, but is again an exile in England, and fills there an exile's grave! WELLINGTON, PALMERSTON, and MACAULAY have dropped the sword, the portfolio, and the pen!

I feel that it is a privilege to have seen such men, and to have known most of them; and it has made me happy during the brief, drowsy hours of a summer vacation to seek relief from the duties of an arduous profession by wandering back into the past in their company.

M. B. F.

NEW YORK, *October*, 1873.

TABLE OF CONTENTS.

PART I.—ABROAD.

CHAPTER I.

CHAPTER II.

CHAPTER III.

CHAPTER IV.

CHAPTER V.

CHAPTER VI.

CHAPTER VII.

CHAPTER VIII.

CHAPTER IX.

CHAPTER X.

PART II.—AT HOME.

CHAPTER I.

CHAPTER II.

CHAPTER III.

CHAPTER IV.

CHAPTER V.

CHAPTER VI.

CHAPTER VII.

CHAPTER VIII.

CHAPTER IX.

CHAPTER X.

CHAPTER XI.

CHAPTER XII.

CHAPTER XIII.

PART I.

ABROAD.

MEMORIES OF MANY MEN

AND OF SOME WOMEN.

PART I.

CHAPTER I.

I WENT abroad for the first time in the spring of the year 1843, and remained absent from America until the month of December in the year 1845. During the intervening period I traveled through all the countries of Europe, except Russia, made the tour of the Seven Churches in Asia Minor, and ascended the Nile as far as the second cataract. I was very young at the time, and my experiences were mostly those of an ordinary traveler. As I am not writing a book of travels, I do not propose giving here any extended account of them. I shall limit myself to a slight, sketchy recital of some trifling incidents connected with distinguished persons whom I happened casually to see.

Mr. Edward Everett was at that time our Minister at the Court of St. James. I was the bearer to him of a letter of introduction from Mr. Benjamin F. Butler, who had been Attorney-General of the United States under President Van Buren. I found Mr. Everett as frigid as an iceberg. His reserve was constitutional. He was as polished as his own writings, but equally cold.

To a young man just out of college, this sort of reception operated like a wet blanket. After my first call, I never ventured upon him again. I feared taking cold.

I had the good fortune to see the famous Duke of Wellington several times on horseback, going to or returning from the Horse Guards, and once in the House of Lords. He was very feeble, and very bowed and bent, and much anxiety was felt on account of his persistent habit of riding instead of driving; but the old warrior was determined to back his steed as long as he possessed the strength to mount him. Every man removed his hat on meeting *the* Duke, and he saluted all in turn with a quick military movement of his forefinger to his own.

He was then Commander-in-chief. I saw him in the House of Lords, and heard him speak. The Peers then occupied their old apartment in Westminster Hall; it was very small, and there was scant room for visitors, and no seats at all for them. When the Duke rose to speak, his tones were so low as to be almost inaudible to me. He hemmed and hawed, after the English manner, and there were painfully long pauses between his sentences. To one who could only see and not hear, it was a disappointing exhibition.

At this time there were iron shutters upon the front of Apsley House, his town residence, which were always kept closed. This was a reminder of ingratitude to the populace, who had stoned his windows on account of his opposition to the Reform Bill. The attack might have had serious consequences had it not been for the gallant interference of Count d'Orsay, who, although a Frenchman, succeeded in shaming the mob.

Our Minister to France at that period was Mr. WM. R. KING, of Alabama, afterward Vice-President of the United States, who, with his accomplished niece, Mrs. ELLIS, dispensed charming hospitality at the Legation. Mr. KING had brought with him from home a negro, whom he made the *major-domo* of his household, and who acquired a surprising ascendency over the other servants and the tradespeople who supplied the family. He was strictly honest himself, and would not permit others to peculate; and this is a terrible hardship to the underlings of a Parisian establishment. He accompanied his master every where. He always coupled his own name with that of Mr. KING, and constantly employed the expression, "Me and the Minister." Mr. KING was a tall, stiff, stately Southerner, and a dignified and high-toned gentleman.

In Paris I attended several meetings of the Chamber of Deputies, and one of the House of Peers. I saw both M. GUIZOT and M. THIERS, and heard the former speak. I recollect one thing he said which raised a terrific storm of indignation—"La France à besoin de se *sentir* gouvernée!" (France requires to *feel* herself governed!)

I never saw the king, LOUIS PHILIPPE; but upon different occasions I saw three of his sons, who are still living. I attended one day in the summer of the year 1843 the races in the Champ de Mars. The DUC DE NEMOURS was then the leading patron of the turf in France, and he had a private stand upon the course. The carriage in which I came was stationed so far off that, although I could make out that this stand was filled with people, I was unable to distinguish any faces. After the first race was over, I alighted from the vehicle, intending to walk across the course and have a look at the Prince, who I was informed was one of the party. When I got to the stand it was empty, and I supposed that he had gone home. Lighting a cigar, I turned back until I reached the centre of the course, where I stood some time, watching what was going on. Near me was a young man, who did not particularly attract my attention, in conversation with an older one. I only noticed that he wore very ill-fitting clothes, and had a very decided lisp in his speech. After a while he took a case from his pocket, and, selecting a cigar, asked me for a light. A few minutes later an officer approached him, bareheaded, and asked when *Monseigneur* would have his guard. I then knew that the young man was the Duc de Nemours.

The Duc d'Aumale I saw the next year, when he returned from the war in Algeria. He made a triumphal entry into Paris at the head of his regiment, if I recollect aright, the Seventeenth Light Infantry, and marched down the Avenue of the Champs Elysées. He was on foot; his uniform was very seedy, and his boots covered with mud. The regiment had camped outside the walls the night before in order to make its entrance in the day-time, and it was said that the Prince, before starting upon the march, had for effect bedabbled his boots in a gutter.

The Duc de Montpensier, who was then not much more than a boy, I saw at a monster concert in the Champs Elysées. Among the pieces performed was the chorus from the opera of Charles VI., "*Jamais l'Anglais ne regnera en France!*" (Never shall the English reign in France!) Feeling between the two nations was running high at that time, and the applause was tremendous. The Prince, by his enthusiastic clapping, split his gloves. His unlucky marriage with the sister of the Queen of Spain was one of the principal causes which led to the hurling of his father from the throne.

I twice saw the late KING OF HOLLAND at the Hague. He was reputed the most daring horseman in Europe; and at the breaking out of the revolution which resulted in the separation of Belgium from Holland, he performed the feat of riding from Brussels to the Hague in a single day. The first time that I saw him was upon a Sunday afternoon, when I was walking, accompanied by a *valet de place*, on an almost deserted street on the outskirts of the town. Presently there came in view a horse, dashing headlong in our direction; and, turning in alarm to my companion, I exclaimed, "There is a runaway!" "It is the King," he replied, and in a moment his Majesty passed us at the same furious gait. He had a foraging cap upon his head and a cigar in his mouth, and, without in the least relaxing his speed, he bowed and touched his cap. Behind him, at a long distance, came two panting and blowing aids, and behind them again two Court carriages. They were all returning from a country palace where they had been dining. It was said that no aid to the King could stand the service more than two or three years at the utmost, and the position was not at all in request.

A few days afterward I was loitering in the Royal Picture-gallery attached to the Palace. Besides myself there happened to be nobody there but a French artist, who was making a very creditable copy of an important picture. Soon I entered into conversation with this gentleman, and while I was so engaged, a door opened and the King walked briskly in. Instead of crossing the room, as we supposed it his intention to do, he came directly to us, and began to compliment the artist upon his picture. He then talked to me for a long time, and tendered me many civilities. At length, offering us each a cigar, he withdrew as he had entered. On one side of the gallery there stood, upon a pedestal, stuffed, the white horse which the King, then PRINCE OF ORANGE, had ridden at Waterloo.

He was a fearful spendthrift. His father was not only a king, but also the most successful merchant and speculator in Europe, and upon his death he left an enormous fortune to his son. The latter managed not only to squander the whole of it in a reign of about seven years, but also to accumulate debts, which compelled the sale, after his death, of his pictures and other effects. He was a very ill-favored man, although the Orange family is noted as an uncommonly fine race. The King was the GRANT of his day in respect of smoking. He was never without a cigar. He even smoked at the opera. When he did this, he occupied a latticed proscenium box, where you could not see him, but whence the odor of the tobacco emerged and impregnated the entire atmosphere of the house. He was a great linguist, and otherwise accomplished; but his reputation as a man was scandalous, and he made the Hague during his reign the rendezvous of some of the vilest characters in Europe.

I was well accredited to Mr. HENRY WHEATON, our Minister at Berlin, and the distinguished writer upon international law. Upon my arrival I sent my letter with my card to the Legation, and the next day the Minister called upon me, and, not finding me within, left for me my own card, with "Mr. WHEATON for" written over my name. It was surprising that such a solecism in manners should be committed by a diplomatist of Mr. WHEATON's experience. Of course, no offense was intended; but I did not return the call.

The KING OF PRUSSIA, elder brother to the present Emperor of Germany, I saw once at Potsdam, as he was entering his carriage. He was a rough, coarse, red-faced German, and wore an immense military cloak of Prussian gray. He afterward became mad, or rather imbecile—from an excessive addiction to champagne, it was said. The present EMPEROR, then Crown Prince, I accidentally met one day upon a by-way in Switzerland. I had left the vettura in which I was traveling to walk to a water-fall, only accessible to pedestrians. I overtook several Germans, with whom I entered into conversation. One of them, who seemed to be the leader of the party, was particularly polite to me. When we again reached the highway, I saw, drawn up on the side of the road, two handsome traveling carriages, with two *fourgons*, or luggage-vans, behind them, and I thus became aware that my chance companions were people of consequence. In the foremost of the carriages were two ladies, and the chief personage, after an exchange of compliments with me, said that he would be pleased to present me to his wife before we separated. Accordingly I handed him my card, and he presented me to the "CROWN PRINCESS OF PRUSSIA." He very cordially invited me to again visit Berlin, assuring me that it would afford him pleasure to be of service to me there. We spoke French together. Had I understood German, which I did not, I might perhaps have learned earlier in our interview the rank of my fellow-traveler.

At Vienna, I saw the EMPEROR FERDINAND, of Austria, a man of low stature and defective intelligence, with the overhanging under-lip of the Hapsburgs; and the EMPRESS, an unusually tall woman, who looked like a giantess by the side of her diminutive husband. The ARCHDUCHESS SOPHIA, mother to the present Emperor (who succeeded upon the abdication of his uncle FERDINAND), was called in those days the most beautiful woman in Austria. Our Chargé d'Affaires in Vienna was Mr. JENIFER, of Maryland. He was an old dandy and beau, and he had pictures of the lovely Archduchess hung in every room of his house. I shall never forget a dinner at which he produced real Johannisberger of the highest grade, presented to him by PRINCE METTERNICH, and other wines of equal fame, all the gifts of titled and distinguished friends.

I saw the great ARCHDUKE CHARLES, the most distinguished adversary of the first NAPOLEON next to the DUKE OF WELLINGTON, at Baden, near Vienna. He was a tall, slender old man, with the unmistakable features of his imperial house, and was walking in the public garden, with his daughter leaning upon his arm, but otherwise unattended. He was himself in plain citizen's dress, and so simple a costume as that worn by the Archduchess would disgust a Fifth Avenue belle. Hats were respectfully doffed to them, but otherwise they moved among the crowd like any one else. And so it is all over the Continent of Europe, but not so in England, unless a great change has occurred there. Members of imperial and royal families are accustomed to walk the streets and frequent public places very much as every body else does. Fancy QUEEN VICTORIA taking a promenade with the PRINCE OF WALES on Bond Street!

I frequently saw the GRAND-DUKE OF TUSCANY in Florence. He was an Austrian Prince, and a plain, farmer-looking person, with a sailor's roll in his gait.

The KING OF SARDINIA at that time was CHARLES ALBERT, the father of VICTOR EMMANUEL, the present King of Italy. Unlike his son, he was of very lofty stature, overtopping most of his subjects by a head. The angle of his forehead and nose was unusually acute, and his face altogether a very peculiar one.

I came upon a very singular personage during my visit to Turin. I was one day sitting alone in the dining-room of my hotel, waiting for my dinner to be served. There were a great many ladies and gentlemen in the room at the same time, either dining or expecting to dine. Presently there entered a very tall young man, dressed, or rather overdressed, in the most *outré* Paris fashion, who seated himself at a round table, hitherto unoccupied, which stood between two windows which opened upon the street. His first act was to roll up a napkin into a ball, and throw it at the head of a waiter in a distant part of the room, for the purpose of attracting his attention. Shortly afterward he was joined by two young officers in uniform, and I observed a deference in their manner toward him which strangely comported with his ill-bred conduct. Every few minutes he would spring from his seat, rush to one of the windows, shout to some passer-by at the top of his voice, and wave a napkin as if in salutation. All the time he talked so loud as to drown all other conversation in the room. I noticed that the ladies smiled behind their fans; but neither their gentlemen companions nor the people of the hotel seemed to pay any attention to his eccentricities. After dinner I went for a walk to the public promenade. I had been sauntering about for some time, when I saw approaching an English drag drawn by four magnificent horses. In the inside were three military gentlemen, and lying upon the roof at full length, his long legs dangling over on the one side, and his head extended beyond the other, was the strange young man whom I had seen at dinner. There was a crowd of pedestrians, and as the drag rolled on he kissed his hand and fluttered a pocket-handkerchief at the ladies. I knew nobody there, and I did not venture to ask who he was. But after I had returned to the hotel, I went straight to the proprietor and inquired about him. He informed me that he was the HEREDITARY GRAND-DUKE OF LUCCA, and nephew to CHARLES ALBERT, to whose pious care his father had intrusted him. The King at first gave him apartments in the royal palace, but he conducted himself so outrageously that it soon became necessary to send him adrift. He was the scandal of all decent people in Turin. He had been turned out of many of the best houses for his shameful behavior. He had ever so many horses of his own, but he seldom drove any but hired ones. He would sometimes come to the hotel at noon, and order a dinner for forty, to be ready at six o'clock. He was both a mountebank and a blackguard.

Some years later this same harlequin made a visit to the QUEEN OF SPAIN at Madrid. The local newspapers were full of accounts of his eccentricities. He would never descend the palace stairs by walking down, like other mortals, but always slid down the baluster, like an untamed school-boy.

Still later, and after he had become GRAND-DUKE, he was secretly assassinated in his capital. The matter was never thoroughly elucidated to the public, but it was supposed that the blow was dealt by the hand of one whom he had grossly wronged.

I went from Marseilles to Civita Vecchia in a French steamer. There was a full complement of cabin passengers from all countries, besides a band of Catalonian peasants in the steerage, who were making a pilgrimage to Rome. At dinner, on the first day out, I chanced to be seated next but one to a middle-aged Birmingham man, who had been ordered to Italy by his physician. I had fallen into a chance conversation earlier in the day with this person, and from his robust appearance should not have taken him for an invalid. He had never before been out of England, and his mind was full of all sorts of insular prejudices.

Nearly opposite to me at table sat a quiet person, whose air, complexion, dress, and manners were those of an English gentleman. As soon as the soup was served, "Brummagem" began to talk in a loud voice, for the benefit, apparently, of all the company. He expressed in the most *ex cathedrâ* manner his dogmatic opinions upon every subject that presented itself to his mind. Finally he slid to the most dangerous of all topics, especially in such a place, the relative merits, or rather demerits, of the different nationalities. He spoke in the freest terms of denunciation of French, Germans, and Italians, and wound up, by way of climax, with the remark that of all blackguards in the world the Spaniards were the greatest! He had hardly uttered these words, before, from the hand of the quiet gentleman opposite, there came a bottle of claret, with such force that it not only struck "Brummagem" in the breast, but hurled him from his seat. The bottle broke, the blood-red liquid saturated his person and his clothing, and there ensued a scene of dire confusion. His injuries were, however, but trifling, and that evening, instead of seeking redress from him, he apologized to his assailant, who turned out to be the Spanish DUKE D'OSSUNA. The Duke, who had been educated in England, and resided there many years, was *en route* for Naples, of which his ancestors had been viceroys, and where his family still had large possessions.

All the frequenters of the Café de Paris thirty years ago, at that time the most fashionable restaurant in the French capital, will recollect the formal and eccentric MARQUIS DE ST. JAGO, who some years later succeeded to the Dukedom of Ossuna. It is still said of that princely family in Spain, that the possessor of the title can travel from Madrid to Naples by land, and sleep in his own house every night.

I saw good old POPE GREGORY XVI. in Rome—the venerable, simple-minded Dominican monk. I had also the advantage of a long interview with CARDINAL MEZZOFANTI, the greatest linguist of modern times. He was short in stature, and extremely coarse in appearance, the last person in the world whom one would have picked out as an eminent scholar. The College of Cardinals was composed of some of the noblest-looking men in Europe; and it was disappointing to see one of the most distinguished of their number fall far short of the average good looks of his order. Some of the Roman nobility were strange-looking old fossils. I shall never forget old PRINCE CORSINI, with his enormous thumb-ring and dirty finger-nails.

I met CHARLES DICKENS in Rome the winter that I was there. I felt very ill-disposed toward him at that time, as did most of my countrymen, on account of his "American Notes," then recently published. We met, as sight-seers do in Rome, every where. I particularly recall the circumstance that at one of the most imposing ceremonies at Saint Peter's, during holy week, I kept my eye upon Mr. DICKENS, who was standing listlessly leaning against a column, apparently paying no attention whatever to what was going on; and yet, in his book on Rome, he gives a most minute and graphic description of that very ceremony. His powers of rapid absorption and of accurate retention must have exceeded those of other men.

During the carnival, I formed one of a party of twelve, composed of LEUTZE and other artists, American and French, who, travestied in the costume of the Neapolitan Punchinello, and armed with twelve hundred pounds of *confetti* in sacks, drove up and down the Corso in an open *char-à-banc*, warring and being warred upon. Our first serious encounter was with the members of the French Embassy, who, less numerous than ourselves, were rash enough to attack us. Them we quickly subdued; and then, upon their proposal, we entered into a treaty with them of offensive and defensive alliance, it being stipulated, among other things, that they were all the time to follow in our wake. It was also agreed that our united forces should bear down upon any person who was obnoxious to any one of us. Presently Mr. DICKENS's carriage came along, descending the narrow street on one side as we ascended it on the other. Mrs. DICKENS and others were inside. Mr. DICKENS, in a blouse, and with a wire screen before his face, was in the rumble. Just as he got opposite, there was a stoppage in both lines. I immediately gave the word for attack, and the weight of the avalanche of *confetti* that fell upon that devoted head nobody could calculate. DICKENS stood it as long as he could, but was finally compelled to conceal his head beneath the seat of the rumble. We were masked, and, of course, unrecognizable. It was fools' play at best, but all the world turns fool at a Roman carnival.

KING BOMBA, of Naples, was a first-class specimen of disreputable royalty. He was obese, vulgar, and filthy to the eye, and was said to be the most ill-bred man in Europe, but of this I had no personal opportunity to form an opinion. Among other stories that were circulated about him was the following: It was said that soon after his second marriage, a court ball was given at the Palace in honor of the event. The Queen had been dancing, and the King pretended to conduct her to a chair; but just as she was about sitting down, he withdrew it, so that she came in confusion to the floor. In her mortification, she turned upon him and said, "When I married you, I supposed that I was marrying a king, whereas I find that I have married a lazzarone!" Whereupon, by way of climax, he slapped her face before the whole assembly! One expects to find a king at least a gentleman, but this is not the fact with all of them.

I once saw the SULTAN ABDUL MEDJID on horseback

as he was going, on a Friday, from the Seraglio to the Mosque of Saint Sophia. His dress was European, even to the patent-leather boots, except that he wore a red Turkish fez upon his head. He was about thirty at the time, but so enfeebled by excesses that he had to be lifted on and off his horse. His features were regular and handsome, his complexion pale, his eyes, hair, and beard jet black. He looked like an Italian (his mother was one), and almost like a gentleman.

In Cairo I often saw old MEHEMET ALI, who, although he looked like a boor, was every inch a king. He was very aged and decrepit, but, like the DUKE OF WELLINGTON, would go on horseback. A party of us, mounted on donkeys, was one day going to Boulac, the port of Cairo. Among us there was a very charming and beautiful young English lady, on her way home with her husband from India. We happened, shortly after leaving Cairo, to meet the old Pasha, followed by a suite. He looked all over our party, and then motioned us with his hand to stop. When we had done so, he called some of his people to assist him to dismount. When he reached the ground, he toddled up to the English lady, kissed her upon the cheek with the utmost gravity, to her equal amazement and confusion, and then, with aid, remounted his steed. As we passed on, he benignantly kissed his hand to the fair Islander, and touched his fez to the rest of us. I also saw in Cairo his two sons, IBRAHIM PASHA, the conqueror of Syria, and ABBAS PASHA, then Governor of Cairo, and afterward Viceroy of Egypt. The latter was a very brutal-looking prince, and possessed but little of the ability of his father and his brother.

I have mentioned that I made the ascent of the Nile.

The river was not navigable quite so far as the second cataract, and we were compelled to strand our boat about a mile and a half before reaching it, and make the rest of the distance on foot across the desert. Just before we arrived at the place of disembarkment, we noticed another boat, flying the Prussian flag, immediately ahead of us, the people from which had just come ashore. Seeing us approaching, they waited for us to land. When we did so, mutual salutations passed, and we started together to walk to the place of our ultimate destination in that country. Gradually we paired off into couples, and there fell to my companionship a stout, middle-aged German, to whom walking was such an effort that we soon dropped behind all the others of the party. As he was getting very much blowed, and as I was younger and more active than he, he asked me for my arm, and so we trudged on together, talking and laughing, until we reached the sandstone rock which projects over the cataract, the Ultima Thule of our journey, and upon which it was the custom of adventurous travelers to cut their names in memorial of their visit. We had provided ourselves with knives for the purpose, and when we two arrived, all the others were already busily engaged in carving their names upon the surface of the stone. My fat friend, to whom climbing was an impossibility, seated himself at the base, while I ascended to a more elevated position. After finishing my work, I came down again and looked at his inscription. He was just completing the last letters of "PRINZ ALBRECHT VON PREUSSEN." I bowed to him, and told him that I had not been aware of the rank of my companion. He laughed, and said that when he left Cairo he had given orders that all recognition of his rank should be dropped. He could see no sense in class distinction in a barbarous land. I found him a downright sensible fellow, and we jogged back together to our respective boats. That evening we supped with him and his companions, and the next morning they breakfasted with us, our cooks vying with each other to produce the most sumptuous feast. We then parted, dropped into the rapid current, and never met again.

On our voyage up the river we stopped, among other places, at Esneh, for the purpose of visiting the ruins of the temple of that name. We found established there a colony of Almés, or dancing girls, at the head of which was SOFIA, a discarded wife of ABBAS PASHA. She was a Circassian, and reputed to be the handsomest woman in the East. I have certainly never seen a more perfect specimen of female beauty in any other part of the world. Her husband had detected her several years before talking to a Greek at the corner of the street. For this offense he condemned her to be put into a sack and thrown into the Nile. But the European consuls interfered to save her, and induced him to commute the barbarous punishment into that of perpetual banishment to this place, situated a thousand miles distant from Cairo. Annually, and upon the anniversary of her arrival there, she addressed a letter to the Pasha, begging that she should be permitted to return. But to none of these appeals did she ever receive a reply. I have in my possession a very pleasing picture of her in colored crayons, taken by Mr. CAMPBELL, an artist, and nephew to CAMPBELL the poet, who accompanied us upon our expedition. When our departing boat drifted out into the stream as we left Esneh, we saw her, in her floating, silken robes, standing, after the Scriptural manner, upon her "house-top," and waving us an adieu. She had discarded the Eastern fashion of veiling the face. Poor creature! she had nothing to gain by adhering to it. I saw some pretty Georgian slave girls in Cairo and in Constantinople; but none of them were to be compared with her for perfection of face and of form, and for attractiveness of manner. She was worthy to be the heroine of one of Tom Moore's Eastern tales.

I happened to be in Athens just after the Revolution of February, 1844, and while there was a large foreign fleet assembled in the bay of the Piræus, and a Constituent Parliament in session in the town. Many of the members of this Parliament were robber chieftains from the mountains, and superb-looking fellows. Not one half of them could read or write. The President was Lord Byron's PRINCE MAVROCORDATO—a stout, intelligent-looking person. The handsomest woman in Athens was the QUEEN — OTHO's wife — and the next handsomest, Miss BÓTZARIS, her first maid of honor, and daughter to Halleck's MARCO BÓTZARIS—not BOTZĀRIS, with the accent upon the A, as he incorrectly places it.

When I was in Madrid, Mr. WASHINGTON IRVING, whom I had known since I was a boy, represented our government at the Spanish Court. I had just come up from Andalusia, and had spent more than a week in Granada, devoting the greater part of the time to the Alhambra, which was then being restored. I was surprised to learn from Mr. IRVING that since he had arrived in Spain in a diplomatic capacity he had never once revisited the subject of one of his earliest and greatest literary triumphs. However, he seemed to take great interest in my account of the condition of the old Moorish palace, and of what had become of those who lived there when he wrote about it. His health was not very good, and he suffered from that overpowering propensity to sleep so common to overtaxed brains. I never saw Mr. IRVING betray any excitement but once in my life, and that was upon an occasion when I dined with him in Madrid. The name of DICKENS happened to be introduced, and he became very heated in telling me about his relations with that author. Finally he could no longer contain himself, and, jumping from his seat, he walked up and down the floor in great apparent agitation. He told me that he had corresponded with DICKENS long before they ever met. That both from his writings and his letters he had formed the highest conception of his personal character. That under these circumstances DICKENS arrived at New York, and he, IRVING, called upon him at his hotel. That immediately after sending in his card he was invited to Mr. DICKENS's parlor, and, as he entered the room, that gentleman met him, napkin in hand. He had been dining, and the table was covered with a vulgar profusion of food, and the table-cloth was stained with gravy and wine. Wringing his hand, DICKENS's first salutation was, "IRVING, I am delighted to see you! What will you drink, a mint julep or a gin cocktail?" "The idea of inviting me to drink juleps and cocktails!" naively exclaimed Mr. IRVING. He found DICKENS outrageously vulgar—in dress, manners, and mind. And none of us young people were then more incensed against him for his "American Notes" and "Martin Chuzzlewit" than was the gentle Goldsmith of American literature.

CHAPTER II.

IN the spring of the year 1848 I made a flying trip to Europe for the benefit of my health; a trip entirely unpremeditated three hours before it was undertaken. I was sitting at the breakfast-table at nine o'clock in the morning, feeling very ill from the effects of overwork, when one present suggested that I should do well to make a break, and take a run across the Atlantic. By twelve o'clock, noon, of the same day, I was steaming down New York harbor on board of a Cunarder, bound for Liverpool. We had a delightful passage, to which the agreeableness of my fellow-passengers largely contributed. One of the most pleasing and entertaining of them was PRINCE LUCIEN MURAT, next to whom I accidentally happened to occupy a seat at table. He was going to France, to derive what advantage he could from the revolution of the previous February. I found him a most good-humored, jovial companion, possessing withal a good deal of a certain kind of wit and shrewdness. He was extremely careless about his person, a voracious feeder, and the most formidable snorer I ever met. Unfortunately for me, his state-room was directly opposite mine, and, as he always slept with his door open, I enjoyed the full benefit of the terrific noises he made in his sleep. More than once, after lying awake for hours, I used in sheer desperation to hurl my boots at his berth, which rather forcible protest he always took very amiably. His proportions were already of the Daniel Lambert order, but they increased considerably afterward. The last time I saw him was in the year 1855, at Paris. He was then in full uniform, and covered with orders and decorations; and the brilliancy of his attire, united to the prodigiousness of his person, made him a sight to behold. What changes his fortunes have undergone. To be elevated from a sort of New Jersey squatter to be a member of the imperial family of France, with at one time a squint at the throne of Naples, again to sink to the position of an offshoot of an outcast dynasty!

The Prince used to wear upon his head a very old, dirty, and dilapidated soft felt hat, which in its best estate could hardly have been ornamental. *Apropos* of this hat, he told me that, before he left home, his wife, who remained in this country to await events, insisted that he should procure a proper black hat as soon as he reached town; that unless he would promise to do so, she declined to accompany him here and see him off. That he told her he could not afford the extravagance, and, if she imposed so unreasonable a condition upon giving him her company to New York, she might stay in New Jersey. He had with him the famous white plume which used to distinguish his father upon the field of battle, or rather the whalebone remains of it, the feathers having long ago fallen victims to time and the moths.

He had acquired a great and somewhat unenviable reputation in New Jersey as a horse-jockey. It was said that he would start off from home for a journey upon the back of a sorry Rosinante, and return, after an absence of several weeks, driving a stylish pair of horses before an elegant carriage; the whole being the result of a series of successful *swaps*. He possessed a great natural taste for mechanics, and, from his conversation, seemed to consider Mr. STEVENS, of Hoboken, the greatest genius of the age.

I was very much amused with a conversation I had with him one afternoon about his uncle, JOSEPH BONAPARTE. I well remembered the ex-king, for as a child I had spent several years as a boarder at the school of the brothers PEUGNET, in New York, distinguished officers of the Grand Army, at whose house JOSEPH was a frequent Sunday visitor. I will try to repeat what the Prince said, as nearly as I can recollect it, in his own words.

"My Uncle JOSEPH was a very estimable man, with one great weakness—his excessive and ridiculous affectation of philosophy and martyrdom. He had been King of Spain; and yet he had become resigned to live in obscurity in a Republic! He used to bore me to death with this nonsense, until one day I lost my patience and almost my temper. 'I am weary of these absurd pretensions,' I said to him. 'You are not half the philosopher I am. Compare for a moment our respective fates. You were born a miserable Corsican peasant. You happened to have a brother who possessed more brains than are frequently allotted to mankind. He grasped the sceptre of the world, and elevated you to the rank of a sovereign. You had not a very quiet time of it in your exalted position, it is true, and you were soon compelled to descend from it. But you came to the ground unharmed—with not a feather ruffled; and while your illustrious brother was completing his destiny on a barren rock in the midst of a distant ocean, you retired in safety to this charming place, where you are living like a prince, surrounded by all the refinements of life, with the comfortable income of sixty thousand dollars per annum. I, on the contrary, was born upon the steps of a throne. My father was shot in Italy; I was condemned to a like fate at Gibraltar; I escaped with extreme difficulty, and with nothing but my life; I got to America, and have been ever since a poor New Jersey farmer. And I take things as they come, without even imagining that I have cause for complaint. To say nothing of martyrdom, I am a hundred times more a philosopher than you are.'"

We arrived at Liverpool on a Sunday—the very day on which the election for members of the Legislative Assembly was to take place in France. Immediately after landing, the Prince and I went together to the Adelphi Hotel, and there learned that, as luck would have it, the election had been postponed one week. The Prince, whose elder brother ACHILLE had died in Florida some years before, and who was consequently the head of the family, believed that if he could reach his father's department in time, he would be sure to be elected. He accordingly started at once for London, crossed the Channel, hastened down to his father's native town, and announced himself a candidate. Other arrangements had been made, and other candidates were already in the field; but the name of MURAT operated as a spell, and he overcame all opposition, and was triumphantly returned. Since then, and so long as the Empire lasted, his fortunes constantly tended upward, with the slight drawback, however, that he was always hopelessly in debt. I called upon him in Paris in 1855. He was not in town; but a few days later he sent an aid to me to invite me to his chateau at Buzenval, near Rueil. Unfortunately for me, my engagements at the time would not permit me to accept this invitation. I subsequently saw him once, as I have intimated, at a public ceremony, but had no opportunity of speaking to him.

It was early in April when I reached England, after the voyage to which I have referred. I think that the most charming weather I have ever known in any part of the world I have found in the British Islands during the months of April, May, and June—particularly the two latter. Nothing can be more strongly contrasted than the London of that period of the year and the London of November. In the month of June particularly, actual night is there reduced to a duration of not more than three or four hours, twilight extending into midnight, and dawn dispelling the brief darkness between three and four o'clock in the morning.

In my opinion the English climate is greatly misappreciated by foreigners. The sun is not always obscured by fogs, as many hasty tourists, judging by their exceptional experience, assert. I am confident that nowhere else can out-door exercise be taken with enjoyment so many days of the year and so many hours of the day as in England. One has always sensations of physical comfort there which one never experiences any where else. This is undoubtedly attributable to the moisture with which the atmosphere is impregnated, and which exercises a most soothing influence upon the nervous system. Here the dryness of the air keeps us constantly strung up above concert pitch. We are all the time under the influence of an artificial stimulus. Our candles burn at both ends. Many of our national peculiarities, both physical and moral, are attributable to this. The reader will please excuse the foregoing deviation from my crooked lane of narrative.

Among my other fellow-passengers was the late GEORGE N. SANDERS, then of Kentucky, going abroad for the first time with the object of negotiating a contract with the French Government for the sale of a large stock of Colt's revolving pistols. When I first noticed Mr. SANDERS walking upon the deck of the steam-ship, clad in a suit of light gray homespun, and with a shapeless fur cap upon his head, his costume, coupled with his features of the Southern Russian type, led me to mistake him for a Kalmuck Tartar. I soon came to know him well, and thus began an intimacy which lasted, with some interruptions, until his death in New York last August. Another passenger was GEORGE W. KENDALL, editor of *The New Orleans Picayune*, and then a sheep farmer in Texas, the forerunner of the ARTEMUS WARDS and the MARK TWAINS who have since made American humor known as a national characteristic. Mr. KENDALL was going to Paris to procure illustrations for a book which he had just completed upon the Mexican War.

As I have already mentioned, we arrived at Liverpool on Sunday. On the next (Monday) afternoon, SANDERS, KENDALL, and myself started by the evening express train for London. As we were all smokers, we desired to obtain a carriage where we could enjoy our weeds without interruption. On all the European railways, except in Germany, there are regulations prohibiting smoking, but their violation is always connived at by the guard (for a consideration), provided that no occupant of the same carriage objects. The first-class carriages contain but six seats, and hence it is not always difficult to make up a unanimous party. In the present instance we feed the official in advance for the purpose of securing a place all to ourselves. Just as he was unlocking the door of a hitherto unoccupied carriage for us to enter, an elderly Englishman, whose high breeding was manifest, and who had lost one arm, came up, and remarking that he did not think he could be mistaken in taking us for Americans, inquired if we had any objection to his joining our party, as he inferred from the cigars already in our mouths that we proposed to smoke. Of course we readily assented, and this was the commencement of one of the most agreeable journeys I ever made by rail. Our accidental companion turned out to be LORD FITZROY SOMERSET, afterward LORD RAGLAN. In his capacity of chief of staff to the DUKE OF WELLINGTON, he had been on a special mission to some of the great manufacturing towns to watch the movements of the disaffected Chartists, from whom a formidable demonstration was expected in London upon the occasion of the presentation of their monster petition to the House of Commons, which was to take place in the course of a few days. It will be remembered that this echo of the Paris revolution of the previous February was looked forward to throughout England, by the orderly classes, with great apprehension.

We arrived at London in the evening, and parted from our distinguished traveling companion with mutual assurances of the pleasure we had derived from our chance acquaintance. My friends had rooms engaged at Morley's Hotel, on Trafalgar Square, and although I, an old *habitué* of London, was only too familiar with that second-class inn with first-class prices, I was unwilling to forego their company, and therefore ordered my cab to the same destination.

I found that nothing else was thought of or talked about at the capital but the Chartist business. There was very serious and wide-spread alarm, in which the Government, to all appearances, largely participated. *Apropos* of this, I will mention a circumstance of comparatively secret history. The DUKE OF WELLINGTON was sent for by the Queen, and requested to take supreme command of the troops upon the occasion. This he consented to do, with the proviso, however, that he should possess an absolute dictatorship for the time being, and be, under no circumstances, subject to receive orders from the Home Department. This condition was acceded to, and there is no doubt that, had an attack upon London been attempted, he would have proceeded to the utmost extremities in its defense. The Court retired to the Isle of Wight a day or two before, and *Punch* and the other wits amused themselves vastly at the expense of PRINCE ALBERT, who, as a field-marshal, should have remained at the post of danger. It was supposed that her Majesty was peremptory upon the subject, and overruled any martial propensities which her consort might possess.

Great preparations were made for the defense of the Bank of England, the Royal Exchange, and other public edifices—especially the Bank, the treasure in which was likely to attract the cupidity of a revolutionary mob. The roof was protected by sand-bags, behind which marksmen could be safely placed. The night before the anticipated outbreak, large stores of muskets and ammunition were conveyed there and to other places from the Admiralty. My friend Kendall came to grief that night from his excessive curiosity. About nine o'clock in the evening he made his way down past the Houses of Parliament to the head of Westminster Bridge, where cannon were planted to rake the insurgents who were expected to come over on the morrow from their camping-ground on Kennington Common. Here he was ordered back in very peremptory fashion. Strolling up Whitehall, he managed in some way to slip by the sentinel and to get into the court-yard of the Admiralty, admission to which was for the nonce prohibited. Here he was pounced upon in short order. In vain he protested that he was only an enterprising Yankee, actuated by no worse motive than curiosity. He was carried off to durance vile, and only liberated the next day upon establishing his identity and his harmlessness.

The most exaggerated rumors were circulated in reference to the numbers of the hostile masses collected on the Surrey side. The general estimate did not fall short of thirty or forty thousand, which was afterward proved to be a grossly excessive one.

The preservation of the peace was primarily intrusted to the police, and, in addition to the regular force, a large number of special constables was enrolled for the occasion. The military was of course only to be called out as a last resort. Some twenty Americans, who lodged at Morley's, myself and my friends included, offered our services as specials, which offers were unhesitatingly accepted. And when the time came, each armed with a formidable club which he had received from the authorities, we were as ready as any of her Majesty's loyal subjects to do battle in defense of law and order. It was rather an interesting and exciting sight as, at nine o'clock on the morning when the demonstration was to come off, I was quietly taking my tea and muffins, and looking out of the coffee-room window upon Trafalgar Square. The whole area was densely filled, principally by a large body of police, who were going through their military evolutions with the precision of soldiers. Among them was a small corps of mounted constabulary, ready for a charge down Parliament Street if occasion should require it. A good many roughs were scattered about, but they gave no indications of any but the most peaceful intentions.

At ten o'clock I emerged from the hotel, and took a short stroll up the Haymarket. The shops were every where closed, and the streets were filled with people. I only remained out about half an hour, and then returned to my quarters.

About eleven o'clock I noticed unusual indications of preparation among the police upon the square, and shortly afterward a dense mass, composed of the lowest class of the populace, came struggling up Parliament Street, and began to pour in upon the open area. They were singing and shouting, and seemed more impelled by the love of a frolic than by any thing more serious. In a moment about a dozen policemen charged at a full gallop, and the mob, by some remarkable power of elastic self-compression, instantly made way for them in every direction, laughing and hurrahing as they did so. This brilliant cavalry *coup* decided, as it were, the fate of the day. The Chartists did not attempt to cross the river, overawed, probably, by the reception which they knew was prepared for them. After that there was nothing but amusing episodes. It was known that London was full of French revolutionary agents, and wherever these gentry showed themselves, they were treated by the populace with any thing but distinguished consideration. I saw one unfortunate apostle of liberty, equality, and fraternity so severely ducked in the basin of one of the fountains of Trafalgar Square, that I was afraid the poor Gaul was taking his last (and perhaps his first) bath.

The rest of the day was a sort of carnival. No one attempted to transact any business, and the shops remained closed. Fun was universal, and the special constables, whose name was legion, paraded the streets with the consciousness that their valor had not been very severely tried. That evening the monster petition was rolled upon a barrow into the House of Commons, and duly presented by its godfather, FERGUS O'CONNOR. The next day I happened to be at the railway station as FERGUS was leaving for the country. Poor fellow, he died insane many years ago, and I am not quite certain that his insanity was then of recent date.

That evening SANDERS and KENDALL went together to the opera. They affected extreme rusticity, and absolute ignorance in regard to every thing pertaining to that or to any other similar performance. They purposely made the most uncouth remarks, and asked the most absurd questions of those who happened to be seated near them. A well-intentioned but officious Cockney wine-dealer came to their rescue—one of those weak-minded cits who so abound in London. Him they at once decided to unmercifully quiz. During the remainder of the performance they poured into his ears the most marvelous stories of American savagery, and they found his credulity quite equal to their united powers of invention. After the play was over they invited him to sup with them at Morley's. He accepted the invitation. They related to him the most horrible stories of Indian butchery until his very hair stood on end. About two o'clock in the morning they began a war-dance, accompanied by the most hideous howlings, when suddenly, brandishing some of SANDERS's sample revolvers, they chased the now thoroughly "demoralized" Briton from the house. The noise which the tormentors made, added to the shrieks of alarm uttered by their victim, aroused every body in the hotel, and came near resulting in the summary and ignominious ejection from it of those who had created the disturbance. The next morning, being gentlemen at heart, they called upon the frightened vendor of imitation sherry, and that very afternoon they all dined together at the Star and Garter at Richmond, upon terms of the most cordial and affectionate friendship.

One or two evenings afterward, the Court having returned to Buckingham Palace, the Queen went in state to the opera. I took especial pains to be there, for I expected an extraordinary exhibition of loyalty. And I was not disappointed. The opera was "Don Giovanni" —a work which calls for the entire strength, both male and female, of the company. The house was packed from pit to dome. Her Majesty entered while the orchestra was playing the overture. In a moment the entire audience arose, and cried with one voice for "God save the Queen!" The orchestra ceased playing, the prompter's bell tinkled, the curtain was drawn up and displayed all the principal artists ranged in a semicircle upon the stage. At a signal from the conductor a prelude was played, and then GRISI advanced to the footlights, and with the glorious voice she then possessed, sang the first verse, the whole house standing, her Majesty included. The chorus was taken up by the other singers and by the entire pit. Then MARIO sang a verse, and then PERSIANI, and then TAMBURINI, and then LABLACHE. I never saw such a scene of wild enthusiasm. It was so contagious that I am confident the Queen had no more loyal subject there that evening than myself. The boxes entirely forgot their usual frigid propriety, and marchionesses and countesses vied with each other in clapping their hands and waving their handkerchiefs.

CHAPTER III.

UPON the occasion of this visit to London I had the pleasure to meet and to make the acquaintance of RALPH WALDO EMERSON, the foremost American philosopher and critic, and the gentlest and most amiable of men. Mr. EMERSON had letters to SIR CHARLES BARRY, the architect of the new Houses of Parliament, not then completed, and we called together upon him. SIR CHARLES received us stiffly, and with but scant courtesy of manner; but he extended to us facilities for visiting and examining this structure, in some respects one of the most remarkable of modern times; although I can not help considering it, in its entirety very inferior to our own National Capitol at Washington. Mr. EMERSON and I also passed much time together in the British Museum, whose varied collections possess an interest for the cultivated mind, hardly, if at all, equaled by those of any other establishment in Europe, and compared with which the best of our own are petty and insignificant. When we parted after a few short days of companionship, I looked upon Mr. EMERSON's acquaintance as a treasure to be preserved and enlarged by me in the future; but in the progress of lives devoted, by chance or inclination, to widely different activities, it has never since been my fortune to meet him. His name already inspired me with awe when we first came together. The simplicity of his nature, and his instinctive abhorrence of all shams, soon dispelled the embarrassment of admiration, and substituted in its stead the ease of familiar and unaffected intercourse.

I have mentioned that I had gone over to England in the pursuit of health. I was the bearer of a letter of introduction from a distinguished physician of New York to the eminent SIR BENJAMIN BRODIE. I called upon SIR BENJAMIN soon after my arrival in London, when he made an appointment for me to come again at nine o'clock on the morning immediately succeeding the operatic *fête* to which I have referred. Punctually at the appointed hour I arrived at his house in Saville Row. The servant who admitted me told me that SIR BENJAMIN was engaged with some ladies, who had come from a long distance in the country expressly to consult him, and that he therefore begged that I would await his leisure. Accordingly I was shown into the library, where I found a cheerful fire, and the morning papers spread out upon a table. Drawing up an arm-chair to one corner of the fire-place, I seated myself, crossed my legs, and was soon deeply immersed in the leviathan columns of *The Times.*

I had been reading perhaps ten minutes, when the door opened, and another gentleman was ushered into the room by the flunky. The stranger was a short, thickset man, evidently a foreigner, and dressed in an irreproachable suit of mourning. I glanced at him furtively from my newspaper, and settled it in my own mind that he must be a German. In accordance with English custom, not the slightest recognition of the other's presence passed between us. He hovered over the table a moment, selected a paper from among several still lying there, settled himself in a chair at the opposite corner of the fire-place, and followed my example by devoting himself to the news of the day.

After a time I became tired of reading, and threw down my journal. The stranger, a few minutes later, did the same thing. I then had an opportunity to more particularly scan his person. He was a heavy, dull, impassive-looking man, and his half-closed eyelids gave a peculiar expression to his face. I observed that his arms and legs indicated great strength, but he did not look like a person of much activity. His arms were very long, and his legs quite short; he stood of low stature, and sat decidedly tall. He kept rubbing the side of his nose gently with his forefinger—a habit which I frequently had occasion afterward to observe in the same person. For some minutes we sat like two fools, or like two thoroughly well-bred Englishmen (by no means convertible terms, however), pretending to gaze at the fire. At length my companion opened the way for conversation by observing that it was a fine day. His accent, which was very marked, struck me as decidedly Teutonic, and confirmed me in the impression that he was a German. I assented to his observation, and, the ice once broken, we soon got on together famously—he taking me for an Englishman, and I taking him for a German. From one subject we passed to another, until he introduced that of the Chartist affair, upon which he talked so well that I became greatly interested. He was unbounded in his praises of the good sense displayed by the English people, particularly the lower middle-classes—meaning the shop-keepers and the artisans. He was happy that he had possessed the opportunity to see so satisfactory and striking an exhibition of this. "A violent revolution will never succeed in Great Britain in this century, at least," he went on to say, "although your institutions are in a state of continuous revolutionary progress, so to speak. There is a vast difference between the classes to which I have alluded here and the corresponding ones on the Continent, especially in France. Every thing continues to move on here in old and well-worn grooves. The London shop-keeper of to-day follows the same business, at the same stand, which his father and grandfather followed before him. He has the sense to comprehend and appreciate the difficulty of making a livelihood amid the competition of so dense a population, should he once get off the track. In a word, he knows that in a general scramble he has more chances of losing than of gaining. Hence, apart from his feeling of loyalty, which is deep-rooted, and impels him toward governmental and dynastic conservatism, his interest, as he understands it, would suffice to induce him to stand by the institutions of the country, should the attempt be made to overthrow them by violence. Your agricultural population is only instinctively, not intelligently loyal. I do not mean at all to imply, by any thing I have said, that your shop-keepers and artisans are not dissatisfied with many things, and do not claim and will not always exercise the right of unlimited grumbling. But at the bottom they know that your Constitution is a self-purifying machine, and that there is a never-ceasing tendency toward improvement. On the contrary, notwithstanding all that experience has shown him since the commencement of the Revolution of 1789, the average French bourgeois can not be convinced that another violent change will not better his condition by some means which he can neither explain nor distinctly comprehend. His hopes always outweigh his fears, and his interests are always subordinated to his passions. He can neither be easily governed, nor can he easily govern himself."

I do not wish to be understood to quote these as the precise words of my interlocutor, but they substantially reproduce what he said.

We must have been talking together at least half an hour, when SIR BENJAMIN opened a door which communicated by a passage-way to his study, and, bowing to my companion, called me in—probably because I alone had an appointment. As soon as we were seated, he asked me if I knew who it was whom I had left behind me in the library. I told him that I did not; that I thought he was a German; that, at all events, he was a remarkably intelligent man, although he did not look at all so. "Well," he said, with a smile, "that is LOUIS NAPOLEON!" This, be it remembered, was a few weeks before the Prince passed over to France to take his seat as a member of the Legislative Assembly. I asked SIR BENJAMIN what was the motive of his visit to him. He told me that he had some trouble about the heart—whether organic or functional, I did not inquire. I never met LOUIS NAPOLEON again until I saw him in Paris, six years later, Emperor of the French.

And here, perhaps, I ought to stop, as my personal reminiscences of the exiled Prince go no farther. But the subject is a tempting one, and, as accident has brought me into contact with several persons who knew him during his first residence in England, the reader will probably excuse me if I draw a little upon the recollections of others.

One of the best friends he ever had on the north side of the channel was BARONESS (then Miss BURDETT) COUTTS. This estimable lady was unceasing in her kindness to him, and, what is still more, she was the first person to appreciate his abilities at any thing like their true value. So high an estimate of them did she form and express, that her friends were both pained and amused at what they considered her good-natured but most unfounded prejudice in his favor. The fast young men of London, whose society he affected, generally pronounced him an idiot. This was especially true of his associates of the notorious Coventry Club, which was afterward broken up by the police. He was also very kindly received at the house of Mr. BATES, of the great firm of BARING BROTHERS, at East Sheene. Mrs. BATES, like most English ladies of the day, held tobacco-smoke in horror; but the Prince, when a visitor, was allowed, as a special favor, to smoke in his own room; and upon such occasions the other gentlemen present were told that if they desired to smoke they might do so in the same place. One evening something occurred to make him very anxious to return immediately to London. He had no carriage of his own with him, and was very reluctant to ask Mr. BATES to lend him one. In this dilemma he went to a friend of mine, who happened to be visiting at the house, and asked him if he minded requesting another gentleman with whom he was intimate to let him have the use of his brougham for a drive to town, without mentioning by whom it was desired. My friend unhesitatingly complied with the request; but the owner of the brougham insisted upon knowing who was to use it, saying that he supposed it was "that bloody fool, LOUIS NAPOLEON," and, if so, that he should not have it. And it was only with great difficulty that he was finally induced to yield the point.

LADY BLESSINGTON and COUNT D'ORSAY were like a sister and a brother to him. The gates of Gore House were open to him at all hours, and he freely availed himself of the tendered hospitality. The only reproach of serious ingratitude of which I have ever heard him accused refers to his alleged neglect of these persons when, during his presidency, they came over to Paris after pecuniary reverses had broken up the Lady's London establishment. So far as D'ORSAY is concerned, it is true that the President tardily conferred upon him the office of Superintendent of the Fine Arts, the honors and emoluments of which he did not live long to enjoy. His neglect of LADY BLESSINGTON, although not excusable, may be partly accounted for by the peculiar position which her ladyship occupied in English society. He may have hesitated to invite her to his balls and receptions, fearing to give too much offense to her countrywomen, who crowded them. At any rate, he delayed a long time before doing so.

LADY BLESSINGTON, besides being a charming woman, was one of the most brilliant wits of her day. Shortly after the breaking out of the Revolution of 1848, a foreign embassador in London asked her what she thought of M. DE LAMARTINE, who was then playing a conservative rôle. "He reminds me," she instantly replied, "of an incendiary who has turned fireman." She had been in Paris for some time, unnoticed by the President, when at last she received an invitation from him to a ball at the Elysée Bourbon. This she accepted, and as soon as the President saw her enter the room he advanced to her, and, extending both hands, said he was glad to see her, and asked her if she purposed remaining long in Paris. "No," she promptly answered; "*Do you?*"

No one in London, it is said, had a more open hand for the future Emperor than MITCHEL, the manager of the St. James' Theatre. It may be remarked that no borrower of money ever more scrupulously returned it than did LOUIS NAPOLEON. When he and the Empress paid the QUEEN a visit in 1854 or 1855—I forget which —he had been but a few hours in London before he sent for MITCHEL, with whom he familiarly conversed for a long time, showing that, with the change in his fortunes, he had not forgotten old friends.

It is related—but of course I can not vouch for the truth of the story—that upon one occasion a wag imposed upon the credulity of the exiled Prince by a forged letter of invitation to dine with the QUEEN at Windsor. Now in those days her Majesty was on terms of great intimacy with the Orleans family, and completely ignored poor LOUIS NAPOLEON, having declined to even receive him at Court. However surprised, therefore, he must have been at so unexpected a mark of royal favor, it would seem that he did not suspect its want of genuineness. Donning a uniform, and arraying his groom in a gorgeous livery, he drove to Windsor, where he discovered that he had been hoaxed; and it is said that the QUEEN was not gracious enough to do any thing to relieve his mortification. If this is not a *canard*, he afterward had an ample revenge: he both visited and received her Majesty while he was supposed to be the most powerful monarch in the world.

I recollect meeting a gentleman who was well acquainted with the Prince in England. He told me that he once went out hunting with him and his cousin, PRINCE NAPOLEON (JEROME). As they were driving to covert, LOUIS NAPOLEON was dull and moody, whereas his cousin was full of excitement about the anticipated sport. But the moment they backed their horses they changed characters; the one became full of energy and daring, the other subsided into quiet, if not timidity.

During the presidency, LORD ABERDEEN, afterward British Prime Minister, went over to Paris with the real, if not the avowed, object of studying the President. He remained there more than a fortnight, constantly in LOUIS NAPOLEON'S society, and dining with him almost every day. Just before he left to return to England, he wrote a private letter to a friend, who afterward showed me the following extract from it: "As to the President, I can make nothing of him but a dismal, dreary creature!" Was he, or was he not, mistaken in his appreciation?

At this time my dear friend, JOHN ROMEYN BRODHEAD, whom I had known from my boyhood up, and whom I only a few months ago followed to his last resting-place, was Secretary of the United States Legation, under GEORGE BANCROFT, as Minister. Poor BRODHEAD, who was one of the most amiable, was also one of the most nervous of men. During his residence in England he had become almost painfully Anglicized, and any departure from English usages and etiquette occasioned him the keenest and most genuine distress. Once I went with him to look for lodgings for a common friend. Among the houses which we visited, in quest of what we wanted, was one kept by a person of very ladylike appearance and manners, and on leaving I saluted her by removing my hat, as we should do upon a like occasion to any respectable woman in America or in France. Seeing my action, BRODHEAD shot off as if he had been exploded from a gun, and at first I was in a state of innocent amazement as to what could have produced this extraordinary exodus. He soon rejoined me, as I was slowly walking away. He was out of breath and panting, and, with an expression of deep injury upon his countenance, he asked me how I *could* be guilty of the solecism of taking off my hat to a lodging-house keeper! "Don't you know," he said, "that it is never done in England?" As I didn't know it, I had to cry *peccavi.* Upon another occasion, BRODHEAD, SANDERS, PRENTISS, and I went to DOLLY'S famous old chop-house in the City to dine. DOLLY'S was a more primitive place than GARROWAY'S, or than NED'S and the other similar establishments which have recently sprung up in the neighborhood of the Royal Exchange. You went there for chops, steaks, potatoes, and beer, which were all served to you in perfection; but for any thing more elaborate and luxurious it was not the habit to call. Some one of the party, however — I forget who — ordered champagne; whereat BRODHEAD, disgusted with our ignorance, incontinently withdrew; and it was only the next day that I learned that to order champagne at a chop-house was an evidence of barbarous bringing-up not to be endured by a civilized man! BRODHEAD afterward held for four years the office of Naval Officer of the Port of New York.

He is best known to the public, however, by his "History of the State of New York," a work of enormous research, written with great care and discrimination, to the composition of which he devoted the declining years of his life, with an assiduity which not only affected his health, but unquestionably hastened his decease. At one time he was sent to Holland by the State of New York to collect documents affecting our early history, and while he was in London he industriously prosecuted his researches in the State-Paper Office. He had in his veins some of our best Colonial blood, both Dutch and English, and he always entertained against the "pestilent Yankees" almost as strong a prejudice as some of his progenitors in New Netherlands.

As I sauntered through the streets of London, I was often struck by the many singular names over the shop doors. You find no such variety of strange patronymics in America. It is well known that DICKENS selected the very peculiar names of some of his characters from real ones, which his ever-observant eyes fell upon as he walked the streets of the metropolis. I noticed upon a sign over a door on St. Martin's Lane the name of "QUILP." I think it was a farrier's shop. This reminds me of a Scotchman of the same trade who used to keep his shop in Church Street, New York, at the top of an alley-way. At the entrance was a sign bearing the following canny inscription:

"SINCLAIR LITHGOW, horse-shoeing smith,
Warks up this close wi' a' his pith.
He dis his wark baith weel and soon,
But likes the *siller* when 'tis done."

I remember a shop near Westminster Bridge, over which was painted, without punctuation,

"TILL late DARKE;"

meaning, as we should express it, "TILL, successor to DARKE." When the words first attracted my attention, I thought that they were intended to indicate that the shop was kept open until late in the evening.

CHAPTER IV.

IN the autumn of the year 1854 I again visited Europe. I stayed in England but a few days, and went thence to Paris, where I engaged apartments in expectation of a prolonged sojourn in that capital. I had no very definite plans for the future, and looked forward to the enjoyment for a considerable period, at least, of rest and leisure. But, as has always happened to me, these expectations were not destined to be realized. I had not been in Paris a week before I was invited by the Honorable JOHN Y. MASON, then our Minister to France, to occupy the position of Secretary of Legation, which chanced to be temporarily vacant. I accepted it without much reflection. I supposed that the office was one which involved but little labor, and the incumbency of which must necessarily be of the most agreeable character. It did not take me long to find out how greatly I had been mistaken. The current work—the answering daily of scores of letters and the transcribing of dispatches—was enough to occupy one industrious person. But, added to this, when I took possession of the place I found every thing fearfully in arrear, and for weeks I was kept at my desk until a late hour in the evening. It was true that we had one or two ornamental attachés, but to do any thing in consideration of having the honor to bear the title upon their visiting cards never occurred to them. Again, all the social embarrassments of the Legation—and they were both numerous and trying—were thrust upon the Secretary. Hundreds of our countrymen, of proverbial modesty, who were entitled at the utmost to have their passports viséd, would ask of us the most unreasonable facilities and the most unheard of favors. Citizens not even accredited by letters of introduction would insist upon private audiences of the Emperor, and, no matter how politely you declined to act as the medium of their laudable ambition, they would anathematize you, and threaten to "go for" your official head immediately after their return to America. Crack-brained inventors would ask you to do the most impossible things for them in connection with the several Departments of the Government, even to bringing them without circumlocution to the fountain of power; and your mildest protests only subjected you to contumely and abuse. I particularly remember one lunatic who had come over with a new projectile, of which he had a wooden model which looked like a rolling-pin tapered down to a point at one end. Of course he did not speak a word of French—they never do—and he pestered the life out of me, until, in an unguarded moment, I yielded, and consented to accompany him to the War Department. It is unnecessary to say that we were politely received, and invited to leave our model with the accompanying explanations, with the assurance that they would be promptly submitted to an artillery commission for examination and report. About a fortnight afterward, my tormentor received an official invitation to call again at the Department and receive the report of the examiners. Of course, I was again badgered into accompanying him. When we arrived, we were conducted to a bureau of the

Department presided over by a captain of artillery. This gentleman proceeded in the most delicate manner to explain to me in French that the same invention had been submitted to his Government so long ago as the year 1827 by a Swedish officer, that it had then been thoroughly tested, and that it was found to be absolutely worthless. At every moment, while he was speaking, my companion impatiently interrupted him by asking me, "What does he say? What does he say?" I waited until the statement was completed, and then translated it into English to the inventor. "Tell him that he is an infernal ass!" he shouted, when I had got through. The French officer smiled, and, resuming, said to me: "I can make every allowance for your friend's disappointment, and, of course, in nowise hold you responsible for his indiscretion, but be pleased to advise him that when he is again disposed to express himself in such unreserved terms toward a stranger, he first make sure that he does not understand English!" Ladies would sometimes be so unreasonable as to ask us to do them the trifling favor of sending over small parcels for them in the dispatch-bag. I remember that once, upon opening the London dispatch-bag, we found in it a corset, which the fair owner had inclosed as a model by which she desired her *corsetière* to fabricate for her a new one. But the greatest calamity to us was when an official ball or *fête* was to be given by some high officer of the Government or by the Municipality of Paris. Whenever this happened we would be hunted down for invitations. Where many asked, the greater number had to be disappointed. The American residents always thought that they had a superior claim upon the Legation, under whose immediate protection they fancied that they lived. The travelers, on the contrary, thought that, because their opportunities were fewer, *they* were entitled to the first consideration. Those who succeeded did not thank you, and those who failed devoted you to the infernal gods. I have particularly in mind a grand ball, which the City of Paris gave at the Hotel de Ville to the King of Portugal. Baron Haussmann, the Prefect of the Seine, sent an early notice of the projected *fête* to our Legation, coupled with the request that we would transmit to him a list of the American ladies and gentlemen for whom we desired invitations. Judge Mason protested that he would have nothing to do with the matter. I was almost in despair. The only device that occurred to me was to post up in the Legation a paper to be signed by those who desired to go. Before the time arrived to make application, the names on that list had swollen to—I should be afraid to say how many hundreds. Conscious of the impropriety which I was committing, I fired the entire catalogue at Baron Haussmann. The next day he returned it to me, with a letter in which he said that, while it always afforded him the greatest pleasure to oblige the United States Legation to the extent of his ability, he was, nevertheless, compelled to inform me that we had asked for more invitations to that ball than could be accorded to all the foreign nationalities united; but that if we would revise it, and send him thirty-five selected names, it would afford him the highest gratification to immediately forward cards to them. To have to select thirty-five out of perhaps eight hundred! I forget how we did it; but the vision of outraged fathers, indignant mammas, and hysterical daughters still floats before me. I am sure that for this one act my memory is still execrated by hundreds of worthy and virtuous citizens of both sexes. Our compatriots in distress, who had gotten themselves into Clichy, or worse, added to the amenities of the situation. So that, as I premised, the position of Secretary of Legation in France did not prove to me to be one of unalloyed delight. Nor is it one that any young gentleman who looks to the office as a stepping-stone to political preferment at home would do well to accept (if only he can get it), at least until he has thoroughly reconnoitered the situation, and become convinced that it is now a seat of more roses and fewer thorns than I found it—pressed into the service and receiving no recompense beyond the consciousness of good intentions, and discharging its duties as long as I did, chiefly it would seem at the bidding of the Nemesis of work, which has pursued me through my life and been the bane of my existence.

JUDGE MASON was a fine specimen of the Virginian of the old school, and in many respects a remarkable man. The day after the presentation of his credentials to the Emperor of the French as Envoy Extraordinary and Minister Plenipotentiary from the United States, the official *Moniteur* announced the event, calling him His Excellency *Johnny*—instead of *John Y.*—MASON. The paragraph must have been written by some traveled Frenchman, who had had a familiar John, to him known as Johnny, and who supposed that John Y., if so the name had first reached him, was the erroneous spelling of some countryman not so well up as himself in English names. The Judge had been on the bench in his native state, and was at one time Attorney-General, and at another Secretary of the Navy. He was a man of commanding presence and of the most generous impulses, which he sometimes indulged to an extent that defied prudence, as he had a large family, and his private means were very limited. His intelligence was of a very high order, and his knowledge of questions of state and of political economy thorough and accurate. He was an earnest advocate of free-trade, and reasoned more cogently in its favor than any one else whom I ever listened to. The Emperor took great pleasure and interest in hearing him talk upon this subject, and many an hour did they pass together *tête-à-tête* at Saint Cloud discussing it. At the same time, Mr. MASON possessed the tenderness and almost the weakness of a woman. His prejudices for and against persons were of the strongest and most obstinate character, and he sometimes indulged them unreasonably and extravagantly. His sensibilities and his emotional character were morbidly developed. In a word, his mind was strong and his moral temperament weak, so that he always reminded me of a powerful steam-engine propelling a feeble and ill-contrived vessel. In spite of all, if you were his friend, you could not help loving him, for his impulses were noble and his affection warm and devoted. If there were any two things in the world that the Judge preferred to all others, they were Virginia hams and Virginia tobacco. A plentiful supply of both was frequently brought over to him by the pursers of the steamers from New York to Havre, and when a fresh provision of hams arrived there was sure to be feasting at the Legation. The Judge had an amiable, accomplished, and hospitable family, and his eldest daughter supplied by her social tact whatever there was of deficiency in that respect in her father's composition.

It was either in the winter of 1854–5, or in the following spring, that CHARLES SUMNER came to Paris to seek medical advice for the injuries inflicted upon him by PRESTON BROOKS, of South Carolina, who, it will be remembered, assaulted him with a heavy cane while seated in his chair in the Senate-chamber, after the adjournment for the day of that body. If there was any thing in the world that Mr. MASON hated beyond all others it was an *abolitionist,* and from what he said about Mr. SUMNER we were all in the direst apprehension lest, if that gentleman should call upon the Minister, a very disagreeable scene might be the consequence. It was in vain that I argued to the Judge that in his capacity of our national representative he was bound to receive with politeness and consideration *any* United States Senator who should present himself. He utterly refused to acknowledge the correctness of my reasoning. It turned out accidentally that Mr. SUMNER called at a time when Mr. MASON happened to be not at home. When the Judge found the card, he declared with emphasis that nothing would induce him to return the call. Two days thereafter, however, the Minister's cards were left at the Senator's lodgings; but the former never knew any thing about it, and the latter was not informed that they came to him without authority.

Mr. MASON's conduct toward HORACE GREELEY, who came to Paris in the summer of 1855, was quite different. It is certain that Mr. GREELEY was as advanced an abolitionist as Mr. SUMNER; but then he did not hold public office. The Judge made just the opposite distinction here to that which appeared to me a natural one. Mr. Greeley told me that when he first called upon the Minister he felt very uncertain about the reception which awaited him; that to his surprise he found his political opponent not only kind, but even cordial. He continued all the time that he remained in Paris to receive marked attention from Mr. Mason. Upon several occasions he spoke to me about this matter, and expressed with much feeling his sense of the politeness of the Minister.

The highest object of ambition of the average American man and woman who came to Paris in those days was a presentation at Court, with a vista of future invitations to the Tuileries. Wholesale presentations usually were accorded at uncertain intervals of time, at which were gathered together representatives of nearly all the nations of the earth. Preceding the arrival of their Majesties, our people were usually gathered together in the same room with the Mexicans and South Americans. Sometimes we occupied an apartment with some of the nationalities of Continental Europe; but never by any chance were we and the English caged together. I presume that the French notion was that under no circumstances could we be trusted to live together in the harmony of a happy family. There were frequently ridiculous and sometimes mortifying incidents at these presentations. I recollect one of them appointed for a Sunday, the usual day for such ceremonies, the notices for which were only issued on Saturday afternoon, and not received by many of the persons interested until the next morning. Gentlemen were required to present themselves "*en uniforme*," and ladies, "*en toilette de ville*"—this latter expression meaning in full visiting dress. The embarrassment which resulted from the tardiness of the notice may be imagined. The men rushed frantically to WOODMAN's, on the Boulevard des Italiens, that accomplished knight of the shears being purveyor-general of court-dresses to Yankeedoodledom in Paris, and constantly keeping on hand an assortment ready made, which he hired out as masquerade-costumers do. Those who were so fortunate as to present themselves on Saturday evening not only had the first choice, but were in time to have the alterations made necessary to give something of a fit; whereas the unfortunates of Sunday morning had to take what was left as they found it.

Such a battalion as presented itself at the Palace at noon could only be compared to Falstaff's regiment, or an old-fashioned country militia company. There were coats too big for their wearers, and coats too small; sleeves too long, and sleeves too short; trowsers dragging under the heel of the boot, and trowsers not reaching down to the ankle-joint; a miscellany of cocked hats, and a confusion of swords that *would* trip up the inexperienced wearers. And all these incongruous articles of attire, apart from their unsuitableness to each individual case, were worn with the awkwardness peculiar to novices in court-dress. The women were more fortunate, being generally provided with all the necessary articles of adornment, as nothing unusual to them was required. Charming as most of them were, there were a few whose appearance was such as to keep their male companions in countenance. You will at any time find in Paris a certain number of peripatetic American ladies, whose whole being is shrouded in mystery—who come no one knows whence, and, after a time, go no one knows whither. They usually travel under the convenient title of widows, and are looking after some important interests which appear to be of a foggy and indescribable character. I remember upon the occasion in question one lady whom nobody knew, or could tell how she got there, and whose appearance attracted some attention. She wore a rusty black silk dress, cut very high in the neck, an enormous shell-cameo brooch, and a Canton crape shawl, which had been originally white in years long past, but which was then, to speak plainly, most disgustingly dirty. After a line had been formed on our side of the room, finding herself inconvenienced by the heat, she removed this shawl, and threw it carelessly upon the back of an arm-chair, of which several were standing in a row opposite. A few minutes later a chamberlain, or aid, lounged into the room, and stood for a moment by the fire-place. Suddenly he glanced at this suspicious-looking garment, and he stuck a glass into his eye to examine it more particularly. Then an expression of horror overspread his countenance, and, stepping upon the points of his toes, he advanced to it with great deliberation, skewered it upon the tip of his sword, gravely recrossed the room with it, and threw it down out of sight in a corner. It was not a pleasant thing to see done, but the owner of the offending article was an "unprotected female," and her ideas of "*toilette de ville*" were evidently not up to the standard of the French Court.

Imagine, then, the American presentees, ranged as at drill, awaiting the Imperial approach. On the other side of the same room was drawn up a delegation of Spaniards, Mexicans, and South Americans. In an adjoining apartment, the door of which was open, were congregated the English and Germans, the greater part of the former (the men, I mean) in scarlet yeomanry uniforms, with an occasional sprinkling of stunning Highland costumes. The British ladies, in general elegance of *mise*, and beauty and grace of person, bore no comparison to our fair countrywomen. Why *are* the English women so unaccountably awkward? why have they such distressingly large hands and feet? and why is their taste in dress so almost universally bad? Beautiful complexions and well-developed forms can not altogether atone for these deficiencies, hardly even kind hearts and cultivated minds.

Upon this particular occasion our Minister, having been taken suddenly ill, was unexpectedly absent. A Secretary of Legation can not present. That most facetious of living humorists, DONN PIATT, then Secretary, was, however, in attendance. A chamberlain was to make the presentations, and before the time arrived he called PIATT to him, and requested him to give him a list of the persons to be presented, in the order in which they stood, and to especially mention for what, if any thing, any of them were distinguished, as the Emperor always desired to particularly notice persons entitled to more than a passing word from him. Heaven only knows what PIATT said about most of the party; but standing in about the middle of the line was a Mr. GROESBECK, and, calling particular attention to him, PIATT told the chamberlain that he was a member of Congress from Ohio.

Their Majesties visited the English and German apartment first. At last they crossed our threshold, the Emperor followed by a male suite and the Empress by a female one. I happened to be standing next the door, and the Emperor stopped directly in front of me, while the Empress passed on to the farther extremity of the line. His Majesty, upon that occasion, merely exchanged with me a few commonplaces, and then addressed himself to my next neighbor. I continued to keep my eye upon him in his downward progress, until he crossed the Empress in her advance in my direction. A moment afterward he accosted Mr. GROESBECK, and the chamberlain at the same time whispered into his ear what he supposed that gentleman to be. "Ah!" said his Majesty, smiling, "I understand that you are a member of Congress from Ohio, Mr. GROESBECK." "No, sir, I am not," answered Mr. GROESBECK; "but I have a cousin who once was." He probably never knew to whom he was indebted for the title. The Emperor bit his lip, and was evidently vastly amused.

This one presentation was but a specimen of numerous others. I will not undertake to describe a certain private audience at which I assisted, which was had of the Emperor at about the same time by the Hon. Mr. WASHBURNE, now our Minister to France, and then a member of Congress from Illinois; the Hon. Mr. GROW, then a member of Congress from Pennsylvania, and subsequently Speaker of the House of Representatives; the Hon. Mr. HARRINGTON, late Minister to Switzerland; and the Hon. Mr. MORGAN, a member of Congress from Western New York.

All the country knows that DONN PIATT is an incorrigible wag. He used to give an account of the reception by their Majesties of a distinguished soldier, which he related with the greatest gravity and the most minute details, and to this day I have never been able to comprehend how much of truth and how much of invention there was in it. I know that I shall fail to do the subject justice, but, nevertheless, I can not refrain from making the attempt.

Immediately after the occurrence of what is known in our diplomatic history as the "Black Warrior Affair," our Government sent to Madrid, as a special bearer of dispatches, COLONEL SUMNER, of the United States Army, who afterward became so famous as GENERAL SUMNER during the War of the Rebellion. The Colonel, upon his arrival at Paris from Washington, made no stay there, but pushed on directly to Madrid. He conveyed instructions to Mr. SOULÉ, our Minister to Spain, to lay the case before the Spanish Government, and to demand an immediate apology, together with reparation. Mr. SOULÉ accordingly addressed a peremptory dispatch to Mr. LUZURIAGA, Minister of Foreign Affairs, and asked for a reply within twenty-four hours. The allotted time passed, and no reply came. Mr. SOULÉ then wrote still more peremptorily, saying that he could detain his messenger, an officer of rank, but one day longer. Before the expiration of this second day an answer came, couched in those terms of extreme courtesy which Spanish officials always employ, but to the effect that, inasmuch as the Government had as yet received no report of the matter in question from its agents in Cuba, it must decline for the present any consideration of the subject. Whereupon COLONEL SUMNER incontinently packed his portmanteau and hurried back to Paris. Having a few days at his disposal before he was compelled to return to

America, he devoted them to seeing the principal sights of the French capital. Among other things, he entertained an ardent desire to have an audience of the Emperor and Empress, and JUDGE MASON, who was usually reluctant to ask these favors, finally consented to do so, and the matter was arranged. The next Sunday, at one o'clock, was the time appointed.

COLONEL SUMNER was stopping with Mr. McREA, of North Carolina, the United States Consul in Paris, who lived somewhere on the Rue de Rivoli, *au quatrième* or *au cinquième.* Now JUDGE MASON knew the Colonel to be a bluff, brusque soldier, who had spent most of his life fighting Indians on the frontier, and who, as PIATT said, while sitting one day with JEFFERSON DAVIS on a log in Mexico, during our war with that country, had been the joint-inventor with him of the inverted chimney-pot which for so many years formed the regulation head-gear of our army. At all events, from his brief communications with him, the Minister did not take him to be a courtly man. So, on the Saturday evening preceding the appointed Sunday, Mr. MASON ordered his carriage after dinner, and directed the coachman to drive to Mr. McREA's residence. When he reached that gentleman's apartment, he found the Colonel in the dining-room in his shirt-sleeves, with an old uniform coat and trowsers, both covered with spots and stains, spread out upon a table, and which, with a sponge saturated with benzine, he was vigorously scouring. At this sight a cold perspiration started out upon the Judge's brow. "Why, Colonel, what is that?" he exclaimed. "That," said the Colonel, "is my uniform, which I intend to wear to-morrow." "You certainly can not think of appearing before the Emperor and Empress in such a frightful suit of clothes as that—all the scrubbing in the world will not remove those spots of dirt; not to mention that it would be shabby, even if clean," resumed the Minister. "Well," rejoined the Colonel, "it is the only uniform that I possess. It is true that it shows the effects of service; I don't think that the Emperor will think any the worse of it on that account. So I *must* wear it, or not go at all." This alternative was, of course, not to be thought of; and, with a very uneasy feeling, Mr. MASON, after a short call, took his leave, promising to return on the morrow punctually at twelve o'clock, to take up the Colonel and convey him to the Tuileries.

The next day the Judge was punctual in keeping his appointment. Indeed, in his anxiety he somewhat anticipated the hour. He climbed up the four or five flights of stairs with much puffing and blowing, and when he entered the Consul's drawing-room he found the Colonel quite ready, ensconced in his rusty blue, and with one of the inverted chimney-pots already referred to upon his head. The Minister gazed at him for some moments in speechless horror, and then broke out with, "I tell you what it is, Colonel, I can stand the uniform, but hang me if I will accompany you to the Palace unless you dispense with that frightful object which you have upon your head." "But what shall I do for a hat?" querulously asked the Colonel. "This is our regulation cap, and if it is good enough to wear in the presence of the President of the United States, it is certainly sufficiently so to wear in that of the Emperor of the French." But the Judge's foot was down this time, and he would not yield. So he and the Colonel and Mr. McREA sat down together, and, after a long consultation, it was decided that the latter should go to a shop and purchase a military chapeau, which should be substituted for the obnoxious article. In the mean time it was getting late, and Mr. Mason was becoming fidgety and anxious. They all descended the stairs together, and while the Minister and the Colonel entered the former's carriage, the Consul dashed on toward the Rue de la Paix in quest of the chapeau, for which the others were to await his return. Mr. McRea was absent a long time; he had to go all the way to the Rue Richelieu; but just as the Judge was about to collapse from utter despair, he returned, triumphantly carrying in his hand an elegant laced chapeau, with a magnificent tricolored plume attached to it. He hastily passed it in through the carriage window, and Mr. Mason ordered the coachman to drive to the Palace. The Colonel held the chapeau in his hands, twirling it from side to side, and curiously eying it. At length he burst out, "Judge, you objected to my hat, but I'll be hanged if I will go before the Emperor with this one." "Why, what is the matter with it?" asked the Minister. "Do you think that I will present myself to him with this infernal tricolored plume?" was the rejoinder. "Well, then, take it out," said Mr. Mason. The Colonel proceeded to tug away at it, but without any success. Either he did not know how to detach it, or else it was too securely fastened for him to do so. Finding that his efforts were in vain, he began to tear out the feathers one by one, and to throw them out of the window, until the vertical whalebone alone remained. While he was thus occupied, the Minister, after some preliminary hemming and hawing, addressed him somewhat as follows: "Colonel, you are a man of the world, and therefore there can be no occasion for me to caution you in regard to your bearing in the presence of their Majesties. But there is one thing which I desire you to keep in mind, and that is that the Empress is a Spaniard, and extremely susceptible upon all questions affecting her own country. The business which took you to Madrid was one of a very disagreeable nature, and, I think that, in conversing with the Empress, you will do well to avoid even mentioning that you have been to Spain." "You are quite right, Mr. MASON," replied the Colonel; "rest assured that I shall say nothing about it." The distance which they had to drive was but a short one, and by this time they had reached the Tuileries. They were promptly ushered into the audience-chamber, and a few minutes thereafter the Emperor entered. Every thing passed off charmingly, and the gentlemen had been for some ten or fifteen minutes engaged in an easy and agreeable conversation, when her Majesty walked into the room, attended by a lady of honor. COLONEL SUMNER was presented, and somehow immediately lost his head. After the first words of courteous greeting, he appalled JUDGE MASON by telling the Empress that he had just returned from a visit to her native land, and regretted extremely that his business there was of such a nature that he was only able to remain in the country two days. "Shall I be indiscreet if I inquire what was the character of the business which compelled so short a visit?" asked the Empress, in her sweetest tones. "Madame," replied the Colonel, in nowise disconcerted, "I took to Mr. SOULÉ dispatches in relation to the *Black Warrior* outrage!" "How, sir!" asked her Majesty, flashing with indignation; "do you call that an outrage—the vessel that took over LOPEZ and his infamous gang of pirates?" "I beg to observe to you, Madame," rejoined the Colonel, "that the *Black Warrior* was not even built until long after LOPEZ had been executed." "It matters not," answered the Empress; "you Americans seem to think that because France is engaged in a war with Russia you can insult Spain with impunity. Permit me to tell you that Spain is abundantly able to take care of herself, so far as you are concerned; that if she is not, France is not so crippled but that she can come to her aid; and that if, notwithstanding all, it shall become necessary to do so, we will liberate the negroes in Cuba, and thus revolutionize your own country!" "Madame!" answered the Colonel, drawing himself up to his full height, "I beg to say, with the highest respect for your Majesty, that we are not afraid of Spain, that we are not afraid of Spain and France together, that we are not afraid of Spain and France together and the niggers in Cuba to boot!" How JUDGE MASON dashed from the Palace, wildly tearing his hair, PIATT used to relate with picturesque details. I do not know whether his story had much, little, or even *any* foundation in fact. *Se non e vero, e ben trovato.*

CHAPTER V.

SOMETIME during the month of December, 1854, we received at the Legation an answer from GOVERNOR MARCY, then Secretary of State, to the famous Ostend dispatch upon the subject of the acquisition of Cuba, which was the result of a conference between Mr. BUCHANAN, Mr. MASON, and Mr. SOULÉ, and had been jointly signed by these three diplomatic representatives of the United States in Europe. This answer not only took issue with almost every proposition enunciated in the triune dispatch, but, more than this, it assailed arguments and conclusions which had not been advanced in it at all. Mr. MASON was at a loss to comprehend this apparent waste of logic, although I do not think that he was personally displeased with the issue of the business. For several days he and I did nothing but read over and talk about this document from GOVERNOR MARCY, and the peculiar animus which inspired it continued as incomprehensible to us at last as it had been at first.

The same mail that brought to Mr. MASON his copy of this dispatch brought two other copies to Mr. BUCHANAN, at London. Of these, one was intended for himself, and the other he was requested to forward to Mr. SOULÉ, at Madrid, by the hands of a confidential messenger—some person of approved trustworthiness and discretion. After keeping it about a fortnight, without finding any such person, he transmitted it to Mr. MASON, informing him of his inability, and begging him to find means to forward it to its destination. Mr. MASON thought that Mr. BUCHANAN did this in order to save the expense of a messenger to the contingent fund of his Legation. However that may be, when Mr. MASON received the document, he was at as great a loss as Mr. BUCHANAN had been to find a person who would undertake the task and to whom he felt justified in intrusting it. For several days Mr. MASON spoke to me about the matter, hovering around nearer and nearer, and at last he ventured to ask me, as a favor to himself and to the Government, to take charge of this dispatch. It was midwinter, and I knew what a journey to Madrid meant at that season of the year. I was reluctant to go, but could not make up my mind to refuse. So it was finally settled that I should leave Paris the next afternoon.

Before I started, Mr. MASON over and over again warned me against the fascinations of Mr. SOULÉ. He represented him to me as a perfect bird-charmer, and, while he desired me to be upon the most cordial terms with him, he was very much afraid that he would absorb me. Had he a recent experience of his own in mind? I can not say. I had never met Mr. SOULÉ, but I went to the encounter forewarned and forearmed.

So far as Bayonne, the journey was a very easy one, being even then performed almost entirely by rail. There was only a short interruption toward its southern extremity, where you were compelled to take the diligence for a few hours. I was so unfortunate as to reach Bayonne the very day after one of the English "Queen's Messengers" had started for Madrid alone in his own carriage. Had I been in time, I am certain that he would have extended to me the courtesy of a seat. As it was, I had to take the Spanish mail—a miserable, dilapidated, rickety vehicle, with accommodations for only two passengers. My chance companion was a young Mexican. We were some seventy-six hours on the road, and esteemed ourselves fortunate that we reached our destination at last without serious accident. We were not robbed, nor even attacked, although we met at Vittoria the passengers of a diligence who had had a serious encounter with highwaymen. It is true that we upset twice, both times at night; but as neither of us suffered any thing worse than slight contusions, we felt that, considering the condition of the road, we had every reason to be thankful. The cold was intense, and we had the full benefit of it, as there was not a window in our crazy conveyance that could be securely closed. I had a good provision of shawls and wraps, which proved, however, so insufficient that one evening, while we stopped at a post-house to change horses, I ran into a small *posada* attached to it, and purchased the blankets from one of the beds.

We arrived at Madrid early in the morning, and I immediately proceeded to the Fonda de la Viscaina, in the Calle Mayor, near the Puerta del Sol. After what the French call a *copious* breakfast, at about nine o'clock I started for Mr. Soulé's house, which was situated at no great distance from my hotel. He was living entirely alone, and in great seclusion. His wife and son were somewhere in the French Pyrenees, and he had quarreled with his Secretary of Legation, Mr. Perry, and removed all the government archives to his own residence. I was at once admitted to his presence, and handed to him my letter of introduction with the dispatch. The former was most cordial. I should have mentioned that before I left Paris, Mr. MASON had stipulated that I should not be detained in Madrid more than two or three days, and this stipulation was incorporated in his letter presenting me to Mr. SOULÉ. After the first compliments, as the dispatch was very voluminous, Mr. SOULÉ observed to me that I had undoubtedly read it, and therefore could acquaint him with its contents. I proceeded to do so, when he turned upon me almost fiercely, saying that I *must* be mistaken, that Mr. MARCY never *could* have given utterance to such views. I quietly assured him that I was *not* mistaken, that I had read the dispatch several times, and that Mr. MASON himself had been very much surprised by it. Finally he told me that he was so overwhelmed by the news that he found it necessary to be alone; at the same time placing his carriage at my disposal, and inviting me to return to dinner at six o'clock. Upon parting from him, I went over to the Foreign Office to call upon my friend the VIZCONDE DEL PONTON, whom I had known in Washington several years before. The remainder of the morning I spent in the Royal Picture-gallery, which I have always thought, every thing considered, the most magnificent in the world —not forgetting Paris, Dresden, Florence, or Rome.

After dressing for dinner, I returned to Mr. SOULÉ at a little before six. I found him just where I had left him in the morning. "If you will believe me, Mr. FIELD," he said, "I have done nothing whatever since we parted but walk up and down this room, and read that dispatch over and over again. I could almost repeat it verbatim. My amazement is without limit. I am stunned. Of one thing only I am certain, and that is, that it is the irresponsible work of Mr. MARCY. The President can neither have inspired nor sanctioned it. You *must* dismiss from your mind all thought of leaving this place for some days. I require time to reflect and determine what course of action it is my duty to take under these most unexpected circumstances."

I dined with him that day, and almost every other day for three weeks thereafter. Our party usually consisted only of ourselves and of a poor priest, whom Mr. SOULÉ had saved from some political proscription by conferring upon him the title of Chaplain to the United States Legation. Notwithstanding the irksomeness of my detention, I can never sufficiently acknowledge the cordiality, kindness, and confidence with which I was treated by the accomplished Minister. It would be out of place here to enter into any discussion of his political principles or his diplomatic career. But I can not refrain from saying that a more delightful companion, or a more thorough-bred man of the world, it has never been my fortune to meet. The life he led at that time was a singularly quiet and domestic one; he seldom left his house unless called out by public business. His relations to the Court were, as they always had been, most friendly and intimate; and if he was not liked by the aristocracy and the press, at all events they respected his courage. During his absence from Spain the previous summer, the newspapers assailed him, day after day, with the bitterest abuse, and with the most violent threats in case he should ever dare show himself again in Madrid. As soon as he returned, they became as silent as the grave, and up to the time of his final departure he was never again annoyed by word or act.

One afternoon I drove with him over the Toledo bridge to the ground of his famous duel with M. TURGOT, the French Embassador, the particulars of which he explained to me upon the spot. A perfect reconciliation never took place between the combatants. It will be recollected that M. TURGOT was severely wounded in the thigh, and rendered a cripple for life. For a long time he was confined to his bed, and when I saw him in Madrid he walked painfully upon crutches. Many months after the duel Mr. SOULÉ had occasion to call upon the Minister of Foreign Affairs. He happened to be occupied at the moment, and Mr. SOULÉ was conducted to the ante-chamber to wait until he should be disengaged. There he found, in solitary possession, his old adversary, whom he had not met since they retired from the field of combat. No recognition took place between them, and the meeting could not fail to be awkward and embarrassing to both parties.

A very intelligent American gentleman, who had resided a number of years in Madrid, explained to me his theory of the origin of the difficulty, which struck me as very plausible. It was as follows: That very decided unpopularity had preceded Mr. SOULÉ to Spain in consequence of his supposed views in reference to the Island of Cuba; that he came there a Frenchman of humble birth, who had left his country at an early age on account of his extreme political opinions, to represent a republic of which he had become an adopted citizen. That he found there, as Embassador from imperial France, a nobleman of ancient lineage, whose family had for centuries been identified with the elder Bourbons, and who had himself but recently left the legitimist ranks. The result was what, perhaps, might have been naturally expected. From the moment that they came together, M. Turgot exhibited a prejudice which he sought neither to control nor to conceal. If Mr. Soulé had been an American, instead of a Frenchman, this prejudice would, probably, not have existed at all, or, if it had, it would have been very much less decided and acrimonious. As it was, it manifested itself in a continuous series of petty slights, each too insignificant to be formally noticed, but in the aggregate extremely galling. Nor did the annoyance stop here. Others took their cue from the Embassador of France, so that the American Minister's position soon became a very uncomfortable one. Mr. Soulé was not the man to brook this sort of thing long. And when he fought M. Turgot, his object was probably as much to right himself generally with society, and earn its respect and fear, if not its love, as to resent the particular insult which brought about the issue. I do not assert the above to be positively true, but it is the surmise of a close observer of the circumstances at the time.

While I was in Madrid there was a Constituent Cortes in session, called into existence by the revolution of the previous June. I had a seat in the diplomatic box, and frequently attended its meetings. I have seen much of both houses of the British Parliament, of the French Chambers, of the Hungarian Diet, and of other deliberative assemblies at home and abroad; but never have I seen elsewhere such an assemblage of dignified, eloquent, and intellectual-looking men as composed that Cortes. Integrity and patriotism seemed stamped upon every countenance. And yet, if what I heard of them was true, such a body of political prostitutes and unprincipled knaves never before sat together in one room.

Every evening hosts of the deputies were visitors at Mr. Soulé's house. They would begin to arrive singly soon after dinner, and would keep on coming until one or two o'clock in the morning. Long after the lights were extinguished in the lower hall, gentlemen, muffled up in their cloaks so as to defy recognition, would ring at the *porte-cochère* of the American Minister. I was never formally introduced to any of these persons, but the next morning Mr. Soulé would inform me that I had met such and such a distinguished member of the Cortes the evening before. They represented all the parties and all the factions, and exactly for what purpose they came there I never could comprehend. Since the *Black Warrior* business, all chances for the acquisition of Cuba by our Government seemed to be at an end. Up to the time of that unfortunate occurrence, Mr. Soulé was very confident that he would succeed in his efforts to negotiate the purchase of the island. If he had only had five hundred thousand dollars secret service money, he felt sure that he could accomplish it. The Cortes, being a constituent body, could do more radical things than an ordinary parliamentary one. He would under no consideration attempt to corrupt the members—certainly not. But he would lend them money upon their own application, and thus as effectually secure their favor for the measure he desired to promote. Such diplomacy, I am happy to be able to say, our Government never resorted to in its better days; and it is to be hoped that it never will do so in these more degenerate times. I believe that Mr. Soulé applied for, or at all events suggested, such a subsidy, but the application or suggestion was not for a moment entertained at Washington. Mr. Soulé was convinced that he had brought the EX-QUEEN CHRISTINA entirely over to his views; but I doubt, after all, whether that very astute lady was not rather the mystifier than the mystified. He told me that he used to spend whole evenings in familiar *tête-à-tête* with her, talking over the Cuban question. His line of agument, he said, was as follows: That Spain was in urgent need of a system of railways, and of other public improvements, in order to develop her resources. That her credit was at so low a point that it was impossible for her to borrow even sufficient money to make a commencement. That the one hundred or one hundred and twenty millions of dollars which the United States were willing to give for Cuba would accomplish this. That in answer to the objection that Spain had a large mercantile marine dependent upon the commerce of her West Indian colonies, and which would be deprived of employment if these islands, especially Cuba, should slip from her hands, he would guarantee that it should be stipulated in the treaty of sale that Spanish and American bottoms engaged in that trade should be upon precisely the same footing for ten years after the treaty should go into operation. So that, from a *patriotic* point of view, he did not see how her Majesty could hesitate. So far as her own *personal interests* were concerned, the case was an equally strong one. She owned a very large property in Cuba. That property should be carefully secured to her by a secret clause in the treaty, and under American dominion it would be certain to increase tenfold in value. This argument *ad hominem*, or rather *ad feminam*, if she accepted the premises, was, I fancy, quite as likely to affect favorably the royal mind as that addressed to her regard for the public interests of her country. However, as I have said, the *Black Warrior* business deranged all Mr. Soulé's combinations. He felt terribly incensed against our Government for their conduct toward himself in that matter. The dispatch which Colonel Sumner had brought to him was very peremptory in its tone. In addressing himself to Mr. Luzuriaga, he adopted the precise language of Mr. Marcy to himself, only changing the formal commencement and ending. He threw down the gauntlet to Spain, as it were. The reply which he received was a snub in civil form—at all events, a refusal to comply with his demand. He entertained no doubt whatever that when news of that refusal should reach Washington, he would be ordered to demand his passports and leave Spain, and that war would follow. He considered it due to himself that, having literally obeyed instructions, he should be thus sustained. Instead of which, after a considerable interval of delay, Mr. Marcy quietly instructed him to re-open negotiations! To him this was an intolerable grievance, for his opportunity in every way had passed.

About ten days after my arrival at Madrid, Mr. Soulé had occasion to request an audience of Queen Isabella for the purpose of presenting an autographic letter from President Pierce, condoling with her upon the loss of I forget what relative. He was good enough to say that he desired me to accompany him upon the occasion. I objected that I had no uniform, which I presumed would be an insuperable difficulty in the way of my admission to the royal presence. But he told me that I had no occasion for concern on that account, as he would let me have one belonging to his son, which would do perfectly, as we were about the same size. A number of days passed, and no notice whatever was taken of the application for an audience. Mr. Soulé became daily more and more impatient and vexed, until he finally threatened to me that he would demand his passports for this personal insult, as he conceived it to be. I had a good deal of difficulty to quiet him, and induce him to refrain from any hasty and ill-considered action; for his mind and temper were for many reasons in a very morbid condition at that time. At last, when I called at his house one morning, he informed me that he had just been notified by the Minister of Foreign Affairs that the Queen would receive him at seven o'clock that evening, and that an earlier appointment had not been made because her Majesty had been indisposed. He promised to immediately look up his son's uniform, and to send it over to my hotel by five o'clock, and he desired me to meet him again, prepared to go to the Palace, at half-past six sharp. At five o'clock, instead of receiving the uniform, I got a letter from him, to the effect that he could not find it, that his son must have taken it away with him, and that I must come to him in an ordinary evening suit, being careful, however, to wear black gloves, as the Court was in mourning, and that he would answer for the rest. I had nothing to do but to comply, which I did with many misgivings.

Mr. Soulé had an engagement to dine that evening with Lord Howden, the British Embassador. He wrote a note of excuse, stating that he had received the Queen's commands to present himself at the Palace. His Lordship replied that he would not excuse him, but should wait dinner until midnight, if he did not come sooner.

Punctually at a quarter before seven o'clock, Mr. Soulé and I entered his carriage to start for the Palace. He wore the Benjamin Franklin costume, which has been so often described, and which became him extremely well. It consisted of a black velvet coat, cut single-breasted, and with a standing collar elaborately embroidered with black silk, black velvet breeches, black silk stockings, shoes with black buckles, a black dress sword, and a black chapeau without plume—every thing as black as Erebus. He looked as Edgar of Ravenswood might have looked upon a state occasion; his black eyes, black locks, and pale complexion completing the fanciful resemblance.

The Palace at Madrid is situated at one extremity of the city, and directly over the Manzanares. It is a very elegant structure, but only one eighth of the size of the building originally projected. No finer apartment than the throne-room is to be found in any palace in Europe.

On arriving, we entered a large vestibule, paved with marble, and flush with the carriage-way in front. Here we found an extraordinarily numerous guard on duty. I never saw any thing like the number at any other similar place. As we passed them we uncovered, and they saluted us with a clang of their muskets which might have been heard to the distance of half a mile. Turning to the right, we commenced, hat in hand, the ascent of the noble marble staircase. When we reached the first landing, a body of halberdiers stationed there, in a uniform of the sixteenth century, rang their halberds upon the stone tiles with deafening emphasis. Bowing our acknowledgments, we proceeded to mount the return flight. At the head of it we found more halberdiers, who did precisely as their companions below had done. We then entered a door to the left, and found ourselves in a spacious ante-chamber filled with officials in uniform, but without side-arms; the inferiority of their grade being thus indicated. These persons bowed to us in the most deferential manner; but I could not avoid observing that my plain black coat was attracting attention, and I began to feel decidedly uncomfortable. Maintaining our dignity by rather haughty and condescending salutations, we moved on into another room, very like the previous one, except that it was crowded with officers of superior rank *with* side-arms. It was evident that matters were arranged upon the principle of a theatrical climax. Hence we emerged into the so-called "Embassadors' Waiting-room," which far excelled in size all the apartments through which we had reached it. It is here that the diplomatic body was summoned when a royal heir or heiress was expected to make its appearance. Tedious hours were sometimes spent there upon such occasions. As soon as the baby was born, it was brought in upon a silver dish and exhibited to the assembled ministers, who thereupon attested the birth with due formalities.

We moved up slowly to the farther extremity of the room, and stationed ourselves to the right of a closed door. Opposite us stood about a dozen of the highest grandees of Spain, headed by the diminutive Duke of Medina Celi, all in gorgeous array, blazing with stars and orders. They had just come from an audience with the Queen. After a moment's hesitation, the little nobleman above named crossed over with solemn deliberation, and, facing Mr. Soulé, bowed nearly to the ground with overpowering gravity. He then turned to me, and saluted me with less formality. All the others in turn went through the same performance. Presently there advanced toward us a brisk, fidgety personage with gray hair. He proved to be the "Introducer of Embassadors," or, as he would be elsewhere called, the chamberlain. Tapping a gold snuff-box, he opened the lid and offered a pinch to my chief, behind whom I was standing, at the distance of a step or two. "I am glad to see you well, Mr. Soulé," he commenced, presenting his hand. "Your audience is, I think, set down for seven o'clock, and I believe her Majesty is ready to receive you."

While he said this, his eyes kept wandering from Mr. Soulé to me, and he scanned me from head to foot.

After a moment's pause, he resumed: "But, Mr. Soulé, you assuredly do not expect this gentleman to accompany you?"

"I beg your pardon; I certainly do," answered Mr. Soulé. "This gentleman is Secretary of the United States Legation at Paris" (I was only so, as I have explained, *ad interim*). "He has come to me with very important dispatches, and for the present is attached to my Legation. There are very peculiar reasons why I am anxious that he should see her Majesty on this occasion."

"It is quite impossible, my dear sir—quite impossible. There are two insuperable objections. In the first place, no audience has been requested for him; and, in the next place, he is not in uniform. It is only the other day that the French Embassador wished to present a gentleman connected with the diplomacy of his country, who *was* in uniform, but for whom an audience had not been asked, and he was not allowed to do so."

"Nothing," answered Mr. Soulé, "would be farther from my wish than to violate the etiquette of her Majesty's Court upon a trifling pretext. This gentleman is not in uniform only because he left Paris in great haste, and brought none with him. As I have already said, I have special motives for wishing him to see the Queen, and, under the circumstances, I must request you to take her Majesty's *personal commands* upon the subject."

There was no answering this; so the unfortunate chamberlain bowed with a rueful countenance, and went to refer the matter to the tribunal of last resort.

As soon as the door closed upon him, Mr. Soulé took my arm, and we slowly paced up and down the room. "It is all right now," he whispered to me; "the Queen is the best-natured person in the world, and I am sure that she will not turn you away."

His prophecy proved correct, for presently the "Introducer of Embassadors" returned, and with a look in his face as if some dire misfortune had befallen the Spanish monarchy, said that her Majesty was ready to receive us both.

Thereupon he preceded us through a passage-way to the open door of a moderately sized drawing-room, upon the threshold of which he bowed profoundly, and then backed himself out of sight.

As we entered by this door, Isabella II. entered by another door from the diagonal corner. The movement seemed to be a simultaneous one. I was a little behind Mr. Soulé, to the right. The instant he perceived the Queen he bowed to the floor, and I followed his example, as he had instructed me to do in all things. At the same instant down came her Majesty in the way that school-girls call "making a cheese." One step with each foot, and the ceremony was repeated on both sides. And so on some six or seven times, until we met at a marble table in the centre of the room. Mr. SOULÉ, holding the President's letter in his hand, then commenced in a low tone a very fluent and elegant little speech in French, at the conclusion of which he laid the letter upon the table. While this was going on, the Queen stood with her right hand resting upon the table, and with a look which plainly indicated that she considered such business a bore. I had an ample opportunity to take mental notes of her appearance. If my impressions were not flattering, they were, at least, unprejudiced, and I must sacrifice gallantry to truth.

"The Innocent ISABEL," as she was styled in her youth, is considerably above the average stature of her sex, and of ample dimensions every way. Her forehead is low, and her nose and chin unmistakably Bourbon. She wore a black dress very *décolletée*, and the charms which it partly concealed were evidently of ponderous proportions. Upon her hands, which are very large, and which looked swollen, she wore lace mitts, not gloves, leaving the fingers bare. Her whole skin was red, and had the appearance of being affected by some cutaneous disorder, which I have understood is the case. I certainly did not fall in love with her Majesty at first sight. I have heard others declare her handsome; but there is nothing about which there is a greater difference of opinion than female beauty.

When Mr. SOULÉ had finished his address, she replied

at less length, in remarkably good French, but with a very decided Spanish accent. This done, she drew a little sigh and paused a moment, and then abruptly asked, in a much louder voice, and with a total change of manner:

"Well, Mr. SOULÉ, and how is MADAME SOULÉ?"

"She was very well, your Majesty, when I last heard from her. She is in the French Pyrenees."

"I thought she could not be in Madrid, for I have missed her for some time. When you next write to her, remember me to her. Ah! Mr. SOULÉ, neither I nor my mother will ever forget your kindness during those horrible days of June."

I can not say that the Queen's eyes were here suffused with tears, but her countenance exhibited much emotion. Her manner during the above dialogue had been as familiar as that of any ordinary well-bred person. In her last remark she alluded to the revolution of the previous June, when CHRISTINA'S life was threatened, and when Mr. SOULÉ alone of the diplomatic body offered her the protection of his house and his flag.

Mr. SOULÉ then kindly turned toward me, and apologized to the Queen for having brought me with him in so unceremonious a manner, explaining that, as I might not improbably see the President before long, he wished that her Majesty might avail herself of the opportunity to send to him any verbal message she might desire. She smiled, and gave me a commission which it is unnecessary to repeat, but which was full of kind and friendly expressions of feeling. She then asked me how much longer I intended to remain in Madrid. I answered only a few days, as I had already overstayed my time. "Oh," she replied, "you must certainly stop for my ball next week. Do you know, Mr. SOULÉ, it will be my first really gala ball since I have been upon the throne?"

"I should be most happy to do so, your Majesty," I replied; "but, in the first place, I have no uniform."

"Oh, Mr. SOULÉ will manage that. Will you not, Mr. SOULÉ?"

"Certainly, your Majesty."

"But then there is another impediment," I went on to say. "I am in the public service, and my instructions are to return to Paris the moment my business here is accomplished."

"Now," she continued, with a smile, "if you were a subject of mine, I would *command* you to wait. But you Americans are an independent and self-willed race. Still I presume that, if you will not obey *my* orders, you will those of Mr. SOULÉ. Mr. SOULÉ, please *order* him to stay."

"I order you, sir, to obey her Majesty's commands."

I bowed, and said I would—but I didn't.

After this *badinage*, there followed a pause of sufficient length to indicate that the audience was at an end. Perceiving this, Mr. SOULÉ backed a step and bowed as he had done on entering. I ditto. Majesty ditto. And so we kept it up, facing each other all the time, until at last both parties disappeared at the same moment through their respective doors.

When we again found ourselves in the Embassadors' Waiting-room, there was the old chamberlain, who evidently belonged to that genus of fossils who believe that a breach of etiquette is sufficient to make the firmament fall. Advancing to me, he put his arm around my neck affectionately, and said:

"Do you know, sir, that an exception has this evening been made in your favor which I venture to say has never before been made in the history of the Spanish monarchy? I am confident that no person was ever before presented to a Spanish sovereign without being either in court-dress or in uniform!"

I assumed an air of offended dignity, as if piqued by the impediments which he had at first thrown in my way, and replied: "I acknowledge the value of the compliment, but I can appropriate no portion of it to myself. It all belongs to my Minister. I counted for nothing in her Majesty's condescension. She did not even know my name."

"Well," he answered, "it was a compliment to both." But I stuck to my original proposition, in which I was unquestionably right.

"We are going," he resumed, "to have a grand ball at the Palace next week, when the Court goes out of mourning. You must come."

"I am much obliged to you," I replied; "but I have already received an invitation from the highest source—from her Majesty herself. If any thing could induce me to remain for the *fête*, it would be her gracious request to me to do so."

Thereupon the old gentleman had nothing further to say, except that he hoped to see me there.

We shook hands with him and commenced our egress, which was accomplished in the same manner that our entrance had been. When we got outside the abode of royalty, Mr. Soulé went to his dinner-party, and I went home.

The most shocking and disgusting—I might almost say incredible—stories were told about the Queen at that time. All classes seemed to vie in speaking ill of her, and the foulest anecdotes about her private life were related to whomsoever would give a listening ear. Indeed, if you believed one half that you heard, all society in Madrid, emulating the example of the Court, was sunk to the lowest depths of social degradation. However that may have been, I saw nothing any where but perfect decorum.

CHAPTER VI.

MR. SOULÉ treated me with unlimited confidence. He threw open his dispatch books to me, and invited me to examine the written history of his mission. I availed myself liberally of his offer. One day I came across a dispatch written by him to the Secretary of State, bearing about the same date as that of the famous Ostend Manifesto. The first paragraph in it referred to that document, and this induced me to read it with care. What was my surprise to find it a sort of "Key to Uncle Tom's Cabin"—an elaboration and explanation of that manifesto! Every point made in the manifesto was cleverly and craftily denuded of all diplomatic reserve in the dispatch, and pushed to the most extreme conclusions; and positions were taken far in advance of any in the joint document. It seemed to say to Mr. MARCY—"We spoke ambiguously, because it would not have been prudent to speak more clearly; we *said* so and so, but we *meant* so and so." Here was the veil lifted from my eyes. I could now understand why Mr. MARCY had written as he had to the three Ministers. He had presumed, or he had affected to presume, that this personal dispatch had been addressed to him by the Minister to Spain after he had submitted it to his colleagues, who were acting with him in the same business. I asked Mr. SOULÉ no questions upon the subject, because I felt that it would be indelicate for me even to suggest the possibility that he had given a personal interpretation to the manifesto about which his associates were not informed. But the incident made a deep impression upon my mind.

While in Madrid I had frequent opportunities of seeing the Duke of Alva, brother-in-law to the Emperor Napoleon, whom I thought he very much resembled in person. I also saw the Duchess several times, at the opera and elsewhere. Although pleasing in appearance, she was not nearly so beautiful a woman as her sister, the Empress. The Opera-house at Madrid was at that time one of the most elegant and comfortable theatres in Europe. The house belonged to the Government, which gave the use of it, rent free, to a first-class, responsible company. It was here that I first heard Verdi's "Trovatore," before it had been produced at all in Paris.

I had been in Madrid more than two weeks, and was becoming very impatient at my prolonged detention, when one afternoon Mr. Soulé invited me to drive out with him. Up to this time I had daily had the exclusive use of his carriage, as he was not himself in the habit of going out. After some preliminary conversation upon other subjects, he told me that he had at last decided upon the course of action which was the best for him to take. That he was more and more convinced that Mr. Marcy was the person exclusively responsible for the change which had taken place in the policy of our Government regarding the Island of Cuba. That he felt sure that the President had not been a participant in the error, or that, if he had been, it would be easy to convince him of his mistake. He also felt terribly aggrieved by the Secretary of State, because he had not sustained him in the action which he took in the *Black Warrior* business, although it was that officer who had himself prescribed that action. Under these circumstances, he thought that, as Congress was then in session, his best plan was to return immediately to Washington, and manipulate that body in the interest of his own policy. There was but one difficulty in the way, and that was to determine to whom temporarily to turn over the Legation. That he had now seen me sufficiently to acquire confidence in my discretion, and he had the following proposition to make to me, viz., that I should accept the position of Chargé d'Affaires *ad interim;* that he would guarantee me the occupation of the office for one year, and that I should have nothing to do but to be entirely inactive, except in obeying instructions to the letter, attending to the routine business, keeping my ears open, and advising our Government fully as to every thing that should occur in Madrid directly or remotely affecting our interests. I immediately objected that, as there was a Secretary to the American Legation then in office, I did not see how he could place its control in other hands. He answered that he had considered that, and that he would be responsible that a satisfactory arrangement would be made as soon as he should reach home. But I had other objections, not necessary here to repeat, which rendered my acceptance impossible. I told him so very decidedly, and he seemed both disappointed and chagrined. "Well," he said, "there is then no alternative left to me but to resign." I felt distressed at appearing so ungrateful for all his kindness, and urged him as strongly as I could to reconsider this determination. But I failed to move him. His mind had evidently been made up to retire from his office in the event that he should be unable to make the arrangement which he had proposed to me.

This one matter settled, there was nothing to keep me longer in Madrid. Accordingly I had myself booked for the first vacant seat in the *Malle-Poste* for France, which was only to be obtained by applying several days ahead. During the interval I made repeated attempts to persuade Mr. Soulé to reconsider his resignation, but all without effect. The last day of my sojourn in Spain I dined with him, and, while availing myself of that opportunity to thank him for all his kindness and confidence, I asked him how much of what I had seen, heard, and read since I had been with him he desired me to consider personally confidential, and how much I was at liberty to communicate to Mr. Mason. He answered that he had no reserve whatever to impose upon me, so far as Mr. Mason was concerned; that I was quite at liberty to speak to him with the utmost freedom about all that I had learned. "However," he said, "rest assured, and do all that you can to keep Mr. Mason in the belief, that the question of the acquisition of Cuba is going to be the principal plank in the Democratic platform at the next national convention of the party. No one can secure the Presidential nomination at that time who shall not be thoroughly committed to that doctrine. If they adhere firmly to it, either Mr. Mason or Mr. Buchanan will probably be the nominee; and Mr. Mason is not the least likely of the two, because Mr. Buchanan has long occupied a position of party leadership which is sure to engender those animosities and jealousies which have so often proved fatal to the aspirations of our most distinguished men. I, being a foreigner by birth, am constitutionally ineligible, even were I, which I am not, so conceited as to believe that, under any circumstances, I might be selected. Besides, these gentlemen are equally responsible with me for the authorship of the Ostend dispatch, and, should they ever weaken in relation to the policy therein enunciated, the world would say that they had been *twisted around my finger;* and, certainly, two gentlemen of such distinguished talents would never permit this to be said of them in respect to so humble an individual as myself!" By the bye, I will here parenthetically remark that I have always understood that the Ostend Manifesto was originally written by Mr. SOULÉ, and that it was then revised by Mr. BUCHANAN; but that it still remained so extreme in its utterances that neither he nor Mr. MASON would have signed it had they not been cajoled into so doing by their astute and specious colleague.

Mr. SOULÉ then handed to me his resignation as United States Minister to Spain, addressed to the President, under cover to the Secretary of State, with instructions to have it forwarded from Paris to Liverpool, and placed on board a steamer there by a messenger, who should not be informed of the contents of the package with which he was charged. He also desired that the fact that he had resigned should be kept a close secret between Mr. MASON and myself. It was, in fact, so kept, and the first knowledge of it in Paris was obtained through the medium of American newspapers.

Mr. SOULÉ accompanied me to the post-carriage, and saw me off. He took leave of me with the same cordiality with which he had all the time treated me. He has been dead now several years, and I never saw him afterward.

My journey back to Bayonne was not so disagreeable

as that to Madrid had been. At least we met with no positive mishaps. My *compagnon de voyage* was a charming young Spanish Marquis, and his agreeable conversation went far to make me forget the discomforts of the road.

I got back to Paris very early in the morning, and at about nine o'clock went over to JUDGE MASON's house to breakfast with him. After breakfast we retired to his private office. I first told him about Mr. SOULÉ's resignation, and handed it to him, and, before proceeding further, he made arrangements to forward it to Liverpool. I then gave him an unreserved and circumstantial account of my visit to Spain. I spoke to him of the private dispatch which accompanied the Ostend Manifesto, assuming that he already knew all about it. But not only did its existence prove to have been unknown to him, but my communication threw him into a paroxysm of excitement and indignation. Nothing that I could say had the effect of quieting him. At first he insisted upon immediately sending to Mr. BUCHANAN a full account of it—that very afternoon. I urged him not to be so hasty, as, with the view which he took of the matter, he might seriously and unnecessarily compromise me with Mr. SOULÉ. With much effort, I succeeded in persuading him to wait a few days. That very evening he was stricken down by a paralytic stroke. A second stroke some years afterward proved fatal to him. I have always surmised that the excitement into which he was thrown by what I told him upon that occasion precipitated the first attack.

CHAPTER VII.

I FOUND upon my return that DONN PIATT the Secretary, was back from America, and my official relations to the Legation were thus terminated. I also found awaiting me an unsolicited commission from his Excellency HORATIO SEYMOUR, Governor of New York, appointing me Commissioner from that state to the Paris Universal Exposition of 1855. There was already in Paris a number of Commissioners from other states of the Union, and the time had arrived to commence the preliminary arrangements. Both the French Government and the Imperial Commission refused to hold official communication with these numerous American Commissioners, and the only course open to us was to organize as a body and appoint officers to represent us. In this manner I became President of the Board of United States Commissioners, and, as their representative, was brought into relations with many distinguished people. I forget how many Commissioners we had in all. Certainly there were as many Commissioners as exhibitors, all of whom received their appointments from the Executives of their respective states, the Federal Government doing nothing in the premises. We had no money at our disposal except our individual means. I was compelled to expend a great deal of money out of my own pocket, for which I never received a return. My labors were very great, and sometimes of the most perplexing character. The greater number of my colleagues had come to Paris for "a good time," and supposed that a passport as Commissioner would aid them in having it; but very few of them had any notion of doing any work. Many of the exhibitors sent us their articles from home, leaving it entirely to us to take care of them, and make all the preparations for their exhibition. The exhibitors who came themselves, or who were represented by agents, gave us a world of trouble in various ways. Some sent articles totally unfit to be shown even in a local country fair. Others, in their unseemly scramble for desirable space, worried and harassed us almost beyond endurance. I remember one of them, who called upon me in regard to an enormous stuffed American eagle which he had lost somewhere that morning in the Exhibition building. He had wandered into it, speaking nothing but English, and with the eagle in his arms, in quest of the temporary office of the American Commissioners. He did not happen to light upon any one to whom he could make himself understood, and, after beating about from point to point, he finally brought up in the Prussian office, where he deposited his eagle without explanations. When he returned for it, he got lost, and could not find the place where he had left it. In his distress he came to me. It took us a long time to find that eagle, but we finally did recover the hapless bird.

The place assigned to us in the Palace of Industry, as it was called, was of large dimensions and most advantageously situated, facing, as it did, the main central entrance to the building. We had a large place upon the principal floor, and also another in the gallery directly over it. No matter how one might spread them out, we had not articles enough to fill all this. Before any arrangements were completed, SIR WILLIAM LOGAN and Mr. STERRY HUNT arrived in Paris with the complete and admirably selected collection of Canadian products. They found that Mr. COLE, the British Commissioner, had omitted to reserve any space for its exhibition, and all the room in the building had been already assigned to the several nationalities. Having no other resource, they applied to me, and I was happy to have it in my power to place at their disposal our space in the gallery, for which we really had no use. As the United States, of all the peoples, made the very worst show for what they *might* have done and *should* have done, so I think Canada made comparatively the best. The inhabitants of the provinces who desired to exhibit were requested to send their articles to Montreal, and then the Government purchased those which it considered worthy to be shown at the Great Exhibition. The Colonial Government was the exhibitor, but the individual inventors and producers received their measure of credit and profit.

The sewing-machine people gave us a fearful amount of trouble. They insisted upon having the most conspicuous places in the main building—and they constantly quarreled among themselves for the choice of these—instead of complying with the regulation of the Imperial Commission, which required *all* machinery to be exhibited in the *Annexe*, or supplemental building. There were only a few of them in existence at that time. What must it have been in Vienna this summer, now that there are myriads of them? Well, they urged and pressed us so that we were finally compelled to allow them to try the experiment, warning them, however, that they would be certain to be driven from their ground as soon as they began to operate. One afternoon, just before the Exhibition was formally opened, the Yankee girls, brought over for the purpose, took their seats at their machines, which were placed upon an elevated platform, and the buzzing and whirring commenced. Just at that moment PRINCE NAPOLEON (JEROME), who was at the head of the Imperial Commission, happened to enter the building upon a tour of inspection. Hearing the sound, he at once searched for the cause. When he perceived it, he rushed toward the unfortunate sewing-machines, and with an expressive gesture shouted to his assistants, "*Balayez-moi tout cela!*" (Sweep all that away!) I did not feel that I could conscientiously protest against this judgment, and so Singer and Grover & Baker and the rest of them were compelled to retire to the machinery hall.

Our people took a great many prizes at the Exhibition in proportion to the number of exhibitors. Perhaps the most creditable exhibition of all was that of GOODYEAR'S articles of vulcanized India rubber. These were comparative novelties then, and were manufactured by Mr. GOODYEAR in France under his patents there, although his inventions had been made and perfected, and originally patented, in this country. After he had gone to a good deal of expense in fitting up the compartment which we had assigned to him, the French Exhibition authorities insisted that he should exhibit with them. This he was unwilling to do, and he desired us to make an energetic appeal. We were as anxious as himself to prevent another nation from appropriating to itself the credit of these admirable inventions. But in vain did I ascend the hierarchy of authority. They were all inflexible. I pointed out to them that in their own list of printed questions which exhibitors were required to answer in writing was this: "Does the exhibitor present himself as *manufacturer* or as *inventor?*" leaving it to be inferred that he had the privilege of exhibiting in either capacity. No; they were determined to have Mr. GOODYEAR, and would not forego their claim to him. After much discussion, I determined to have recourse to PRINCE NAPOLEON himself, and, with this object in view, I addressed him a letter, asking him when it would suit his convenience to grant me an audience. A reply promptly came, making an early appointment at his residence at the Palais Royal, or, as it was then called, the Palais Impérial.

PRINCE NAPOLEON, as all the world knows, is the son of JEROME, the youngest brother of the first Emperor, by a daughter of the King of Würtemberg. A previous marriage of his father, contracted in extreme youth in this country, with Miss PATTERSON, of Baltimore, was annulled; and it has been decided, after litigation in France, that the rights of the issue of that marriage are limited to the use of the family name. The Prince has one sister, the beautiful PRINCESS MATHILDE, who separated from her husband, the Russian PRINCE DEMIDOFF, on account of his alleged cruelty. This allegation seems to have been well-founded, inasmuch as the EMPEROR NICHOLAS espoused her cause, and compelled him to pay to her a handsome annuity as long as he lived. PRINCE NAPOLEON—or, as he is familiarly called, *Plon-Plon*—is tall and portly, but round-shouldered, and somewhat awkward in his gait. His head is of the unmistakable BONAPARTE type, common to every member of the family I have ever seen, except the late Emperor, who did not possess the faintest trace of it. So marked is this type, that any one familiar with it could not fail to instantly recognize it whenever he accidentally met one of the blood in any part of the world. It is a curious fact that the beautiful antique bust in the Vatican, at Rome, of the EMPEROR AUGUSTUS when a youth, might perfectly serve for that of the EMPEROR NAPOLEON I. at the same age, and bears a strong likeness to all his family, with the single exception above mentioned.

The Prince was in his youth a good deal under the tutelage and guidance of his Imperial cousin, who treated him as a spoiled child, and whom he was as unlike as possible. Although a man of genius, and one of the foremost orators of Europe, he has always been looked upon as a sort of *enfant terrible;* and with good cause, if one half of the anecdotes related of his indiscretion and violence are true. It was rumored that terrible altercations frequently took place between himself and the wearer of the purple, to which he was heir-presumptive, until the birth of the Prince Imperial put his nose out of joint for the succession. The story goes that he once so far forgot himself, after an angry discussion with the Emperor, as to tell him that he was nothing but "a kite in an eagle's nest." This is said to have occurred previously to the Crimean War. It will be recollected that the Prince served in that war, but returned to France some time in the winter of 1854–5, before the surrender of Sebastopol. A few months later the Emperor made up his mind to assume command of the army in person, and went so far as to have his baggage forwarded to Constantinople. The Prince, who has a considerable taste for intrigue, was very anxious to remain in Paris during his cousin's contemplated absence; but this by no means accorded with the Imperial views. The Emperor is said to have told him that if he went himself he would insist upon his accompanying him, to which the Prince flatly refused his consent. Thereupon it is reported that the Emperor put an end to the conversation by telling him that he should take him with him, if he had to take him in irons. The contemplated expedition never took place, so there was no occasion to execute this threat.

Apropos of the Prince's Crimean campaign, his reputation for courage has never stood high with his countrymen, and many reports to his disadvantage were circulated during the war. I happened accidentally to see a letter from Sebastopol, addressed by an officer of high rank to a friend in Paris, and describing one of the engagements—which particular one I can not now remember. Among other things, he said: "Le Prince, à ma *grande surprise*, s'est conduit à merveille" (The Prince, to my *great surprise*, behaved admirably). Great weight was attached to this reluctant testimony by those who knew the writer.

The Prince at that time affected extremely radical political opinions, aspiring to the leadership of the French Democracy. These pretensions did not then receive much recognition; indeed, he was decidedly unpopular with the very class that he desired to conciliate. He could not show himself at one of the Parisian theatres without meeting with a very cold reception. The people seemed to have no confidence in his sincerity, and were indisposed to excuse certain acts of glaringly bad taste in his private life. The publicity with which he seemed to take pains to surround his relations with a distinguished tragic actress, long since dead, offended the popular sense of propriety. The French are very particular about external decencies, and this extends even to those among them who are very liberal about private morals. They think, with the Spartans, that detection, and not crime, should be visited with punishment. Particularly, they can not endure that persons in high station should parade their immoralities before the public. Now it was said that the Prince used to drive at all hours to the residence of the lady referred to in an Imperial carriage, with servants in the Imperial livery, and that the carriage would frequently be left standing at the door a very long time, to the great scandal of the neighborhood. They said that upon one occasion he was notified some time after he had entered the house, by a superior officer of police, that an indignant mob was collected outside, and that, unless the carriage was dismissed, he could not be responsible for the consequences. Many will undoubtedly recollect with what severity *Charivari* used to handle the alleged relations between the late Duke of Orleans, father of the Count of Paris, and the same lady many years ago.

To return to my interview with the Prince upon the subject of the exhibition of Mr. GOODYEAR's India rubber. I had to wait a long time in the ante-chamber, as he was closeted with somebody else when I entered. This ante-chamber was a plain room, ornamented, however, with two objects of art (there were no others) which attracted attention. These were marble busts of RACHEL, the one as Tragedy and the other as Comedy, placed on pedestals in diagonal corners of the room.

After a while I was admitted to his presence, and I had no difficulty whatever in persuading him that I was right in my controversy with his official inferiors. The necessary orders upon the subject were given by him the next day, and they were peremptory and final. This matter disposed of, we fell into a general conversation about a variety of subjects. All the time that it lasted the Prince was incessantly smoking cigarettes. Among other things, he asked me if I knew that when CHARLES X. escaped from France to England, after the revolution of 1830, he crossed the Channel in an American ship?

I told him that I never knew it, or, if I had known it, had forgotten it.

"Yes," he said, "she was called the *Charles Carroll*, and a remarkably fine vessel she was. The King was accompanied, among others, by a French Admiral and several naval officers, and he was standing surrounded by them on the quarter-deck shortly after they got under way. He had been silent for some minutes, when, looking up to the Admiral, he remarked, 'This is a magnificent ship.' 'She is, indeed, Sire,' was the reply. 'Have we any equal to her in our commercial marine?' asked the King. 'We have not,' answered the Admiral. Here the King was again silent, and for some time kept his eyes fixed upon the deck. After a while he drew a sigh, and said, 'Ah! that was the greatest mistake ever made in the history of the French monarchy!' 'To what do you refer, Sire?' inquired the Admiral. 'To the espousal by my brother, LOUIS XVI., of the cause of the American Colonies against Great Britain,' he answered. And that is my opinion, too," said the Prince, laughing, and slapping me playfully upon the leg.

He was quite right, in so far as the fate of the BOURBON family was concerned. They joined us in our struggle, not because they loved us, but because they hated England. The establishment of a republic upon this side of the Atlantic precipitated the revolution of 1789 in France, cost the reigning monarch his head, and has cost his successors their crown.

CHAPTER VIII.

DURING the months of May and June, 1855, PRINCE NAPOLEON had receptions at the Palais Impérial every Saturday evening. At these receptions were gathered together all the most distinguished people who happened to be in Paris. The number of invitations was very limited, there being never more than two hundred and fifty persons in the rooms at one time, so that there was no crowd. The apartments are very fine, much finer than those which were used for similar purposes at the Tuileries. The Prince, who was then a bachelor, did the honors, assisted by his sister. His father was only occasionally present. At my first visit, I was accompanied by the Mexican Secretary of Legation, Mr. ESCANDON. When we got to the first door, an usher on duty asked our names and titles, that he might announce us. My friend handed him his card. Not happening to have one with me, I wrote my name upon a piece of paper, and under it, in French, "President of the Board of United States Commissioners to the Universal Exposition." What was my dismay and mortification to hear called out, as I made my entrance, "The President of the United States!" Whether it was stupidity or malice, who could tell?—probably the former. Fortunately for me, the Prince was standing with only one or two persons in the outer apartment. He laughed meaningly as he gave me his hand, but made no allusion in words to my discomfiture.

There was a most extraordinary galaxy of celebrities present that evening. Among others, I may enumerate the ex-Queen Christina, of Spain, with her husband, the Duke of Rianzares, and her three beautiful daughters, the eldest of whom was the dashing Princess Czartoriski; Prince Lucien Bonaparte, from Rome; the late King of Portugal, and his brother, the Duke of Oporto, the present King, the latter not being more than fourteen or fifteen years of age.

The King was a slight, fair-haired, German-looking boy (his father was a Coburg), timid as a girl, and blushing whenever he was spoken to. He wore a pair of gloves immensely too large for his hands, which (his hands) he seemed to be in continual distress what to do with. He was almost swallowed up in the broad ribbon of a Grand Cross of the Legion of Honor of France, which etiquette required him to wear, the Emperor upon the same occasion wearing the broad ribbon of the Tower and Sword of Portugal. The Duke of Oporto was a rosy, plump, cool little fellow, incased in the oddest little dress-coat imaginable, the skirts of which were a mere apology for covering.

Besides the foregoing, there were the late Duke of Brunswick, with thickly painted face, wearing a black silk wig, a black silk dress-coat, of extraordinary cut and of his own manufacture—and of which no civilized tailor would have been guilty—and solitaire diamonds, of enormous size and value, for waistcoat buttons; the Duke of Holstein, and I know not how many others. It will be remembered that when the Duke of Brunswick was many years ago driven from his throne and his dukedom, he took the precaution to carry the crown-jewels with him, and for the rest of his days he was famous as the greatest collector of diamonds in Europe. He was said to know more about them than any person engaged in the trade. His numerous other eccentricities were well known to the people of London and of Paris, in which two capitals, at different times, he resided nearly half a century.

I had been for about an hour wandering from room to room, unintentionally overhearing at one time a very curious conversation between the PRINCESS MATHILDE and the DUKE OF BRUNSWICK at the *buffet*, when the Emperor and the Empress arrived. After making a tour of the apartments, her Majesty seated herself upon a sofa in the largest of them, with a lady of honor at each side of her. I never saw her look so charming as she did that evening. She was, as usual at that time, most becomingly dressed. I say at *that time*, because when she first arrived from Spain she indulged in the strong colors and decided contrasts which the ladies of that country, when not in faultless black, affect, and the French dressmakers had great difficulty in correcting this bad taste. When she first took her seat, as I have mentioned, I was standing, at some distance, directly opposite the sofa; and I found it so agreeable an occupation to look at her, and was so protected from the appearance of exceptional intrusiveness by having others near me similarly employed, that I did not move. I noticed that the Emperor was standing at her right, conversing with the Papal Nuncio, but, after observing the fact, I bestowed no further attention upon him or his movements. A few minutes had thus passed, when somebody, whose approach I had not seen, said good-evening to me in

French. I hastily turned, and to my amazement recognized the Emperor. I understood perfectly that he must have some particular reason for addressing me, one of the very least distinguished or conspicuous persons present. After a few commonplaces, he remarked that he had that afternoon walked through our department of the Exposition (this was just before it was opened to the public), that he had seen many things there which interested him, but that nothing had so much pleased him as Mr. GOODYEAR's vulcanized India rubber. That among Mr. GOODYEAR's articles, however, he had noticed something which had *intrigued* him then, and continued to *intrigue* him ever since. That he very much regretted that I was not present at the time of his visit. Here I interrupted him to say that I very much regretted it myself, and that, if he had sent me an intimation of his purpose, I would have been certain to attend. "Well," he answered, "in one corner I saw, stacked as one sees them in an artillery-yard, a pile of vulcanized India-rubber cannon-balls! There was nobody there to answer the inquiries which I desired to make. Perhaps you can explain the matter to me." I had not even seen the balls in question, and had to say so. "I can not imagine," resumed his Majesty, "how any preparation of India rubber can be used for *projectiles*. It has often occurred to me that, in combination with other materials, it might, from its quality of elasticity, be made useful for *defensive purposes*—for instance, in breastworks." I was compelled to admit that it was equally mysterious to me how Mr. GOODYEAR could have seriously thought of making cannon-balls of it. After so unsatisfactory an interview, the Emperor probably did not think that it would be civil to immediately leave me. So he asked me if I took much interest in military matters. I answered that I did not any more than civilians usually do. He then asked me if I had noticed the new cuirasses which he had just given the Imperial Guard. I told him that I had; but that I knew nothing of the difference between them and the old ones, except the appearance. "Well," he said, "I will tell you. They weigh so much less," stating a very long fraction, "and their power of resistance is so much greater," mentioning one that was equally long. He then went on to explain to me various matters of military detail, and finally asked me if I had heard the news of a French success in the Crimea which had that afternoon reached Paris. I replied that I had. "*Eh bien!*" he said, stroking his moustache and smiling; "*C'est encourageant, mais nous sommes encore assez loin de Sébastopol!*" (Well! it is encouraging; but we are still far enough off from Sebastopol!) With this observation, which would have affected the stock markets of Europe had it reached the Bourse, he bowed and withdrew.

I was at that time residing in the Champs Elysées, very near the Palace of Industry. The next morning I went over before breakfast for the purpose of obtaining information upon the subject which had so *intrigued* the Emperor. I went directly to Mr. GOODYEAR's compartment, and, sure enough, found the balls there, just as they had been described to me. It was too early for me to expect to see Mr. GOODYEAR himself, but there was a person in charge. I asked him what in the world he expected to do with India-rubber cannon-balls. "They are not cannon-balls," he answered; "they are footballs!" I am sorry to say that I never had the opportunity to set the Emperor right upon the subject.

Among my fellow-Commissioners to the Exposition was my good old friend HORACE GREELEY. It was at that time in Mr. GREELEY's career when he still affected very old white overcoats and equally old white hats. This peculiarity of summer attire caused him to attract more attention on the street in Paris than would have been attracted by a score of Japanese, Chinese, and South-Sea Islanders. Of this he appeared serenely unconscious. I remember one high-priced or gala day at the Exhibition, when all the fashion, elegance, and distinction of Paris were assembled there. While I was standing in our own part of the building, HORACE entered in his usual costume. Telling me that he wanted to show me something, and seizing me by the arm, he started off, with his peculiar plowman's lope, dragging me along through a space which the astonished visitors opened for us on either side. Wonder was expressed upon every face. All the way down the principal gallery we went, until we reached its farther extremity, a distance which I would be afraid to express in feet. What he desired to show me was well worth seeing. It was some specimens, in the Austrian department, of printing and book-binding, executed at the Imperial Press in Vienna, which excelled every thing else of the same character to be found in the Exposition.

A very droll circumstance happened in connection with this visit of Mr. GREELEY to Paris, which he has but partly described in his "Recollections of a Busy Life." I will only relate what occurred under my own personal observation.

I had issued invitations for a dinner to my fellow-Commissioners and other distinguished gentlemen from the United States, to take place at the *Trois Frères Provençaux* on Saturday evening, June the second, at six o'clock. I arranged with Mr. PIATT to come to the Legation at half-past five, when he was to drive me down to the restaurant. My own residence was in the immediate neighborhood of the Legation, and Mr. PIATT occupied an apartment in the same building with it. At a little before the appointed time I started from home to keep the engagement. As I turned into the street upon which the Legation building was situated, I saw an ordinary *fiacre*, or street-cab, drawn up before the door, and PIATT standing, in his shirt-sleeves, talking to its occupants. They were three in all, two of them upon the back seat and one upon the front seat. As I approached nearer, I recognized one of those upon the back seat as HORACE GREELEY, who was to dine with me that day. The other two were very ordinary-looking Frenchmen. All were talking and gesticulating violently, and as Mr. GREELEY spoke no French, and Mr. PIATT very little indeed, and the two Frenchmen no English, the whole was a Babel of unintelligible jargon. The moment that Mr. GREELEY saw me coming, his countenance, which had hitherto worn an expression of the deepest distress, was illumined by a ray of hopeful satisfaction. When I got near enough to hear him, he explained to me that he had been arrested at the instance of a French sculptor, who had sent a statue for exhibition to the World's Fair at New York, of which Mr. GREELEY was one of the managers, because this statue, which he valued at fifteen thousand francs, or three thousand dollars, had been returned to him in a mutilated condition. He claimed that the managers had guaranteed the safety of all the articles exhibited, and that therefore Mr. Greeley was responsible to him for his loss. Hence he had commenced a civil action for damages against him, and had obtained an order for his arrest. That he was taken before the judge who had granted the order, and that the magistrate had consented that the *huissiers*, or bailiffs, who had him in charge should accompany him to the American Legation, and had ordered that, if the officers thereof would agree to become responsible for the amount, in case judgment should go against Mr. Greeley, he was to be forthwith released. I translated this statement to the bailiffs, who admitted its correctness in all respects except as to the conditions for the release. They said that the judge's instructions to them were not to let Mr. Greeley go unless some gentleman of the Legation would consent to make a *deposit in money* of the sum at issue. When I told this to Mr. Greeley, he emphatically denied its accuracy, and made an effort to elbow himself out of the cab, in order to enforce his explanations to me more at his ease. Seeing this, the bailiffs supposed that he was endeavoring to take sanctuary within the Legation, where, by international law, it would be impossible to arrest him. So they shoved him back with some show of force, and, getting out themselves upon the sidewalk, tied their tricolored scarfs around their waists. At this proceeding Mr. Piatt laughed sarcastically, which threw them into a terrible passion. They desired to be informed if he intended "to ridicule the colors of France." Piatt's hilarity continued, and it was all that I could do to bring matters back to the basis of quiet discussion. In the mean time, Mr. GREELEY, paralyzed by the efforts which he had made, was sitting back in the cab with the most woe-begone look of martyrdom upon his face that can be imagined. Finally, finding that the officers were inexorable in carrying out the judge's order, as they understood it, I offered to draw my check for the amount involved. This proposition they discussed for a moment between themselves, and then declined it as unacceptable, upon the not unreasonable ground that, as it was long after bank hours, it would be impossible for them to ascertain that night whether the check was good or not. There, therefore, remained nothing farther to be done. When I communicated to Mr. GREELEY the failure of all my efforts to save him from Clichy, the apathy of despair overcame him, and he exclaimed, in that piping treble which we all remember, "Take me to jail! take me to jail!" As he was about to be driven off, we assured him that every thing possible would be done to effect his liberation upon the morrow. The bailiffs re-entered the cab, and it drove away.

By this time it was nearly half-past six, and Mr. PIATT was not yet dressed. The first thing done was to dispatch a messenger to Mrs. GREELEY, at their residence somewhere outside the Arc de l'Etoile. Then Mr. PIATT made a hasty toilet, and we started for the *Trois Frères*. A roomful of angry gentlemen was awaiting me, indignant that the host was not only not present to receive them upon their arrival, but had actually kept them waiting three quarters of an hour after the time appointed for dinner. This necessitated a public explanation from me of the cause of my delay, which I made upon the spot. In this way the most prominent Americans then in Paris were informed that their expected fellow-guest and distinguished countryman, HORACE GREELEY, was to spend that night behind the bars of the debtors' prison of the Rue de Clichy.

With this single drawback, the dinner passed off, I believe, to the entire satisfaction of all present. Among the *convives* were Mr. O'SULLIVAN, Minister to Portugal; Mr. BELMONT, Minister to Holland; GENERAL THOMAS, Assistant Secretary of State; CHARLES ASTOR BRISTED, ESQ.; several United States Consuls; and all my fellow-Commissioners—whose name was legion. The Hon. A. C. DODGE, the newly appointed Minister to Spain, left for the Peninsula that morning, and thus deprived me of the expected pleasure of his company. Mr. MASON was too ill to attend, but he sent me a very feeling and complimentary letter of apology. The authorities so little understood American gentlemen that they had expressed some anxiety, which had reached my ears, lest the opportunity should be availed of to ventilate revolutionary doctrines, and possibly insult the Imperial Government. The difference does not yet seem to be every where understood between the orderly and elevated republicanism of the United States and the pandemoniacal red republicanism of Continental Europe. Thank Heaven! they have nothing in common.

The next, Sunday, morning, without any unseemly hurry, I went to the Clichy Prison, at about ten o'clock. Upon presenting my card, I had no great difficulty in gaining admittance into the warden's room, and thence I was gradually forwarded to the interior of the prison, after a series of innumerable checks and receipts. The prisoners were allowed to receive their friends on Sunday, but it was almost as difficult to get into the place as to get out of it. It seemed that during all the previous hour there had been a constant stream of visitors for Horace Greeley, and the prison authorities were bewildered to imagine who their singular-looking but evidently distinguished new charge could be. Finally I penetrated to the large common room in which the prisoners and their friends were assembled. It presented altogether a singular scene. In one corner squatted a laboring man in his blouse, surrounded by his wife and children, who had brought him some delicacies for his Sunday dinner. In another corner lounged a fashionably dressed young gentleman, evidently of the genus *fast*, in earnest conversation with a still more fashionably dressed young woman, as evidently of the genus *faster*. The room was filled with the most strangely contrasted groups. Standing in the middle of it, wearing his old white overcoat, and with his hat on the back of his head, his countenance wreathed in smiles, flanked on either side by a United States Minister, stood Horace Greeley. To refrain from laughing was impossible. "Mr. Greeley," I said, "you irresistibly remind me of Parson Adams in jail!" His lassitude and alarm were all gone, and he was in the very highest spirits. "Field," he replied to me, "this has been one of the most fortunate incidents in my life. Without it, I doubt if I ever should have had the opportunity to see *good society*. You know that I know nothing about it at home. I have never associated with the people who compose it there. I dare say they are very good people, but they are not *my* people. Now we have two classes of inmates here—aristocrats and plebeians. Scarcely had I arrived last evening, when I was waited upon by a delegation of the aristocrats, and invited to join their mess. Of course, I accepted. *We* breakfast at ten and pay three francs, and dine at half-past six for four francs. *The plebeians* breakfast and dine earlier, and at much lower prices. Last evening at dinner we had a prince at the head of the table, and I was flanked on one side by a count and on the other side by a baron. If I only remain here long enough, I shall not only learn the French language, but good manners into the bargain." And so he ran on, his auditors hardly knowing whether they were laughing with him or at him. All our efforts to get him out that day were, however, fruitless. We sent for lawyers in every direction, but all the lawyers were amusing themselves, and none of them could be found at home. On Monday Mr. GREELEY was restored to liberty.

When Mr. PIATT used to tell the story, *more suo*, he related that as soon as Mrs. GREELEY heard what had happened, she immediately proceeded to pack Mr. GREELEY's luggage, which consisted of a fine-tooth comb and a night-shirt, and then incontinently rushed to the prison. That the moment she was introduced to the presence of her husband, she frantically threw up her hands and exclaimed, "Why, father!" to which he responded, with a like gesture, "Why, mother!" I fear that this was an apocryphal joke of PIATT's.

At the trial of his case, Mr. GREELEY came off victor.

CHAPTER IX.

THERE was a very odd fish in Paris during the summer of 1855. He came from somewhere on our western frontier, and crossed from New York to Havre in the *North Star*. He dressed in a complete suit of furs, and during the voyage slept on deck every night. He appeared to be a very intelligent man, and had plenty of money, but was very eccentric, and even disgusting, in his habits. He stopped at Meurice's Hotel, in Paris, and soon became the wonder of the crowds of cockneys who frequented that house. Standing in the centre of the court-yard, and describing around him a magic circle of tobacco-juice, he would tell the most marvelous stories, with a look which plainly said, "You had better not express any doubts, if you do not want a bowie-knife between your ribs." A highly cultivated friend of mine, who had made his acquaintance, was once guilty of the imprudence of inviting him to walk. After a time they arrived at the Cathedral of Notre Dame, which they entered. As soon as they had done so, the frontier's-man began to look about, as if anxiously searching for something. Presently he espied a marble font, or receptacle for holy water. His face at once lit up, and, advancing to within six feet of it, he with the most accurate aim discharged a stream of tobacco-juice directly into it. A sacristan, who happened to be passing, came up, full of exasperation at the sacrilege. It was difficult to persuade him that the stranger thought the font was intended for a spittoon.

The American students—*humanes* they called themselves—in the Latin quarter were a queer set. Among them were two young medical men from Louisiana, who had come over to enter the Russian service, but had never got farther than Paris. One of them carried a card, which he seriously presented to every Frenchman to whom he was introduced, on which was engraved for a crest a device of two alligators fighting with their tails, and beneath that the name *Le Baron d'Attakapas.* The crest of the other was a stalk of sugar-cane, and he sported the name of *Le Comte de Plaquemine.*

I met in the street one day an acquaintance from New York, and not a very young man either, who was making his first visit abroad. He was delighted to see me, for I spoke French and he did not; and I was supposed to know all the ropes, whereas he had just arrived. The first business to be attended to, as is usually the case with traveling Americans, was a visit to the tailor. This was dispatched. Then came the bootmaker's turn. This was likewise attended to. Then some pocket-handkerchiefs were required, which it was desired should be very elegant. So I took my friend to DOUCET's, on the Rue de la Paix. When we entered the shop, it so happened that neither M. DOUCET nor any of his assistants were in; they had retired temporarily somewhere into a back room. Lying on a counter were some beautiful specimens of cambric, each elaborately embroidered in one corner with a coronet and initials. They at once attracted my friend's attention and admiration. He asked me what the coronet meant. I explained to him that it indicated that the owner was a nobleman. This he doubted; he fancied that the coronet might be only an unmeaning ornament. He had a great mind to have some handkerchiefs similarly embroidered. I begged him not to think of doing any thing so ridiculous, and just then M. DOUCET, who spoke English, re-entered the shop. "Whose handkerchiefs are these, M. DOUCET?" I asked. "They belong to Prince P——, a Russian," was the reply. I supposed that this explanation would silence my companion, and so for a time it did. At length a happy thought seemed to strike him, and he abruptly asked the tradesman if he could not embroider an *American Eagle* upon some handkerchiefs for him! DOUCET could hardly keep his countenance. He replied, with as much gravity as he could command, that it might undoubtedly be done, but that he was not acquainted with the peculiarities of our national bird. Thereupon my friend triumphantly drew a silver dollar from his pocket, and threw it upon the counter! The handkerchiefs were selected, and the order was booked, and, I presume, executed; but I made no inquiry, and registered a mental vow that from that day forward I would never again allow myself to be persuaded to accompany an American upon a shopping expedition.

And yet I once unintentionally broke my vow. I had turned from the Boulevard des Italiens into the Rue de Richelieu one day, when I was overtaken by an American Envoy Extraordinary, who had just reached Paris on his way to his residence. He was a man of gigantic stature, who had been a Senator from one of the Western States. On his right shoulder he carried a horrible baby, about a year old, clad in an abominable pink flannel dress! Of course, the distinguished diplomatist spoke no French, or he never would have been appointed to represent the Stars and Stripes any where upon the Continent of Europe. He was in quest of a trunk, and he forthwith pressed me into the service of aiding him to effect the purchase of one. The attention which that unhappy baby—which made itself heard as well as seen—attracted to us was enough to drive a civilized being mad. The father, however, accepted it with the utmost serenity.

I have been unsuccessfully trying to recall the name of the Italian shoemaker who fired at the Emperor on the Champs Elysées some time in the spring or early summer of the year 1855. He was an emissary from London, but died, if I recollect aright, without disclosing the names of his confederates. He had provided himself with two pistols—one a revolver, and the other an ordinary double-barreled pistol. He fired two shots from the side of the road at his Majesty, who was on horseback and quite near him, but neither of them took effect. I happened to be in a carriage with some friends at a distance of only a few hundred yards in the rear, near enough to see the puffs of smoke. I then noticed the immediate gathering of a group of people, and observed a man being dragged into a cab. We were on our way to the Bois de Boulogne, and, anxious to ascertain what had happened, we ordered our coachman to drive on rapidly. When we reached the Barrière de l'Etoile, we stopped a moment, and, in answer to our inquiries, were informed that the Emperor had been fired at, that he had escaped any injury, and that he had pushed on for the Bois, escorted by his aids, Ney and Fleury, on horseback. We were also told that the Empress and her ladies, in two Court carriages, had preceded him some ten minutes, and could as yet know nothing of the occurrence. With the hope of overtaking him before he reached the Bois, we put our horses to the top of their speed. But he must have ridden very rapidly, for we saw nothing of him until we came to the lake, when we observed the mounted party, followed by the carriages, coming toward us on their return. We at once reined up on the side of the drive, and, standing uncovered, awaited their approach. The Bois was very crowded that afternoon, but the news of the occurrence had evidently not yet reached there. As Napoleon passed us, we saluted him, and in so significant a manner that he could not doubt that we knew of the attempted assassination. He bowed in return, and I shall never forget his look. His teeth were closely set, and his face was literally of the color of old parchment. That this indicated *fear*, I do not for a moment believe. The man did not know what fear is. It only exhibited the strong emotion under which he was laboring. When the Empress came up, she was smiling and chatting with the lady on her left, and was evidently entirely ignorant of the fact that her husband's life had just been in imminent peril. As soon as the *cortége* passed, we wheeled into line and tried to keep up with it. But we could not do so—our horses were not equal to the task; and when the Imperial party reached the Triumphal Arch, we were already a long way behind. By this time the news had spread through Paris like wild-fire, and the Avenue of the Champs Elysées was one dense mass of human beings. Every where as the Emperor appeared he was vociferously cheered, and he had not proceeded far before the pressure became so great that he was compelled to dismount from his horse and walk the rest of the way to the Tuileries.

Among the many talents which the Emperor possessed, he was said to be unsurpassed as a judge of horses. As a rider, I never saw his equal, unless it was the late King of Holland. Insignificant on foot, he was superb on horseback. From the length of his body, he looked like a tall man when mounted, and he and his steed composed a perfect centaur. To see him thundering along at a review with the *cent gardes* at his heels was a magnificent spectacle.

It was not very often that he was seen in a carriage. Occasionally he got himself up in gorgeous attire and accompanied the Empress for a drive. And sometimes of a morning you met him driving with his own hands a pair of spanking bays up the Avenue of the Champs Elysées, accompanied by a single groom. But he went mostly on horseback. He commonly wore, when riding for pleasure, an old blue frock-coat, the seams of which were white from wear, and he indulged in a pair of old linen or cotton gloves distressing to behold.

His tact was great, and he sometimes did things very gracefully. When the Russian war was over, he determined to make GENERAL BOSQUET a Marshal. Accordingly he invited him to a grand dinner at the Tuileries. After the cloth was removed, the Emperor requested all present to fill their glasses for a toast. He then proposed the health of *Marshal* BOSQUET, who was taken entirely by surprise.

While the works for the completion of the Louvre were going on, the Emperor used often to stroll there, cigar in mouth, to watch their progress. Upon one occasion he had not been there long when he noticed a group of stone-cutters talking together earnestly. Presently one of them, cap in hand, advanced toward him in a hesitating and abashed sort of way. "My Emperor," said the man, "I have made a bet of five francs with one of my companions that you will permit me to light my pipe from your cigar." "You have lost, my friend," answered his Majesty, laughing; "but here is the money to pay your bet and treat your friends besides," at the same time placing two golden Napoleons into his hand. He thus managed to preserve both his dignity and his popularity.

When QUEEN VICTORIA was in Paris, the Emperor was particularly attentive to the Prince of Wales, then a boy. This made the Queen very uneasy. She was afraid that her son might be badly influenced—that he might be induced to smoke cigars, or do something still more horrid. It is related that one day, after both families had been lunching at the Palace of the Elysée Bourbon, the Emperor suddenly disappeared with the Prince, whereat the maternal anxiety and distress were most acute. It turned out that they had gone by themselves for a two hours' drive.

I am sure that he was never fond of this country. I have some reasons for so thinking which I do not consider myself at liberty to mention. But he was very civil to our countrymen in Paris, and sometimes very patient with them.

I know a Spanish gentleman of rank who was once sent to the States upon a special mission. He had been a friend of the Empress in Madrid, long before she aspired to a crown. On his return from America he stopped in Paris. Immediately after arriving, he addressed a note to her Majesty, requesting the honor of an interview. He received a prompt reply, in which she said that she regretted that, in consequence of the absence of her husband at Boulogne, she could not see any one; but that he would be back in a fortnight, when she would be most happy to receive my friend. Accordingly, after the delay indicated, an invitation came to him to *take tea* at Saint Cloud. He went, and spent the evening *en petit comité* with their two Majesties. The Emperor did not talk much. He was reading the newspapers, or more likely pretending to read them, nearly all the time. The Empress was very particular in her questions about this country. Were the women so handsome as she was induced to believe by the beauty of some whom she had seen in Paris? Was there so much luxury in the great cities as she had been told? Was New York so fine a town as she had heard? I am justified in believing that my friend gave a pretty favorable account of every thing. Finally, her Majesty asked him, all things considered, which he preferred, Paris or New York? "Paris, of course," he replied. Hereupon the Emperor withdrew his head from behind his paper, and, with a grim and ironical smile, exclaimed, "*Quel mauvais gout!*" (What a bad taste!)

I had the honor of knowing M. Guizot at this time. After translating into French for publication the President's Annual Message to Congress, and also some of the accompanying documents, I was requested to do into English an address which M. Guizot delivered before the Academy of Moral and Political Sciences upon the intellectual activity of the United States. This circumstance brought me into personal contact with that eminent statesman. His character and the tone of his mind are rather English than French, and so, indeed, is his appearance; but when he speaks, although remarkably sober in gesticulation for a Frenchman, he could not possibly be mistaken for any thing else. He is a Protestant, as is well known, and, after the downfall of Louis Philippe, under whom he was Prime Minister, he was offered the professorship of modern history in the University of Oxford, which he declined. I spent many hours in his library at his modest residence. He was an old man then, and must be an octogenarian now.

I also saw much of that strange character, M. ALEXANDRE VATTEMARRE. Originally a physician, and finding that he could not support himself in that profession, he turned "*prestidigitateur*," or magician, and, under an assumed name, being very skillful, became famous all over Europe. Having accumulated a moderate fortune, he retired to private life, and devoted the remainder of his days to promoting literary exchanges between the different countries of the world. In this last pursuit he was enthusiastic and indefatigable, and deserved great credit for his self-sacrificing industry. At his house I met the elder DUMAS, who was his friend, and several other literary celebrities. I exchanged cards with M. DE TOCQUEVILLE, the distinguished political writer, but had not the good fortune to meet him.

EX-PRESIDENT VAN BUREN was also in Paris at the time of the Exposition, and I had the pleasure of being a great deal in his company. He was quite as courtly, and almost as active, as when he was President of the

United States some fifteen years earlier. I have a number of letters which he addressed to me in May, 1855, written in that slanting manner across the paper which is so familiar to those who corresponded with him during the last years of his life. His favorite son, MARTIN, on account of whose health Mr. VAN BUREN came abroad, died in Paris, and the remarks of the ABBÉ COCQUEREL at the grave were as eloquent as any to which I ever listened. All Mr. VAN BUREN's sons except one have now passed away. JOHN and ABRAHAM and MARTIN are dead; SMITH, the youngest, alone survives.

The engineer officers commissioned by the United States Government to examine and report upon the military operations in the Crimea were also in Paris at about this time. They were MAJOR DELAFIELD, MAJOR MORDECAI, and CAPTAIN (since GENERAL) GEORGE B. McCLELLAN. I had the pleasure of meeting them several times. I particularly recall one occasion when they were all in uniform, with those extraordinary regulation caps to which I have referred upon their heads. They were just getting into a cab, and their appearance attracted a crowd of *gamins* to the spot. These caps were the only peculiar thing they had about them, and must have been the principal cause of the gathering. They did not receive those facilities for visiting the French camp in the Crimea which they had the right to expect. Indeed, I understood that they were treated with scant courtesy by all the belligerents except the Russians.

I was one day walking up the Avenue of the Champs Elysées when I met Mr. THACKERAY, the author, whom I had last seen in America. He joined me, and we had proceeded some distance when he recognized a young gentleman on the other side of the street. The stranger, a tall and uncommonly handsome person, immediately crossed over to meet him, and I stepped aside. I overheard THACKERAY ask him what had brought him to Paris. He answered that he had come for pleasure. "And have you found it?" drawled THACKERAY, with a slight sneer in his voice, as if pleasure, as a pursuit, was an unworthy object for any man's ambition. When they parted, and THACKERAY again took my arm, he said to me, "Of course you know the young man with whom I was just speaking?" I answered that I did not. "You don't mean to tell me," he continued, "that you, who have been so much in London, don't know him?" I assured him that I had no recollection that I had ever before met the gentleman. "Why," he said, "that is the MARQUIS OF FARINTOSH." "And *who* is the MARQUIS OF FARINTOSH?" I pursued. "Why, the MARQUIS OF BATH, of course," he replied. This led to a conversation about several other characters in his books. He told me that his own mother was the prototype of HELEN PENDENNIS, but that the copy fell very far short of the original. He also told me who had sat for the portrait of HARRY FOKER, but all the town knows about that.

I then remarked to him that he must have been intimately acquainted with many French families of the best class; that his French characters were more accurately and delicately drawn than those of any other English writer whom I had ever read—and to this opinion I still adhere. He assured me that, on the contrary, he had never in his life been intimate in a single French family. This is very surprising, for he has exhibited in his books the most profound knowledge of the nature of the French, as well as of their manners, and he has dissected the former and depicted the latter with the most wonderful skill, and without any false deductions or tendency to caricature.

A few days afterward I called upon him at his lodgings in company with my old college classmate, DONALD G. MITCHELL, better known to the literary world as *Ik Marvel*. Upon receiving our cards, Mr. THACKERAY invited us to come in, but we found him in one of those moods of surly incivility in which I have seen him a number of times. He was probably busy writing, although, if my recollection is correct, we saw no evidence of it; and, after remaining a very few minutes, we beat a retreat. I regretted very much that Mr. MITCHELL, who had never before seen him, was so unfortunate as to drop upon him when he was in this unamiable state of temper.

The reader will long since have observed with what little plan or system I wander from subject to subject, like an old woman and some old men. And yet, perhaps, if he be one of those who like to let conversation flow in its natural bent, and who dislike the use of stilts in books as much as on dry land, he will find no great fault with my discursiveness.

To return to the Exposition. The heads of the various Commissions organized themselves into a body for purposes of mutual conference and protection, and we used to meet every Thursday evening at the residence of BARON JAMES DE ROTHSCHILD, the Austrian Commissioner, and who was also Austrian Consul-General. The Baron was a portly Hebrew gentleman, with light hair and complexion, and a tendency to redness about the eyes. He was very abrupt and brusque in his manners, as was natural for a financier who held the purse-strings of monarchs, and he made himself extremely disliked by some of his associates. Upon one occasion he kept us waiting for him more than an hour after the appointed time, without any explanation whatever, and it was all that a few of us could do to prevent the Commissioners from leaving the house in a body. When he did join us finally, he merely casually mentioned that he had friends to dinner, but without taking the pains even to couch the statement in the form of an apology. At these meetings the Commissioners received the refreshment of a cup of tea. The Baron spoke a number of times with me of several persons in New York, but his object was apparently rather to learn about their financial standing than the social consideration in which they were held.

The old BARON SALOMON DE ROTHSCHILD died in Paris during the summer of 1855. The following is a translation of the invitation to the funeral which I received, and which can not fail to be curious to my American readers:

SIR,—The BARON and the BARONESS ANSELME DE ROTHSCHILD, the BARON and the BARONESS JAMES DE ROTHSCHILD, the BARON and the BARONESS NATHANIEL DE ROTHSCHILD and their children, the BARON and the BARONESS ADOLPHE DE ROTHSCHILD, the BARON and the BARONESS WILLY DE ROTHSCHILD and their children, the BARONS ALPHONSE, GUSTAVE, SALOMON, and EDMOND DE ROTHSCHILD, the Misses LOUISE and ALICE DE ROTHSCHILD, and the BARONS NATHANIEL, FERDINAND, and SALOMON DE ROTHSCHILD, the BARON AMSCHEL DE ROTHSCHILD, Madame WORMS, Madame SICHEL, Madame MONTEFIORE, Madame BEYFUS, the BARON and the BARONESS LIONEL DE ROTHSCHILD and their children, the BARON and the BARONESS ANTHONY DE ROTHSCHILD and their children, the BARON and the BARONESS MAYER DE ROTHSCHILD and their children, the BARON and the BARONESS MAYER-CHARLES DE ROTHSCHILD and their children, Mr. and Madame ADOLPHE BEYFUS, Mr. and Madame S. SICHEL and Mr. J. SICHEL,

Have the honor to inform you of the irreparable loss they have experienced by the decease of the BARON SALOMON DE ROTHSCHILD, who died at his hotel, No. 17 Rue Lafitte, the 27th of July, 1855, at the age of eighty-two years, their well-beloved father, father-in-law, grandfather, great grandfather, brother, and uncle;

And invite you to attend the funeral on Tuesday, the 31st of July, at nine o'clock.

The funeral will take place from the residence of the deceased.

Before the Exposition came to a close, I was called away from Paris by private business. The United States made but an indifferent show at this great World's Fair. Still a comparatively large number of medals and diplomas was awarded to our exhibitors. Among ourselves matters worked harmoniously, and nothing scandalous was ever charged upon our unpaid Commission. If our services received no particular acknowledgment at home, they were amply recognized upon the spot. Our fellow-citizens in France exhibited their appreciation of them in every way open to them, and the Emperor awarded to some of us the Cross of the Legion of Honor. Before the year expired, the permanent position of Secretary of the United States Legation in France was tendered to me by PRESIDENT PIERCE; but the office had lost many of its charms for me, and I respectfully declined the offer.

CHAPTER X.

TOWARD the close of the year 1855 I again went abroad, and took up my temporary residence in England. I became very fond of England, as I think there is reason that every intelligent American should. Very few of our people, however, are accustomed to stop there any considerable time, in their hurry on their arrival to reach the Continent, and on their return to get home. Paris is the American man's, and especially the American woman's, paradise. But, after all, for a *home*, I prefer England to France, and London to Paris. English society is a cold and repulsive mystery to us at first. Our gregarious habits, like those of the French, render it natural for us to make and to desire to make chance acquaintances. This you can not do to any great extent in England, although you may do it with the English when they are traveling in other lands. You may reside in England many years, and *know* nobody. But if you have a proper introduction to one person, it carries with it the acquaintance of all belonging to the circle in which he moves. The English, so cold and reserved with strangers, are the kindest and most cordial people in the world with their friends. According to my experience, an American is always especially favored by them. They hardly look upon him as a foreigner. I have frequently heard this form of phrase, "Oh! there were two or three Americans and half a dozen foreigners." And friendship in England means a vast deal more than it does in some other parts of the world. Many of their social usages are the reverse of ours, and have a better foundation in common-sense. For instance: here Brown and Jones are walking upon the street; they meet Robinson, who is a friend of Brown, but not acquainted with Jones; forthwith Brown introduces the two strangers to each other, and they affectionately shake hands; after a brief conversation, they part without shaking hands; and the probability is that Jones and Robinson will never meet again, or, if they do, will forget that they had ever met before. In England, however, no introduction ever takes place casually. If made, it is with a purpose, and with the assumption of responsibility as to its suitableness in all respects. When persons previously unacquainted are introduced, they do *not* shake hands. But they do on parting, and whenever they again meet and separate. Giving the hand is looked upon as a pledge of friendship, not as a mere expression of civil recognition. Almost every thing is deeper, stronger, and heartier in England than with us. All is surrounded there by a thick rind, hard to penetrate, but when you have once got within it, you come upon a rich, fruity core. Shams and superficialities are not so abundant there as elsewhere, notwithstanding the satirizing of themselves by their native Juvenals.

I remained in England upon this occasion until some time in the month of July, 1857. I had not been there very long, when I received a call one day from a mulatto sculptor from New Orleans, who had exhibited some very creditable and promising works at the recent Paris Exposition. By some chance the Duchess of Suther-

LAND had been attracted to his studio in Paris before the opening of the Exposition, and it was indirectly through her agency that my attention had been originally called to him. I am not quite certain of his name, but think that it was WARBERG. The poor, foolish fellow, having exhausted his means, had come over to London to find his Duchess, hoping that she would relieve his wants and give him the advantage of her protection. Upon going to Sutherland House, he was informed that the Duchess was then in Scotland, and would not return to town for several weeks. He also learned that Mrs. HARRIET BEECHER STOWE was with her Grace. In his disappointment he looked me up, having, I believe, not a single other acquaintance in the great city. To make matters worse for him, he had brought with him a charming little quadroon wife, of whose existence I had hitherto known nothing. They were residing in a wretchedly squalid place on the Surrey side, and were in imminent danger of starvation. I did the little that I could to relieve their immediate wants, and gave him an order for a bust. I had not the honor of Mrs. STOWE's acquaintance, nor have I ever since met the lady. But I took the liberty of immediately writing her a full account of my *protégé*, knowing that it would be laid under the Duchess's eye. At that time I had some doubts about Mrs. STOWE's sincerity in the cause of the negroes. I was not sure that she was any thing more than a writer of sensational fiction. An answer soon came, to the effect that the Duchess and herself would be in London in a few days, when the matter should have attention. When these ladies did return, they associated with themselves in their benevolent purpose LADY BYRON, and, for aught I know to the contrary, some others. Shortly thereafter they took a nice suite of apartments for WARBERG, as I shall call him, and his wife, in the artists' quarter, on one of the streets leading into Bedford Square, paid the rent in advance, and furnished them with every comfort. After a further interval of time, WARBERG informed me that the same ladies had arranged to send him to Italy, that he might have the opportunity of pursuing his studies in the studio of a famous sculptor. Never since that time have I doubted Mrs. STOWE's sincerity in the great work of African emancipation.

It was not my fortune to personally meet LADY BYRON; but in the eyes of many people her eccentricities and restlessness were evidences of a deranged mind. It was said that she let her house (on Park Lane, I believe), furnished, for a year or longer, and almost immediately tried to rescind the bargain and re-enter into possession. Failing in this, she hired another furnished house, of which she became tired in the course of a month or so. She managed to get rid of this one, and then took another. And so on to the end of the chapter. Some people who knew her, did not hesitate to call her downright mad. Under these circumstances, it is not unreasonable to believe that the horrible revelations which she made to Mrs. STOWE, in relation to the cause of the separation between herself and her poet-husband, were but the hallucinations of a diseased brain.

It was at about this time that I received an invitation to breakfast with Mr. MACAULAY, who was not yet elevated to the Peerage, at his chambers in the Albany. I found him a bluff, downright sort of person, not at all like my preconceived ideal of the author of the essay on MILTON. I am not quite sure whether he was or was not at that time in the Ministry. Our breakfast was *tête-à-tête*, and my host did all the talking. He had no "brilliant flashes of silence," as SYDNEY SMITH remarked of him upon another occasion. We were together about an hour and a half, and most of the conversation turned upon the institutions of this country, and their probable future fate. Mr. MACAULAY shocked me by prophesying with the utmost confidence that slavery was certain to break up our Government within ten years from that time, and that in the no very distant future two divided confederacies would, by their own weight, and from the operation of other causes, drop into half a dozen broken states, with military despotisms ruling over them. This was an extraordinary prediction to an American ear in the year 1856. At that time we none of us thought of the possibility of an impending crisis. Slavery brought us to a civil war, within even less than the limit of MACAULAY'S prophecy. He was mistaken in foreseeing a dissolution of the Union, as immediately involved in the struggle which that institution provoked. And it is to be hoped that he was equally in error in his vaticinations in respect to our ultimate fate. I tried to persuade him to reduce what he had said to writing, and permit it to be read before the New York Historical Society; but he declined, excusing himself on account of his overwhelming engagements.

He spoke to me of the Chartist demonstration in 1848, about which I have already written, and told me that the number of the disaffected collected on Kennington Common, which had been popularly supposed at the time not to fall short of thirty or forty thousand, did not, in fact, exceed seven thousand. He said that the Government had resorted to the photograph in order to accurately estimate the number. That knowing the area of the Common, and computing the number of people who could stand on it side by side, and possessing a picture showing to what extent the space was covered with human beings, and in what closeness of proximity they stood, they were thus enabled to determine how many they were.

I used to see a good deal of Mr. THACKERAY. He was living at that time in his new house in Brompton, which he told me he had purchased, together with the furniture contained in it, from the proceeds of his lectures in America upon the Four Georges. When I found him at home he was sometimes engaged in dictating to his daughter, and my calls upon these occasions were necessarily brief. His health was not very good, and he often dictated lying upon the bed, while Miss THACKERAY sat upon a chair at its side, with a table before her upon which she wrote. I dined with him one day at the Reform Club. He was a great *gourmet*, although not a great eater, and that day he was suffering from a severe headache. After the soup and the fish had both been removed, he told me that the next dish would be one of his own invention. It proved to be a boiled pheasant, with a *soubise* sauce, and it was really delicious. Between us we could not eat more than half of the bird, and he sent what remained with his compliments to a friend who was dining on the other side of the room. Such a proceeding would look odd in one of our New York Clubs, but I presume that it could not be unusual there.

After dinner we withdrew, or rather ascended, to the smoking-room, where Mr. THACKERAY introduced me to several members of Parliament, and, excusing himself on account of his headache, retired, leaving me to be entertained by them. I have always found it a severe ordeal to be left to the tender mercies of a member of Parliament. They are so well informed about this country, so familiar with the *Federalist* and other writings of the Fathers, and so thoroughly versed in our more recent history, that it is not very easy to hold up one's own end of the rope in a conversation with them turning upon these subjects. And these are the subjects upon which they naturally desire to hear an American talk.

I was one day walking with Mr. THACKERAY, when something was said by me about Mr. DICKENS. Thereupon THACKERAY, in the most naive manner in the world, remarked to me that it was very strange, but nevertheless a fact, that DICKENS's publishers sold five copies of any one of his books for one copy which *his* booksellers sold of any of his. It did not appear to me so very singular, but I did not say so. The one appealed to only the cultivated class, the other to all classes. The one was a great humorist and moral anatomist, and the other a great humanitarian. I then referred to the rumor, at that time in general circulation, that DICKENS was in pecuniary embarrassments by reason of his extravagant living, and was contemplating a flight from England to avoid his creditors. THACKERAY with great warmth denied this story as a gross calumny. He said that he was acquainted with DICKENS's affairs, and that, so far from exceeding his means, he had always lived within them. He complained very much of the annoyances of notoriety. He said that he could not walk a foot in London without being recognized, and that he found this a great penalty for literary fame.

I once saw the famous dramatic author, Tom Taylor, at the theatre, while I was in England at this time. He wore his hair long, and combed behind his ears, and was much changed in appearance since I saw him at Trinity College, Cambridge, in the year 1843. He was then studying for holy orders, and was private tutor to one of my particular friends. I remember that he gave me a delightful breakfast there, and that, notwithstanding the gravity of his contemplated profession, he was one of the most amusing and jocular personages that I fell in with. Sheridan Knowles exchanged play-writing for the pulpit, and Tom Taylor discarded clerical robes for the pen of the dramatist.

One of the most delightful houses which I visited in London was that of Mr. S. C. Hall and his accomplished wife, who both held high positions in the world of letters as well as socially. Mrs. Hall had the faculty of bringing together in her drawing-rooms people the most distinguished in all the walks of life. I met there one evening Professor Owen, Jenny Lind, Lover, Hawthorne, Miss Poole, and I don't know whom besides. Professor Owen looked like one of his own pre-Adamite fossils reanimated. I had not seen Jenny Lind since we parted in America, after her extraordinary musical tour through this country. She looked thin and wan, very unlike the vigorous Swedish peasant-like woman whom I had so well known. As I entered the room, she crossed it to meet me, and we seated ourselves upon a sofa, and had a long chat about old times upon this side of the Atlantic. LOVER sat down to the piano and *warbled*, as TOM MOORE is said to have done, rather than sang, "The Low-backed Car," and others of his own compositions. I had heard him many years before in the old Burton theatre on Chambers Street, in New York, but the drawing-room, rather than the stage, was evidently the proper place for him. HAWTHORNE'S superb head was by all odds the finest in the room. He looked genial, and, *mirabile dictu!* appeared at his ease. To me, who had not seen him since he lived at Lenox, in Massachusetts, this transformation appeared marvelous. I sat down by his side, and he talked brilliantly for half an hour, without exhibiting any of the shyness which for years had made him a perfect recluse. It was said that he was still unapproachable in his Consulate at Liverpool, but he appeared completely humanized at Mrs. HALL'S. Miss POOLE sang still more charmingly than she used to do in New York, I fear to say how many years ago, when she was the delight of Metropolitan audiences.

I was a very frequent attendant at the meetings of the two Houses of Parliament, and had many opportunities of listening to some of the most eminent statesmen and orators of Great Britain. Among them there were very few who were eloquent, as eloquence is understood in this country. There were many good, sensible, downright talkers—men with no nonsense about them. Indeed, there are very few persons to whom eloquence would be permitted in the British forum. Bosh and humbug have become the national aversion, and if a man has any thing to say, they wish him to say it in the simplest manner; and, if he has nothing to say, they do not want to hear him at all. The truth is that both the Commons and the Lords meet for business, and not for buncombe. I heard a great many more good speakers in the Lords than in the Commons. This seems natural enough when we remember that nearly all the Lords have had a preliminary training, and sometimes a long one, in the Commons before being called to the Upper House.

The only man in either House to whom I listened, who possessed the unmistakable gift of eloquence, as we in America understand it, was the late EARL OF DERBY. He was fluent, forcible, and imaginative; and his invective and sarcasm were very powerful. He had a strong tendency toward liberalism in his youth, and his father sent him to this country to cure him of it—a remedy which in his case proved effectual, for he *hardened* in his politics as he advanced in life. I recollect one occasion when the BISHOP OF OXFORD, afterward BISHOP OF WINCHESTER—the same who was killed last August by a fall from his horse—one of the most fluent and forcible speakers in the Whig ranks, had been addressing the House at considerable length upon some question which I do not at present recall. He was followed by the little DUKE OF ARGYLL, one of the Whig leaders, who has an amazing gift of language, in a bitter harangue of half an hour's length, every word of which was directed at LORD DERBY personally. When the Duke sat down, the Earl arose, and, advancing to the woolsack, made a powerful speech in reply to that of the Bishop, without noticing the Duke, as if he was an adversary unworthy of his attention.

Among the other speakers in the House of Lords who

pleased me most were the dyspeptic and bitter LORD GREY and the MARQUIS OF CLANRICARDE among the Whigs, and the bluff EARL OF HARDWICKE among the Tories. LORD CLANRICARDE, who married the daughter of PRIME MINISTER CANNING, was said to be the most ill-favored man in the United Kingdom. He was at one time Embassador to Russia, and at another Postmaster-General. Notwithstanding his lack of good looks, he was the most noted man in Great Britain for his gallantries, always excepting the EARL OF CARDIGAN. I heard the young EARL OF CARNARVON, of whom great things were expected, make his maiden speech, and although at its close LORD DERBY complimented him, as in duty bound (he is a Tory), it appeared to me both in manner and in matter an effort that would have been unworthy of an American school-boy of fifteen. In the Commons I heard very little agreeable speaking, hardly any from the leaders. Mr. DISRAELI has much of the English stammer and stutter, and his tones are deep and monotonous. EARL RUSSELL, who, as LORD JOHN, was then in the Commons, is tedious to a degree that is almost unendurable. Mr. GLADSTONE is impressive, but his sentences are so involved that it is painful to follow him. LORD PALMERSTON was fearful with his hesitations and his mumblings, and his ohs and his ahs. There was nothing remarkable in his speeches except his skill as a tactician. I never knew him to meet an argument squarely, and endeavor to answer it. His usual manœuvre was to attempt to turn his enemy's flank, raise a side issue, and, if possible, get up a laugh at his expense. There was something about him, however, which always carried the House with him. He was prodigiously magnetic. He always appeared to me the incarnation of John-Bull-ism; and it was from this fact, I believe, that he acquired much of his popularity. He was the average Englishman, as Abraham Lincoln was the average American. He was that sort of a man that, if he happened to be shaving in his bedroom in his shirt-sleeves, and heard a row in the street below, would be very likely to drop his razor, and with lathered face rush down stairs to take a part in the *mêlée.* He generally sat on the front ministerial bench, with his colleagues on either side of him, and his hat drawn down over his eyes. Occasionally he would jump up suddenly, and go off into the wine-room for a glass of sherry, or into the lobby for a chat; but while he sat in the House, he never moved or spoke until he arose to close the debate. There was that in his character and in his appearance which made you recognize him as an *old boy* as long as he lived. At this time he was in deep mourning for Lord Cowper, Lady Palmerston's son by a former marriage.

English travelers have said a great deal about the indecorum of our Houses of Congress. At the time, *ante bellum*, when arguments were sometimes enforced by revolvers, and when violent epithets were occasionally launched in debate, there was a good deal of truth in their strictures. *Mais nous avons changé tout cela.* In the British Houses of Parliament the disorder and indecorum which prevail affect foreigners very disagreeably. The wearing of hats, the free and easy attitudes, sitting and lounging, indulged in by the members, and the unpleasant noises which sometimes prevail, the English are so accustomed to as to be unconscious of their singularity. I venture to say that to-day, unless there has been a great change in that regard on the other side of the water, the American Senate and House of Representatives are far more dignified and orderly bodies than the British Houses of Lords and Commons.

Of all the speakers to whom I remember to have listened in the House of Commons, Mr. WHITESIDE, the Tory barrister, pleased me most. He is an Irishman, and for an Irishman to secure an attentive audience in that forum, he must speak uncommonly well. Mr. WHITESIDE had a short time before written a book on Italy, which has not its equal in the English language—not even excepting Mr. HILLARD'S. I believe that he is now Lord Chief Justice of Ireland.

During a part of the time that I resided in England, the relations between that country and our own were very much disturbed by complications and embarrassments growing out of the Central American and enlistment difficulties, as they were called. The Government at Washington had proceeded to the extremity of dismissing Mr. CRAMPTON, the British Envoy, together with the Consuls at New York, Philadelphia, and Cincinnati. This action produced a very deep feeling in England. *The Times* thundered from day to day in ominous tones. Every body was talking about the possibility of war with America, not flippantly, I must own, but with deep feeling and sincere regret. Mr. APPLETON, of Maine, our Secretary of Legation in London, and afterward Minister to Russia, applied to *The Times* unsuccessfully for a hearing in its columns. What was refused to him was conceded to me. This was probably because he was an official and I only a private citizen. I wrote two long letters advocating the American side, which were printed, and upon each occasion *The Times* devoted its leader of the succeeding day to an answer. The immediate question just then was, should Mr. DALLAS be dismissed from London in retaliation for Mr. CRAMPTON's dismissal from Washington? Almost every body thought that he would be.

At this juncture I met one morning, in a Bayswater omnibus going to the city, the venerable GENERAL CAMPBELL, our Consul in London at that time. There were one or two other persons in the 'bus who were acquainted with the General, and conversation naturally turned upon the subject of the impending difficulties between the two countries. Finally one of the other gentlemen courteously asked the General how he thought a war would result, if it should unfortunately occur. The days of spread-eagleism were not yet over, and the General, who was an old war-horse, immediately answered, with more force than politeness, "Such a war, sir, which God forbid, would never cease until the American flag was waving over the Tower, at one end of London, and Buckingham Palace at the other!" The subject of conversation was immediately changed.

At last *The Globe*, the evening ministerial journal, announced that, at a Cabinet Council, it had been decided to tender his passports to Mr. DALLAS. Every body considered that announcement as official. As soon as I read it, I called upon my friend, ADMIRAL WALCOT, member for Christchurch, for an order to the House of Commons for that evening. There was already a great rush for seats, and the Admiral requested me to meet him at the House upon the opening of the session, when he would do the best in his power for me. I went early, but every seat in the gallery was already disposed of. The Admiral succeeded, however, in seating me in the compartment reserved for the Peers; but I was in danger of being compelled to vacate the position at any moment, if required by one who was legitimately entitled to it. For several hours, during the time when committee business is usually disposed of, there was a thin House. At length the members began to drop in by the dozen at a time, from their clubs and their dinners. Mr. McGregor, the member from Glasgow, whom I knew, and who afterward came to so sad a fate, had been dining altogether too freely. He was in a great state of excitement, and kept rushing from his seat to me to inform me of the rumors which were floating through the House, and which other members brought to his ear. Then ensued a very uninteresting debate upon some unimportant question, which I thought would never come to an end. At length it closed, and there was a division of the House, and all who were not members were compelled to leave for the nonce. It appeared to me a very long time before we were permitted to return. Soon after I had resumed my seat, however, Mr. Disraeli arose, amid profound silence, and begged to ask what decision, if any, her Majesty's Government had arrived at in respect to the retention or dismissal of the United States Minister. When he resumed his seat, Lord Palmerston got up, and in a low voice, and with a manner which seemed to me to indicate infinite disgust, said that, after due consideration, it had been decided to take no present action in the matter! Mr. Disraeli and his Tory adherents looked thunderstruck; they evidently had made up their minds that Mr. Dallas would be dismissed, and had prepared to avail themselves of what they thought would prove a political blunder. I rushed out of the House, took the first cab, and ordered the driver to Mr. DALLAS's residence, on Portland Place. I wanted to be the first to convey the important news to him. But I failed in this: a more expeditious countryman had got there before me.

I afterward heard, upon pretty good authority, that it *had* been decided, at a Cabinet meeting, to send Mr. DALLAS home, the only vote in the negative being that of Mr. VERNON SMITH. That, in the mean time, MADAME VAN DE WEYER, the wife of the Belgian Minister, and the daughter of Mr. BATES, and one of the Queen's favorite friends, had been to her Majesty upon the subject. That thereupon the Queen had sent for LORD PALMERSTON, and ordered a reversal of the decision. That the Government did not care to go to the country upon the question, and had therefore withheld their resignations. Whether this is true or not, we Americans hardly know what a good friend the Queen has always been to us. In more instances than one the weight of her prerogative has been thrown in our favor. Mr. CRAMPTON deserved his dismissal for his action in the enlistment business; but I hope that the occasion may never again arise which will require so harsh a proceeding on the part of the American Government toward a diplomatic representative of Great Britain.

PART II.

AT HOME.

PART II.

CHAPTER I.

THE first man, famous or infamous, in the annals of our country whom I recollect seeing is AARON BURR. I was a mere child, and he was already a withered old man, who used to walk up and down Broadway, with his eyes bent upon the ground, never raising them for recognition. He was at that time residing upon Staten Island, where he afterward died, equally barren in friends and fortune.

The late JUDGE AARON VANDERPOEL, of New York, described to me a party, or rather an orgy, that BURR had at his house, at Richmond Hill, on the night before his duel with ALEXANDER HAMILTON. BURR was up nearly or quite all night, and was among the gayest of the gay. This, "parva componere magnis," recalls the incident of the DUKE OF WELLINGTON's presence at the DUCHESS OF BRUNSWICK's ball in Brussels the night before the Battle of Waterloo. The venerable JAMES A. HAMILTON told me that his father lingered until some time in the afternoon of the day after that on which he was shot, and that he was the last person to whom the great Federalist spoke.

Another almost daily walker in the same street in those days was the noble-looking, half-civilized chief of the Seneca Indians, RED JACKET. He carried his head aloft, except when occasionally compelled to let it droop from an over-dose of the white man's fire-water. He derived his name from an elegantly embroidered jacket which was presented to him by a British officer during the Revolution, and he wore upon his breast a silver medal, the gift of GENERAL WASHINGTON.

The next of our distinguished public men of whom I have any remembrance is GENERAL JACKSON, then President of the United States, upon the occasion of his visit to New York in the year 1833. I was but a small boy at the time, and I remember standing upon the steps of the American Museum, where the *Herald* building is now, to see the procession on its passage up Broadway. The President was on horseback, and wore upon his head a white hat almost covered by an enormous "weeper," with pendant bands, such as mutes wear at funerals in England. This was for Mrs. JACKSON, then recently deceased. I had never before seen one of these strange emblems of mourning, which were peculiar to the South and Southwest of the country. As he was passing from Castle Garden to the Battery, the bridge which then connected them broke down, and, although he reached *terra firma* in safety, several of those who followed him were precipitated into the water. Many years afterward I saw PRESIDENT PIERCE, as he rode at the head of a procession to take part in the inaugural ceremonies of the New York World's Fair. There was a pouring rain, and he protected the Presidential head with an umbrella. I do not know which impressed me as most odd, GENERAL JACKSON's "weeper" or GENERAL PIERCE's umbrella.

I saw Mr. VAN BUREN in the summer of the year 1840 at the Executive Mansion. To me, at that time a student at Yale College, a President of the United States was an object of awe—an awe which I regret to say, on my own account, soon passed away with advancing years. I can see him in my mind's eye now, as I then saw him in the flesh, dressed in faultless black, with natty boots, sitting before a sea-coal fire, which he vigorously stirred during the pauses in the conversation.

On my return from that, my first, visit to Washington, I stopped in Baltimore. The Democratic National Convention was in session, and in vain I went from hotel to hotel in quest of lodgings. I finally brought up in a second-class hostelry called the "Fountain Inn," which may or may not still exist, and there I was so fortunate as to find a vacant billiard-table, upon which I was permitted to pass the night, but not to sleep. I was terribly "demoralized" the next day, and started for New York by the first train. I was strangely impressed by the roughness and coarseness of a majority of the delegates and others who attended that Convention.

It was years after this before chance threw me into contact with any of the persons who have played leading parts in our national history. Early in the month of August, of the year 1852, provided with a letter of introduction from CHARLES O'CONOR, I sought at Concord, New Hampshire, where he resided, FRANKLIN PIERCE, then recently nominated by the Democratic National Convention as their candidate for the Presidency at the ensuing election in November. Not finding GENERAL PIERCE at home, I followed him to Rye Beach, a watering-place upon the coast, where he was passing a few days with his only child, a boy of thirteen, who was delicate, and required the tonic of sea-bathing. After securing a room at the hotel, I inquired for the General, and was informed that he was not then within. Presently there came into the hotel office, where I was standing, a slender, smooth-faced man, apparently of middle age, very carelessly dressed, with rumpled linen and a shockingly bad white hat, who was pointed out to me as the person of whom I was in quest. I delivered to him my letter, and he received me with great cordiality, immediately inviting me to accompany him to his own room. I had a very long and delightful conversation with him. He was entirely unaffected, and a remarkably picturesque talker. He told me how surprised he was at his own nomination, and the circumstances under which he had received the news of it. He was stopping, with Mrs. PIERCE, at the Tremont House, in Boston, at the time of the opening of the session of the Convention. There was balloting after balloting, and it was not until just before the thirty-fifth that his name was at all mentioned, it then being introduced by the delegation from Virginia. It was not at first received in a manner to indicate the probability of its adoption. But the moment she heard that it had been brought forward, Mrs. PIERCE, who was an invalid, became very nervous and alarmed lest he should be finally selected. GENERAL PIERCE did not explain to me *why* she was apprehensive, but, in common with every body else, I understood it. She had persuaded him some years before to resign his seat in the United States Senate, where he was conspicuous for one unhappy personal habit. And she feared that if elected President he might again relapse into the same habit, a possibility the thought of which was unendurable to her sensitive mind. He went on to say that one afternoon, while the action of the Convention was still undecided, he ordered a carriage for a drive to Mount Auburn. As he was descending the steps of the hotel to enter the carriage, into which Mrs. PIERCE had preceded him, he purchased an extra edition of a newspaper which was just issued. Casting his eye over the head-lines, he saw that no choice of a candidate had yet been made, and a telegram predicted that all the chances were in favor of one of his competitors. Entering the carriage, he placed the newspaper in his wife's hand, and, pointing to this paragraph, told her to read it, and it would set her mind at ease. He then directed the coachman to drive on. About an hour after they had left the hotel, and while they were driving within the inclosure of the Cemetery, they were overtaken by a mounted messenger, who brought the news that the General had been nominated on the forty-ninth ballot. Mrs. PIERCE fainted upon the receipt of the intelligence, as if a disaster, instead of a triumph, had come to her husband.

He asked me if I knew NATHANIEL HAWTHORNE, the author, his class-mate at college, and life-long friend. Upon my answering in the negative, he gave me a whimsical account of the eccentricities of that great genius. He said that it was several years since they had met, when only two days before HAWTHORNE called upon him at the hotel where we then were. The General happened to be in his room at the time. HAWTHORNE, upon entering, wrung his hand, and then, without a word of salutation, abruptly threw himself upon a lounge at the other side of the room. Here he lay for several minutes, without speaking, and tangling himself into all sorts of contortions. At last, with an expression of sympathy and woe upon his countenance, he gazed upon the General's face, and exclaimed, "FRANK, I pity you! Indeed, I do, from the bottom of my heart!" In the moment of triumph, the object of his sympathy, probably, did not appreciate the regrets of either his wife or his friend. After more of this light talk, Mr. PIERCE finally entered upon the domain of politics. He was sure that he would be elected, and he gave me unequivocally to understand that to Mr. CHARLES O'CONOR he intended to offer the portfolio of Attorney-General in his Cabinet.

We had been together some two hours when I got up to take my leave. He asked me how long I intended to remain at the Beach, and I replied that it was my purpose to go by the early morning train to Boston. He told me that I must abandon that idea, that CALEB CUSHING was coming in his yacht from Newburyport the next day, that they were to have a chowder party, and that he would be pleased to have my company. I had really no occasion for haste, so I thanked him, and, without demurrer, accepted the invitation.

I met him at breakfast the next morning, and soon after breakfast accompanied him to the beach for his son's bath. I never saw more tender watchfulness exhibited by a parent. He dressed and undressed the child himself, and while the boy was in the water his attention was so engrossed by him that it was impossible to pursue any conversation. Alas! in less than a month from that time the poor lad was dashed to pieces upon the rocks by a railway accident, leaving his father's heart crushed and desolate.

It was not until eleven o'clock on that morning that Mr. CUSHING's "yacht," as he called it, or "fishing-sloop," as it might with more nautical propriety be designated, cast anchor off the beach. That gentleman came ashore, and after remaining a few minutes, during which I had the pleasure of being introduced to him, he re-embarked, accompanied by the future President and myself. No time was lost in getting under way, and we all began to catch fish for the chowder which was the pretext for our expedition. The mackerel were running in innumerable shoals, and we soon had a supply far in excess of our expected wants. An expert in a red-flannel shirt then commenced, with fish, salt pork, potatoes, and biscuits, the preparation of the savory dish, which was soon steaming under our watering mouths. I had never tasted chowder before, and have never tasted it since—at least, not the genuine, simon-pure article, served up to appease appetites sharpened by the sea-air. The meal disposed of, there was much private talk, doubtless upon matters of politics, between the General and our host, in which I was not invited to participate. We remained out all the afternoon, and the shades of evening were approaching when we again stood off Rye Beach. The wind had been freshening, and by this time there was such a surf rolling that the "yacht" could not approach very near the shore. She ran in as close as she could, and then a small boat was lowered to convey Mr. Pierce and myself to the beach, Mr. Cushing intending to sail home without landing. We got on well enough until we were near the shore, when a huge wave rolled in and upset our boat. The water was up to our necks, but we struggled along until we reached dry land. As we were shaking ourselves like water-dogs, I begged the General to remember, if he should ever become President, that there had been a time when he and I were "alone in the same boat."

I may as well go directly on and relate what afterward happened between this peculiar man and myself. He was always so amiable, so friendly in his manner, so *affectionate* even in his demonstrations, that I never could continue angry with him forty-eight consecutive hours, although the provocations which he gave me were frequent enough and gross enough to make me break with him forever. I presume that my own experience was similar to that of thousands of others. He was so absurdly false to his promises, that, where it did not cut too hard, it was positively ludicrous. And yet I never in my own mind accused him of insincerity. He was a weak, imaginative, almost brilliant, undetermined man, who said in the morning that he would do something, and when he said it meant it, but who changed his mind in the afternoon if the smallest obstacle interfered with his purpose. He was no more to be relied upon than Horace Skimpole or Micawber. He had no fixed will of his own, and all through his administration he was battledored and shuttlecocked about by JEFFERSON DAVIS and WILLIAM L. MARCY, the master minds of his very able Cabinet. Most of the state-papers which appeared under his signature were attributed to the pen of Mr. CUSHING, who became his Attorney-General instead of Mr. O'CONOR. He exhibited the same vacillation to all. Besides the instance just cited, he offered to GENERAL DIX, whom he had at one time intended to make Secretary of State, the mission to France, and then appointed Mr. MASON. As I believe, this arose not from duplicity, but from unsteadiness. But whatever theory in the premises be the correct one, he succeeded in alienating from himself the personal support of many of the very best members of his party.

I had the audacity at that time to aspire to the office of United States *Chargé d'Affaires* at the Court of Sardinia. From personal observation, I had satisfied myself that there was a great future in store for that little country. Besides, there was the opportunity to negotiate a treaty of commerce, which might largely extend our Mediterranean trade. So, armed with the very best vouchers and recommendations, I began my experience as an office-seeker by going to Washington on the second day of March, in the year 1853, two days before the inauguration of PRESIDENT PIERCE.

On the morning of the third, I called upon him in that drawing-room which forms the south-east corner of Willard's Hotel, and which has been the reception-room of so many incoming and outgoing Presidents. When I entered, there were already probably twenty persons assembled there, about a dozen of whom were standing in a row, and with them the General was then engaged. The moment he saw me he advanced with both hands outstretched, after the manner of the French, and, telling me how delighted he was to see me, drew me away from the crowd to one of the windows. He proceeded to say that he most especially desired to see me at the Executive Mansion the next day, immediately after the inauguration—that I must on no account fail to come, and under no circumstances be later than four o'clock. He made no explanation of the reason which impelled him to urge so early an interview, but left me with a very decided impression that I had the good fortune to enjoy his highest favor.

I repeated his request to an older and more experienced friend, who advised me, notwithstanding it, not to be so precipitate in making my first call upon the new President. He said that he could not fail to be very fatigued after the inaugural ceremonies; and that it certainly would be in bad taste, as well as impolitic, to intrude upon him at such a moment. I thought the advice good, and followed it. I allowed two days to pass before I presented myself at the White House. When, at last, I did so, I was without delay ushered into the Presidential presence. I reminded Mr. PIERCE of his invitation to me to call sooner, and explained to him the reasons of delicacy which had prevented me from doing so. He was "delighted," "charmed" to see me, and invited me to a seat. He sat down by me, and chatted with me in the most agreeable manner about almost every thing in the world; but not one word did he say personal to myself. I was all the time expecting it, but it never came. Finally, when it would have been indecent to remain any longer, I left. He accompanied me to the outer door, and begged me to "call again to-morrow."

I did not go again the next day, but allowed two or three days to intervene before I once more sought an interview with the "head of the nation." Upon this occasion I was received as before, "with effusion." By this time I had made up my mind that, if the mountain would not come to Mohammed, Mohammed would go to the mountain. So, having brought with me all my documents, I determined to force the fighting, and began at once to explain, without circumlocution, what I wanted. I asked the President to read my papers; but this he declined to do, saying that my original letter to him from

CHARLES O'CONOR answered every purpose, and that it would afford him the very highest satisfaction to comply with my wishes. I would please file my papers in the Secretary of State's office, and give myself no further concern upon the subject. There might be a little delay in announcing the diplomatic appointments, as some of the more important ones at home first required attention; but mine was his personal affair, and, under all circumstances, should be made. I think, then, that I was justified in considering myself booked for Turin for the next four years. The President asked me to dine with him that day, which I did.

The next day I called upon GOVERNOR MARCY, the Secretary of State, handed him my papers, and explained to him what the President had said. He was always friendly to me, and he expressed, and I have no doubt sincerely, his gratification, and his perfect acquiescence in the President's proposed action. I recollect, as an amusing incident, that in the course of our conversation he insisted that Genoa was in Tuscany, and not in Sardinia. As far as I was personally concerned, I saw no reason to remain longer in Washington; but the incoming of a new administration is always full of excitement and interest, and there was besides much in our New York matters in which I felt a deep concern.

In those days the New York Democracy was divided into two factions, severally known by the euphonious titles of "Hunkers" and "Barn-burners," or "Hard-shells" and "Soft-shells." I was affiliated with the "Hunkers." Between those two factions there was a fierce struggle waging for the possession of the Federal offices in the city of New York. And even within the ranks of each there were competing candidates. For instance, both Mr. John J. Cisco and Mr. Augustus Schell desired to be made Collector of the Port. It was claimed in behalf of the former that, upon the occasion of his declining a nomination for the office of Mayor, it was arranged that he should have the unanimous support of his faction, the "Hunkers," for the Collectorship; and that Mr. Schell, who belonged to the same subdivision of the party, was committed to the transaction. But when the time came to make the appointment, Mr. Schell, who seems not to have considered himself so committed, allowed his friends to press his own name for the same position. The result was that Secretary Marcy cut the knot by having his old friend, Mr. Heman J. Redfield, who happened to be accidentally in Washington, after spending the winter in Florida, made Collector of the Port of New York. At the same time, to Mr. Cisco was tendered the office of Assistant Treasurer of the United States in that city, which he was at first very reluctant to accept. Fortunately for the country and for himself, he finally was induced to yield to the persuasions of his friends, and to take the position. He continued to hold it until the first day of July, in the year 1864, when he peremptorily resigned it, his health having become seriously impaired by so long a term of arduous official service. For eleven years, and under three successive administrations, he had discharged the at all times severe, and during the war overwhelming, duties of his office with the greatest ability, fidelity, judgment, and delicacy. He several times before his final withdrawal had tendered his resignation, but no President or Secretary of the Treasury, even although of opposite politics to his own, had consented to accept it.

At a later period, under Mr. BUCHANAN, Mr. SCHELL became Collector of the Port, and discharged the duties of the office in a manner entirely acceptable to the Government. He was very vigilant in regard to smuggling, and the wags used to say that his name should be changed from AUGUSTUS SCHELL to AUGUSTUS SEIZER.

Before any final decision was arrived at by GENERAL PIERCE and his Cabinet in regard to the New York Collectorship, Mr. MARCY sent for me to inquire whether the late Mr. JOHN M. BRADHURST, who was then an old man, still retained the vigor of former years, telling me that, if I could give a satisfactory answer to the question, the office would be placed at his disposal. I was compelled to tell him that the gentleman to whom he referred had been prostrated by a stroke of paralysis some time before, and that the condition of his health rendered it impossible for him to discharge any laborious duties.

All the Federal appointments in the city of New York were simultaneously announced. They were about equally distributed between the two factions. On the same day, and after they had been made public, I was dining at Willard's Hotel. Mr. MARCY, who was temporarily stopping there, occupied a seat at the same table, opposite to me. I had a bottle of hock, and I asked the Secretary to take wine with me. As the waiter was filling his glass, he facetiously exclaimed, "Hic, hæc, hoc!" "All right, Governor," I replied; "something neuter will not hurt you after the very decidedly masculine and feminine appointments which have just been made!" He laughed; and I then asked him whether he had recommended them, or simply acquiesced in them. As some of them were known to be very objectionable to him, he did not vouchsafe any reply. He was an inveterate snuffer, and was constantly to be seen with his long forefinger and thumb applying a pinch to his nose, his head in the mean while cast down in deep meditation.

About this time he received a letter which afforded him immense amusement, and which he showed to every body whom he met. It was from a person in West Troy, New York, who begged to remind him that he had been a private in a company commanded by the Governor, when he marched to the Canadian frontier in the year 1813. He supposed that he might have long since forgotten his very existence, and he therefore took the liberty to inform him that, after the war was ended, he had settled in West Troy as a mechanic of some sort, had married, and had reared a family of children. He had been reasonably prosperous all his life, and had until recently been in the enjoyment of uninterrupted domestic happiness. But since the election a strange and insane passion had taken possession of his wife. She was unalterably determined to be the wife of the Postmaster at West Troy, even if, in order to be so, she were compelled to commit bigamy! Under these circumstances, he appealed to his old commander to save him from a life of future wretchedness, and his wife from destruction, by getting him appointed to the office. The Secretary enjoyed the joke so hugely that, after some inquiries about his correspondent's fitness, he went to POSTMASTER-GENERAL CAMPBELL, and had the commission made out for him.

Having received renewed assurances from the President that my matter was finally settled, I returned home to await results.

Weeks passed away without any action in relation to the foreign appointments. I was confined to my bed with a severe attack of inflammatory rheumatism, when one day the morning newspaper was brought me to read. It contained a complete list of the new diplomatic appointees, and my name was not included. A gentleman from Virginia was to go to Sardinia.

After a while I returned to Washington. The President received me with open arms, as he had always previously been accustomed to do. I remember that he wore a stunning dressing-gown of black velvet, lined with cherry-colored silk, which some admiring lady had sent to him. He used to wear it not only in his private apartments, but also in the executive rooms, when he received the dignitaries of the Senate and others upon business. Before I could begin the speech of mild reproach which I had prepared for the occasion, he cut me off by telling me that, notwithstanding his interest in my behalf, it had been determined, for reasons which I could better comprehend than he could explain, to send Mr. AUGUST BELMONT to Holland, and that this rendered it impossible to accord another position of the same character and grade to the city of New York. It was believed that Mr. BELMONT had contributed largely of his means toward the election, and Mr. DANIEL E. SICKLES had been in Washington ever since the inauguration in the interest of that gentleman, as was supposed.

The President went on to say that I had arrived at Washington at a very opportune moment, and that it was within my power to do a great favor to himself, as well as to Mr. BUCHANAN, then lately appointed Minister to England. Mr. APPLETON, of Maine, who had been commissioned as his Secretary of Legation, for private reasons had suddenly been compelled to abandon the thought of accompanying him. Mr. BUCHANAN was besieged by applicants for the place, and would be delighted to be spared further annoyance by having a suitable appointment made for him. "I expect BUCHANAN here," he said, "every minute." In a word, he offered me the office. At first I positively declined, and urged many objections. Among others, I mentioned that I had no personal acquaintance with Mr. BUCHANAN, that the compensation was very small, and that I did not possess sufficient private means to enable me to live as the Secretary of the American Legation in London ought to live. He pooh-poohed all this; told me that as Mr. BUCHANAN was a bachelor we could keep house together, and thus reduce expenses, and finally insisted that I should go directly to Mr. MARCY with directions from him to make out my commission. I was carried away by him as by a torrent; and before I hardly knew what I was doing, I found myself in the presence of the Secretary of State, who listened to my statement with evident surprise. "What can the President mean," he asked, "by saying that he expects Mr. BUCHANAN at the Executive Mansion every minute? I have no reason to think that he even intends to visit Washington again before sailing for England." He then went on to say that he doubted much whether Mr. BUCHANAN would be so pleased as the President supposed at an appointment made without previously consulting him; that he was one of the leading statesmen of the country, and that, in his judgment, it would not answer to saddle a Secretary of Legation upon him, as might be done in the case of some of "those other fellows." That he would make out the commission, as directed; but that in the mean time he advised me as a friend to go to Wheatland, and have a conference with Mr. BUCHANAN upon the subject.

Thereupon I went directly back to the President. He told me that he did not intend to be understood as expecting Mr. BUCHANAN every minute at the Executive Mansion, but in Washington. He urged me to take the first train for Philadelphia, and thence to Lancaster. He was certain that I would find it with Mr. BUCHANAN just as he had told me. He sat down and wrote a very strong letter to him, of which I was to be the bearer. I took leave of him, and very foolishly, and against my own better judgment, started for Wheatland.

When I arrived there, I found the old statesman at home. He received me courteously, and carefully read my letter of introduction. He then told me that he had already been treated with such gross discourtesy by the President that it was very doubtful whether he would not throw up his commission, and not go to England at all. That, at all events, he did not intend to return to Washington. That about a fortnight before he had written an important letter to the President, which required, and should have received, a prompt answer. That no reply coming, after the interval of a week he had addressed him another, and, in decided language, requested that it have immediate attention. And that the first word which he had since received from the Executive was the letter which I presented to him, and which in no way referred to the subject of his two communications. As to the Secretaryship of Legation, he went on to explain to me that, before Mr. APPLETON was appointed, the office had been influentially solicited for two gentlemen, one of them a friend of his own from Pennsylvania, whom, he admitted, he did not consider competent to discharge the duties, and the other a South Carolinian, who possessed every necessary qualification for the position. That he had not again heard from either of them since Mr. APPLETON had declined, and that, under all the circumstances, he was not yet prepared to definitely express himself. Of course, I felt, for the time, infinitely disgusted with the President, although I had no occasion to find fault with Mr. BUCHANAN. He assured me that he would give the subject his best consideration, and communicate with me before he sailed, if he sailed at all. I parted from him, and never saw him again. The thousands who knew him will never forget his white neckcloth tied awry, and his head perched on one side like that of an inquisitive bird.

I returned home, and shortly afterward went to Stockbridge, Massachusetts, for the summer. While there I received a civil letter from Mr. BUCHANAN, telling me that he had selected for his Secretary of Legation a gentleman of great abilities and unquestionable fitness. A few days later, Mr. DANIEL E. SICKLES was gazetted as the appointee. I have always understood that Mr. MARCY, with whom Mr. SICKLES was not a favorite, declined to sign his commission, and that it was finally signed by Mr. DUDLEY MANN, the Assistant Secretary of State.

I again went to Washington late in the summer. The President took me to his heart as usual. It was impossible to entertain malice against him. There was a new Consul to be appointed at London, and, notwithstanding my past experiences, I ventured to ask him for the appointment. I must do him the justice to say that upon this occasion he gave me an evasive answer. He insisted, however, that I should come and dine with him that afternoon. I accepted the invitation, and was received by him in the Blue Room at the appointed hour. There was but one other guest, a very old gentleman, with an enormous ruffle to his shirt, whom he introduced to me as GENERAL CAMPBELL, of Texas. At dinner we were the only three persons present. Mrs. PIERCE never came down when there was company. I noticed that the President took no wine, but placed his hand upon his glass every time the butler passed him. The conversation was neither very interesting nor very dull, and was rendered very formal by Mr. CAMPBELL introducing the word "sir" between every three or four words that he uttered, after the old-fashioned American habit. After dinner, we again returned to the Blue Room, and in a few minutes rose to depart. The President followed us, with one arm around the neck of each. He then turned to the old gentleman, and told him that he did not wish him to consider his introduction to me as a casual one; that he had intentionally brought us together, as we were both among his dearest friends, and that he hoped we would ourselves become very close friends. It is unnecessary to say that we were both surprised at this effusion, and I, at least, failed to comprehend the occasion for it. As we went out it was raining. GENERAL CAMPBELL had an umbrella, but I was unprovided with one. The venerable gentleman insisted upon accompanying me to

Willard's Hotel, although his own road led in the opposite direction. The next day he called upon me soon after breakfast. A few days later it was given to the public that GENERAL ROBERT S. CAMPBELL was appointed Consul to London, and the mystery of Mr. PIERCE's conduct was solved.

Once more, and only once, I visited Washington during the time of his administration. This was in the year 1854. I called to take leave of him, as I was going abroad as a private citizen. He seemed to love me even more than ever. He told me that I did quite right to go, and that he would "jump" me into the first diplomatic vacancy that should occur in Europe. These were his very words; but I knew him thoroughly by this time, and placed no reliance upon his promise. The position of Secretary of Legation in France was, however, formally tendered to me in the year 1855, to be declined.

I saw Mr. PIERCE but once again. This was after the expiration of his official term, and just after his return from a visit to Europe. I accidentally met him on Washington Street, in Boston. He wore a flaming scarlet neck-cloth, and a suit of clothes of some very light material, which ill became a man of his years and position. He was as affectionate as of old, and apparently as serenely unconscious that I ever had any cause to complain of him. Certainly if I had, I did not treasure it up, and I remember no more delightful chat than the one I had with him that afternoon about old times.

I have written the foregoing pages not to ventilate the wrongs of a disappointed office-seeker, but to illustrate some of the peculiarities of a man who once held the first position in our country.

CHAPTER II.

AT this time General "Sam" Houston was one of the United States Senators from Texas. He was, physically, a magnificent specimen of manhood. His dress was extravagantly *outré,* suggestive of both the frontier's-man and the Indian. He possessed a great mind and a great heart, and his many peculiarities were harmless and endearing, rather than repulsive. His courtesy to women was remarkable, and he never addressed one otherwise than as "lady." "Good-morning, *lady*," was his invariable salutation to any fair friend whom he met at the breakfast-table or elsewhere during the earlier hours of the day. He resided at Willard's when in Washington; and although his room was replete with the appliances of civilized life, he discarded, or pretended to discard, the use of many of them. Buffalo robes were spread upon the carpet, and upon these he slept in preference to using the bed. He had a printed poster upon the wall bearing the words, "My hour for retiring is nine o'clock." This was a silent monition to visitors to withdraw when that hour arrived. But it was the popular belief that the restless old warrior was in the habit of nightly pacing the floor until the small hours of the morning, before he sought repose upon his extemporized couch of skins.

The eccentric, able, honest, and cynical "Mike" Walsh was then a member of the House of Representatives from New York. Mike was the perpetrator of many practical jokes, which furnished subjects for Washington gossip. A fellow-member of the House, whose private avocation was that of a hotel-keeper, rose to make his elaborately prepared maiden speech. As he proceeded, Mike, whose seat was distant from his, would, at every pause, call out in his deep, bass voice, loud enough to be heard by those in his immediate neighborhood, but not so loud as to reach the orator's ear, "John, a pitcher of ice-water to No. 122!" "William, answer the bell of No. 139!" etc., etc. Upon the same fellow-member he played the rather rough joke of sending him an invitation, in the name of the President, to dine at the Executive Mansion. That there might be no occasion for an answer, the invitation was only delivered an hour before the appointed time for dinner. The victim, suspecting nothing, arrayed himself in evening dress, and started for the White House. He was closely followed by Mike, and half a dozen of his cronies whom he had let into the secret, for the purpose of witnessing the discomfiture of the unexpected guest. As the President had happened to go to Baltimore that very afternoon, this discomfiture was complete. Whether the then somewhat unsophisticated sufferer ever discovered or not who had played this "Heathen Chinee" trick upon him, I am not aware.

I saw Daniel Webster under the following circumstances. In the month of November, in the year 1851, I accompanied Mr. Augustus Schell to Washington, for the purpose of persuading Mr. Webster, then Secretary of State, to consent to deliver a Memorial Address before the New York Historical Society on the twenty-third day of the next month. Mr. Webster had previously declined a written invitation to do so, but we were successful in overcoming his objections. Accordingly he came to New York at the proper time, and took lodgings, as he always did when in that city, at the Astor House. At about seven o'clock of the evening appointed for the address, Mr. SCHELL and I called there with a carriage for the purpose of conducting Mr. WEBSTER to Niblo's Theatre, the place selected for its delivery. He kept us waiting a long time in his drawing-room, while he was dressing in his bedroom. When he at last came out to us he looked wan and exhausted, and appeared almost inanimate. He was accompanied by his private secretary, Mr. ABBOTT; and while we were driving from the hotel to the theatre, hardly a word was spoken by any of the party. Once only Mr. WEBSTER opened his mouth, and, in those deep, sepulchral tones which those who have heard them will never forget, asked, "ABBOTT, what is that quotation from EURIPIDES?" When we arrived at the theatre, the distinguished orator was met by a committee of the society and conducted to a private room, that he might rest and refresh himself before presenting himself to the public. Knowing his habits at that time, they had provided a bottle of excellent old brandy for his use, which, with a pitcher of water and a tumbler, stood upon a table in the room. Advancing to it, Mr. WEBSTER almost filled the tumbler with the spirit, and then, tempering it with about a table-spoonful of water, drank it down in two or three gulps. The bottle was then put aside for future use; and almost immediately thereafter Mr. WEBSTER was conducted to the stage and presented to the audience by the president of the society, the late EX-LIEUTENANT-GOVERNOR LUTHER BRA-

DISH. He was, of course, received with vociferous applause, and without delay commenced his address. At first his voice was so low as to be scarcely audible, his utterance was hesitating, and his choice of words frequently unhappy. Gradually, as the stimulus of the brandy operated upon him, he warmed up and became fluent and eloquent; and when he had finished, it was conceded that he had made one of the most masterly and successful of his later efforts. By this time he was again exhausted and overpowered by the weariness and listlessness which had become habitual to him. He was reconducted to the committee-room, that he might take some more of the brandy before returning to his hotel; but, unfortunately, in the mean time some toper had scented the bottle to its hiding-place, and there was not a drop left in it. Mr. SCHELL and myself accompanied him home, and left him more apathetic than we had found him.

He had been persuaded to remain in New York another day, for the purpose of presiding at a meeting to be held the next evening in honor of the then recently deceased novelist, JAMES FENIMORE COOPER. I had known Mr. COOPER during the later years of his life, and used to see him occasionally when he visited New York. He was an amazingly fluent talker as well as speaker and writer; and he affected an intense bitterness against the institutions of his native country in his conversation as well as in his writings. I can see him now, in my mind's eye, standing with his back to the fire-place in my office, with his legs apart and his coat-tails under his arms, pouring out diatribes which did not seem half in earnest.

The following preliminary notice appeared in the New York newspapers of the day:

"At a meeting of friends of the late JAMES FENIMORE COOPER, held in the City Hall, in the city of New York, pursuant to notice, the following gentlemen were appointed a Committee to make the necessary arrangements for a suitable demonstration of respect for Mr. COOPER's memory:

WASHINGTON IRVING,	GEORGE BANCROFT,
GULIAN C. VERPLANCK,	LEWIS GAYLORD CLARK,
JOHN DUER,	JOHN A. DIX,
JAMES K. PAULDING,	GEORGE P. MORRIS,
JOHN W. FRANCIS,	SAMUEL OSGOOD,
RICHARD B. KIMBALL,	CHARLES ANTHON,
FRANCIS L. HAWKS,	CHARLES F. BRIGGS,
WILLIAM C. BRYANT,	MAUNSELL B. FIELD,
WILLIAM W. CAMPBELL,	PARKE GODWIN,
FITZ-GREENE HALLECK,	JONATHAN M. WAINWRIGHT,
RUFUS W. GRISWOLD,	DONALD G. MITCHELL,
CHARLES KING,	N. P. WILLIS.

"At a subsequent meeting of the Committee, held at the Astor House, on the 25th of November, it was reported by a special Committee that negotiations were in progress with Mr. H. GREENOUGH for a monument to Mr. COOPER; that Mr. BRYANT had consented to pronounce a discourse on the life and genius of Mr. COOPER, on the evening of the 24th of December, at Tripler Hall; and that DANIEL WEBSTER had consented to preside on that occasion.

"WASHINGTON IRVING, *President.*

"FITZ-GREENE HALLECK,
RUFUS W. GRISWOLD, } *Secretaries.*"

The meeting was a crowded and a brilliant one. Mr. WEBSTER, in his opening address, faltered and hesitated, and talked as if he did not know the difference between FENIMORE COOPER and MUNGO PARKE. Mr. BRYANT's discourse was, as was to be expected, an appreciative and elegant essay, but his delivery of it was, as is usual with him, without animation. Then followed some of the most brilliant and magnetic speeches to which I ever listened. Rev. Dr. BETHUNE, one of the finest orators of any country or any time, made the room ring with applause at his eloquent periods. GEORGE BANCROFT, the Rev. Dr. OSGOOD, Dr. JOHN W. FRANCIS, and Mr. G. P. R. JAMES, followed with feeling tributes to the memory of the great novelist. Mr. WEBSTER, who had been half asleep, became aroused. When all the speakers of the evening had concluded, he arose from his chair, advanced to the edge of the platform, and delivered a short closing address of marvelous elegance and appropriateness, his glowing and admirably constructed paragraphs falling upon the audience like a magnificent funeral dirge after lighter music. Stimulus was essential to his wearied faculties, and whether it came in the form of brandy or of eloquence, it served alike to vivify them into temporary animation.

And this was the last of the COOPER movement, so well initiated and so successfully carried on to this point. There is no monument in Central Park or elsewhere, so far as I know, to the spirited, wayward romancer, any more than there is to the gentle IRVING. Shame upon New York if statues of both do not soon adorn that magnificent pleasure-ground of which its citizens are so justly proud!

I never saw JOHN TYLER when he was President of the United States. A very good story was told of him at the time that he succeeded as Vice-President to the Chief Magistracy upon the death of PRESIDENT HARRISON. It was said that he commissioned his Irish coachman to purchase a carriage for him. After searching Washington a day or two, Pat came to his master and reported that he had found a very handsome one for sale, but that it had been used a few times. "That will never do," answered Mr. TYLER; "it would not be proper for the President of the United States to drive a second-hand carriage." "And, sure, what are you but a second-hand President?" was the prompt and unanswerable reply.

I saw Mr. FILLMORE, another "second-hand" President, in Washington, but had no acquaintance with him. He *looked* the President better than any man whom I have ever seen who occupied the office. It was somewhat singular that a lawyer who never held more than a secondary rank at a provincial bar should attain so eminent a position. He certainly was one of the most discreet Presidents we ever had, and his administration was an eminently successful one. Mrs. FILLMORE died a few days after the inauguration of Mr. PIERCE, in one of the same rooms in Willard's Hotel which that gentleman had just quitted. I saw the venerable ex-President in Albany last spring, upon the occasion of the delivery of a eulogy upon the late Mr. SEWARD before the New York State Government by Mr. CHARLES FRANCIS ADAMS. Mr. FILLMORE looked the same fresh, dignified gentleman that he did when at the head of the nation. It is a subject of congratulation that our Chief Magistrates, after their retirement, have always comported themselves in a manner to do credit to themselves and the country.

I knew the late JOHN VAN BUREN, as who did not? There never lived another man in this country who wasted such opportunities and such talents. His power to adapt himself to all sorts of people and to all kinds of occasions was simply marvelous. His faculty of ready and apt speech, his equal happiness as a stump and an after-dinner orator, his brilliant wit, and his occasional cynicism, united to make him a remarkable character. He was an indifferent leader, but an admirable executive. When he led a portion of his party at Buffalo, in the year 1848, to repudiate the nomination made by the National Convention of GENERAL CASS for the Presidency, simply on account of the disappointment of his father, the unsuccessful competitor of CASS, he did much to wreck his own political fortunes, although he unwittingly planted a germ there which grew to be a powerful agent in the regeneration of the country.

Speaking of GENERAL CASS reminds me of a pun which was once perpetrated upon his name. It will be recollected that he was United States Minister to France while Louis Philippe was king. When he returned home from his mission, he wrote and published a rather weak book, under the title of "France: its King, Court, and Government." Somebody was ridiculing the book in the presence of a wag, who thereupon remarked that it was impossible for *Cass* to cross the sea (*c*) without making an *ass* of himself.

But to return to JOHN VAN BUREN. During the autumn of the year 1851 there was a terrible contest waging between the "Hunker" and "Barn-burner" factions of the dominant party in the city of New York. An excellent but very young gentleman, afterward a member of Congress, and now holding a high office under the municipal government of that city, happened to be the "Hunker" candidate as delegate from the Fifteenth Ward to the State Convention to be held at Syracuse, in opposition to JOHN VAN BUREN, who was the "Barn-burner" nominee. There was a great deal of excitement at the polls, possibly some "ballot-stuffing." The result was that the gentleman anonymously referred to was returned, and received the certificate of election, while VAN BUREN announced that he would go to Syracuse to contest the seat.

Accordingly, the day before the convention was to assemble, I with several others started for Syracuse in company with our candidate. We arrived at Albany in the evening, and went to Congress Hall for supper. When we entered the dining-room, whom should we find there but JOHN VAN BUREN seated at the head of the table, and flanked on either side by several of his prominent adherents. Our man and ourselves took seats at the same table, somewhat lower down, and Mr. VAN BUREN, who knew me, saluted me. This was like waving a red flag at an enraged bull. Our candidate, who sat next to me, at once began to abuse VAN BUREN to me in very savage terms. Presently the latter, who knew him as well as he knew me, turned to me, and in his usual drawling tone, but in quite a loud voice, said, "FIELD, who is that young man who sits next you?" "That, Mr. VAN BUREN," I answered, "is Mr. ———." "Oh! that is Mr. ———, is it?" he rejoined; "well, please give him my compliments, and tell him that he is a confounded young politician." Hereat my friend waxed only the more angry and violent in his expressions.

When we arrived at Syracuse, our infuriated candidate threatened to take personal vengeance upon VAN BUREN in case he attempted to contest his seat. The convention at its first meeting appointed a committee of three on credentials, composed of two "Hunkers" and one "Barn-burner." They were to meet that afternoon in the hotel where we lodged. At the designated time we watched them as they went up stairs to their room, and saw both ——— and VAN BUREN follow separately after them. An hour passed, and we became very uneasy. We feared that a personal encounter might actually take place between the contestants. Shortly afterward, to our great surprise, we saw VAN BUREN and our friend coming down together, VAN BUREN having his arm around the other's neck, and both laughing in the best of humor. It appeared that VAN BUREN told the committee that he did not think that, under any circumstances, he could expect the seat to be awarded to him by a tribunal so constituted, and therefore declined to present his claim. He made a funny speech, and by his inimitable facetiousness appeased the angry feelings of his opponent, and hence the tableau which we witnessed. Friendship between them was cemented over several bottles of champagne, and their personal animosities were buried for all time.

CHAPTER III.

IN the spring of the year 1842 I was returning North, after spending the winter in Cuba and New Orleans. I stopped a day or two at Cincinnati for the purpose of visiting an old college friend. Upon my arrival there, my friend informed me that Mr. CHARLES DICKENS was in town, and was to hold a levee at his hotel that morning. He was going to it, and asked me to accompany him. At that time I had that admiration, almost hero-worship, for DICKENS which was common to all young men in this country immediately after the publication of his earlier works. I therefore readily accepted the invitation, and we were soon in the presence of the distinguished novelist. There were not many persons in the room when we entered. Immediately behind us followed a small English gentleman of subdued and timid manners. Mr. DICKENS was standing in front of the fire-place, with his coat-tails under his arms, gorgeously attired, and covered with velvet and jewelry. Mrs. DICKENS was lounging upon a sofa at the farther end of the room. We were duly presented by an usher, or master of ceremonies, and, after exchanging a few words with the author of "Pickwick," retired to give place to the little Englishman who was behind us. Upon being introduced, this gentleman deferentially remarked, "I had the pleasure of meeting you, Mr. DICKENS, at Mr. LOVER's, in ——shire, two years ago." DICKENS looked him steadily in the face for a minute, and then answered in a loud voice, "I never was there in my life!" "I beg your pardon," replied his interlocutor, overcome with confusion; "it was in the winter, and" (naming several persons) "were there at the same time." DICKENS again gave him a withering look, and after a pause repeated in a still more elevated tone, "I tell you, sir, I never was there in my life!" Here Mrs. DICKENS interposed, and, addressing her husband, said, "Why, Charles, you certainly were there, and I was there with you; don't you remember the occurrence?" Mr. DICKENS glared at her almost fiercely, and, advancing a step or two, with his right hand raised, fairly shouted, "I *tell* you, I never was there in my life!" I had never been so disenchanted in all my days. The unfortunate Englishman withdrew without another word, and I and my friend retired disgusted. I then for the first time reluctantly appreciated the fact that a man may be a great author without being a gentleman, a conclusion which I have frequently seen verified in my more mature years.

I became acquainted with Mr. G. P. R. JAMES very soon after his arrival in this country in the year 1850. His initials stood for GEORGE PAYNE RAINSFORD, but some wag had once dubbed him *George Prince Regent*, and this was believed to be his real name by many who did and many who did not know him. His original intention in coming to America was to settle in Canada, but he abandoned that purpose after he had been here a short time. He had three sons, none of them then grown to manhood, and he thought it better for them to cast their fate in a new country than to remain in Europe.

He had recently, too, met with very severe pecuniary reverses. He had contracted with a London bookseller for the publication of a uniform edition of his novels, to be illustrated with steel engravings. The engravings were all ordered and in course of execution, when, after the appearance of a few of the volumes, the bookseller failed. The engraver brought an action against Mr. JAMES as a partner with the publisher in the contract with him, was successful in his suit, and the author, whose fortune in this instance was similar to that of SIR WALTER SCOTT in another, was compelled to pay several thousand pounds sterling. This was a severe blow to him, and although he had excellent and powerful friends at home, such as the late DUKE OF NORTHUMBERLAND and the present DUKE OF WELLINGTON, Mr. JAMES, who was then residing at Heidelberg, in Germany, made up his mind to turn his face westward. He came to London before sailing, and among other leave-taking calls made one upon the DUKE OF NORTHUMBERLAND. I have often heard him relate with much emotion what occurred upon the occasion. He told the story of his misfortunes and his purposes to the Duke, who listened to the recital with close attention. When it was finished, his noble auditor exerted himself to the utmost to dissuade him from carrying out his intention of leaving Europe. Finding that his arguments failed of the desired effect, the Duke asked to be excused for a moment. Presently he returned, accompanied by the Duchess, and holding in his hand a check upon his bankers to Mr. JAMES's order, signed, but in blank, begged him to accept it and fill in the amount. The Duchess added her own entreaties to those of her husband. Mr.

JAMES firmly, but with overflowing heart, refused to accept any thing, even in the form of a loan. The Duke and Duchess had no children, and could afford to be, as they were, munificently liberal. The Duke, better known by his earlier title of LORD PRUDHOE, was an unsung Macænas to artists and literary men.

Mr. JAMES was a gentleman by birth, and a Tory—of a very mild form, however—in politics. His father was an officer in the British Navy, and commanded the frigate which bombarded New London in the War of 1812. Young JAMES was originally in the army, and after a short service upon the Continent during the Napoleonic wars, was wounded, taken prisoner, and detained upon parole in France until after the battle of Waterloo. An incident which occurred during his confinement there cast a gloom upon the rest of his life. For some cause which he never explained to me, he became engaged in a duel with a French officer. He escaped unhurt himself, but wounded his adversary, who died after lingering for months. I have still in my possession the old-fashioned pistols with which this duel was fought, which my deceased friend presented to me at the time of our early acquaintance. It was during the period of his captivity that he devoted himself, for want of other occupation, to thoroughly reading up French history, and storing his mind with that mass of details upon which he was accustomed to draw for his future novels without having to refer to books.

After the pacification, he returned to England with the intention of devoting himself to a diplomatic career. His father had some interest with LORD LIVERPOOL, then Prime Minister, and he secured from him the promise of an early vacancy for his son. Shortly afterward LORD LIVERPOOL informed CAPTAIN JAMES that he could give his son the position of Secretary to an Extraordinary Embassy about to be sent to China, but that he did not advise him to accept it, as it was only of a temporary character, and would not necessarily lead to preferment, whereas he expected to be able soon to find for him a position in the regular corps. Following this advice, the proffered place was declined, and a week thereafter LORD LIVERPOOL suddenly died of a stroke of apoplexy.

In the mean time young JAMES had written "Richelieu," his first work of fiction. He had kept his manuscript concealed from his father, who belonged to the old class of the LAIRD OF AUCHINLECK, who considered it a degradation for a gentleman to print a book. He managed, however, to obtain an introduction to SIR WALTER SCOTT; and, taking his manuscript with him, he went to Abbotsford, and with the temerity of a fledgling, asked SIR WALTER to read it, and give him his opinion of it. This the great man promised to do. Six months passed, and no news came from Scotland. One day JAMES was riding in Bond Street, when his horse shying, pressed against the side of a carriage which happened to be passing. There was but one person in it. Putting out his head to see what was the matter, this person, who happened to be SIR WALTER, who had just come to town, recognized the young author, and invited him to call upon him at his hotel the next morning. JAMES went, of course, and, to his surprise and delight, received from SIR WALTER the warmest encomium of his book. He was further so kind as, at his request, to reduce to writing what he had said of it. Possessed of this, Mr. JAMES easily found a publisher, to whom, however, he sold his copyright for a song. "Richelieu" was immensely successful, and his next books, of which he retained the ownership, brought him very large prices for those days.

When Mr. JAMES first came to New York, he took lodgings with his family at the New York Hotel. He had not been here a week before I began to see him almost daily. For some time he was busy presenting his letters of introduction. Among others, he had one to HORACE GREELEY, and he personally called with it upon the philosopher. He found him within, and directly after his interview with him, he came to me. He summed up the impression produced upon him by Mr. GREELEY by saying that he had "the head of a SOCRATES and the face of a baby!"

Mr. JAMES soon found a residence in a hotel incompatible with the prosecution of any literary labor. So many people constantly called upon him that he had no command whatever of his own time. Accordingly he desired to find a place, a little out of town, if possible, where he could be comparatively free from intrusion. After some looking around, he was offered and finally made an agreement to hire Mr. CHARLES ASTOR BRISTED's house at Hell Gate, opposite Astoria. The house, which originally belonged to Mr. BRISTED's grandfather, the late Mr. JOHN JACOB ASTOR, was not adapted to winter occupation, and was only partly furnished. After he had removed to it, JAMES came to me with a plaintive account of his difficulties in getting into it, and of his discomforts when he got there. A day or two thereafter he sent me the following amusing lines, and was to finish the story of his mishaps in a second "fytte," which, however, I presume he never wrote, as it never came to hand.

THE JOURNEY TO HELL GATE.

Dear Field, I will give you a picture, in verse,
Of disasters it grieves my steel-pen to rehearse,
As trotting fast on the high-road to the devil,
All cookless, and manless, with coachman uncivil,
We set out by some strange arrangement of Fate,
To make our abode just outside of Hell Gate.

But first let me show you the course of the packing,
The cramming, the jamming, the wracking, the cracking;
With boxes too few to contain all our store,
And each minute bringing some thingumbob more;
While Walter, and Courtney, and Florence, and I,
To put gallons in pint-pots laboriously try,
And Charlie himself must have finger in pie.

The scene was the parlor, the whole was dramatic,
And wanting in naught but a little salt attic:
In her own quiet chamber, hard by, "Stabat Mater,"
And first of the histrions, "loquitur Pater."

G. P. R.—"Come bustle, come bustle, come bundle the traps,
Come pack up the bonnets and poke in the caps!
The porters are damning,
The doors are all slamming,
Portmanteaus are cramming;
Come, fill up the gaps!"

C.—"Oh, dear me! oh, dear!
How marvelous queer!
Here's Whipple's oration got in the slop-pail!"

G. P. R.—"Leave it there,
And don't stare,
It will very well fare.

One half the world's verse,
More than half of its prose
Is slop, and at last to the slop-pail it goes."

F.—"Here are EVERETT's speeches; oh, where shall they go?"

G. P. R.—"On Fame's highest platform, where clouds are below,
And sunshine above them, and clearness around,
And flowers few, but lovely, bespangle the ground—
But I'm thinking of tropes, when I should think of locks,
For CICERO, printed, must go in a box—
Put him in beside SUMNER—"

F.—"They'll never agree."

G. P. R.—"Jam them tight,
They can't fight,
At least for one night,
However opposed to each other they be."

W.—"Here are IRVING and LOWELL and HAWTHORNE and HOLMES,
And BRYANT and TUCKERMAN, too;
And hundreds of vagrant poetical tomes—
Oh, dearie me! what shall I do?"

G. P. R.—"Put IRVING and ADDISON close side by side,
And GOLDSMITH as near as may be;
Three such kindred spirits may well take a ride,
E'en were it to Eternity.
'Tis but to Hell Gate,
And the fiat of Fate
Has decreed that they should not go in:
For the devil himself,
Though a covetous elf,
Would not suffer such spirits within.
The English poet would preach peace
To damned souls longing for release;
The Irishman would teach simplicity
To knaves condemned for earth's duplicity;

And tears and smiles at IRVING's voice
Would deck the face of hard remorse,
Till, all forgetful of the curse,
Hell's tenants would themselves rejoice,
And RIP VAN WINKLE's solemn souls,
With laughter cheer their game at bowls.
Put them in! put them in!
'Tis a traveling sin
To waste time in packing a box to a pin.
If the binding is hurt,
'Tis but the bard's shirt;
He himself will be found
All immortal and sound
Whatever may happen to damage his skin."

C.—"Here's Mr. THACKERAY."

G. P. R.—"He rhymes to quackery."

W.—"Here's CHARLIE DICKENS,
And his whole brood of chickens."

F.—"Here are HALLAM and HUNT,
And JOHNSON and BLUNT,
And a score or two more
Lying round on the floor."

G. P. R.—"Cram them in! cram them in!
'Tis a traveling sin
To waste time in packing a box to a pin."

W.—"Here are papers,
And tapers,
And rapiers,
And capers,
And things from the drapers."

C.—"Here are pistols,
And crystals,
And rifles,
And trifles,

And holsters,
And bolsters,
And beds made of osier,
And things from the hosier,
And boxes of furs,
To say nothing of curs,
And poor little Frizzy."*

G. P. R.—"You make my head dizzy.
Cram them in! cram them in!
'Tis a traveling sin
To waste time in packing a box to a pin."

W.—"They're all in at last!"

C.—"Don't get on so fast!
Here are lucifer matches,
And a box for dispatches."

F.—"A pair of nail-nippers,
An old pair of slippers
That came from Morocco,
And lots of rococco."

G. P. R.—"All presents from friends I shall never see more,
Till the journey of life, like this journey, is o'er;
But their gifts still to fancy shall call back their faces,
And yield the dead present the past's living graces.
Oh! put them by safe, for an hour oft may come
When I long for some sight to remind me of home—
Of that home o'er the waters, where hope's early sight
First presented the world all resplendent and bright;
Where memories crowd, and the flowers of past years
Blossomed forth in life's morn to be watered by tears:
Like the lily, that opens its breast for one day,
And closes forever at evening's last ray!
The dear ones around us the present may cheer,
But we can not forget there were others as dear.

* A certain traveled and highly accomplished spaniel—a friend of the family.

Kind friends may be near us—bright skies overhead—
But we still must remember the land of our dead;
And, though this new world my dead ashes may share,
One half of my heart is, at least, buried there!
On, on with your work

W.—"It is done"

C.— "Oh, what fun!
We shall get there ere nightfall, as sure as a gun!"

G. P. R.—"But the cart's breaking down with the weight of the packages."

W.—"Ere 'tis home, there will be a rare number of crackages."

G. P. R.—"And the wine's left behind, t'other end of the city;
We must temperate dine—"

C.—"Dear me, what a pity!"

G. P. R.—"Well, you all get into the carriage and go,
And I will run off to the stores down below;
Of barrels and bottles make speedy purveyance,
And follow you fast in some other conveyance."

'Tis all done—
They are gone,
Wife, daughter, and sons,
Cart, carriage, and boxes, beds, bolsters, and guns;
While, like a sea-weed on some oyster-bed thrown,
I am left on the *pavé* of New York alone.

[Ye end of ye Firste Fytte.]

It will be seen from the foregoing specimen that Mr. James wrote capital squibs. I find a copy of another transcribed in my scrap-book, where two were concerned, and where I am not sure that James came off with the highest honors.

On the 25th day of December (Christmas), 1840, when the excitement in diplomatic circles upon the subject of the so-called Eastern question was at its height, he dined with SIR HAMILTON and LADY SEYMOUR in Brussels. SEYMOUR'S note of invitation ran: "Will you and your wife come and eat a turkey with us?" The dinner was a very good one, but there was no turkey; and on the following day Mr. JAMES sent to him the lines below:

"ON THE NOTORIOUS BREACH OF POLITICAL FAITH COMMITTED BY SIR G. HAMILTON SEYMOUR, G. C. H., ETC., ETC., ETC., HER BRITANNIC MAJESTY'S MINISTER PLENIPOTENTIARY AT THE COURT OF BELGIUM, ON THE 25TH OF DECEMBER, 1840.

"Most perfidious, most base of all living ministers,
You deserve to fall back to the rank of plain misters;
Your star taken off, and your chain only serving
To fetter your ankles *selon* your deserving.
Don't think that my charge is some trumpery matter
Of Court etiquette. It is greater and fatter;
Fit cause throughout Europe to spread conflagration,
Set king against kaiser, and nation 'gainst nation.
'Tis a fraud diplomatic—a protocol broken—
The breach of a treaty both written and spoken—
A matter too bad for e'en Thiers's digestion—
The loss of an empire, the great Eastern question!
In vain would you move my ambition or pity—
In vain would you offer me province or city—
Neither Bordeaux, nor Xeres, nor eke all Champagne,
Can make me forgetful of promises vain.
Such pitiful make-weights I send to perdition;
'Twas *Turkey* you promised—at least a partition.
'Twas *Turkey* you promised—you've broken your word.
'Twas *Turkey* you promised—and where is the bird?"

To the above, SEYMOUR sent the following answer within an hour after he received it:

"Of Eastern affairs most infernally sick,
No wonder I failed to my promise to stick.
With the subject of Turkey officially crammed,
If Turkey I dined on, I swore I'd be d—d.
But, at least, my good friend, and the thought should bring peace,
If I gave you no *Turkey*, I gave you no Greece!"

While Mr. JAMES was residing at Hell Gate, a gentleman of wealth, and of the best social standing in New York, came to see me, and requested me to appoint a time when I would drive there with him and introduce him to the novelist. A day and an hour were decided upon sufficiently far ahead to enable me to notify Mr. JAMES about it. When the time arrived, we went there in my friend's carriage, and the desired introduction took place. After the usual words of salutation had passed between them, the visitor observed to Mr. JAMES that he was a great admirer of his novels, that he believed he had read all that were published, and that there was one among them which he vastly preferred to all the others." "And which is that?" asked JAMES. "The Last Days of Pompeii!" was the answer. "That is BULWER's, not mine," replied the mortified novelist. It was awkward enough for all present, and JAMES never forgave that man, as few in his place would do. I am in the habit of meeting him in the street almost daily, and I never do so without thinking of his unpardonably absurd mistake.

I once heard something which was so good that I could not forbear repeating it to the creator of the "solitary horseman." It ran thus: A lady spending the summer in the country was thrown upon the not very extensive resources of a village circulating-library for books. She was one day pleased to find there, and took home with her, a copy of an English edition of one of JAMES's novels in two volumes. She read them through with delight, and only after finishing discovered that she had been perusing the first volume of one work and the second volume of another! Nothing but our great intimacy could excuse me for telling this to JAMES, but he winced under it. Mr. JAMES passed the next summer at Stockbridge, Massachusetts, where he hired the Ashburner House furnished. I had already spent several successive summers in that lovely spot. There was no neighborhood in America at that time so distinguished for its literary society. The SEDGWICKS were the most conspicuous family, and their influence had done much to attract cultivated people there. Mrs. SUSAN SEDGWICK, widowed daughter-in-law of THEODORE SEDGWICK, some time Speaker of the House of Representatives of the United States, resided in the old manor-house at Stockbridge, and Mrs. HENRY SEDGWICK lived in the same village. Mr. and Mrs. CHARLES SEDGWICK, and Miss CATHARINE SEDGWICK, the authoress, resided at Lenox, five miles off. With them Mrs. PIERCE BUTLER, *née* FANNY KEMBLE, was a frequent visitor, until she purchased a residence for herself in the vicinity. Doctor OLIVER WENDELL HOLMES had a summer-seat near Pittsfield, in the same county. HERMAN MELVILLE, the author of "Typee" and "Omoo," occupied a fine old place between Pittsfield and Lenox. NATHANIEL HAWTHORNE resided in a little box of a house, which looked like a district school-house, near the Lenox Lake. GEORGE WILLIAM CURTIS frequented Lenox, as DARLEY, the artist, and DAVID DUDLEY FIELD did Stockbridge, where MRS. FIELD owned an old family residence; CYRUS W. FIELD was a frequent visitor there, and the Rev. Dr. ORVILLE DEWEY made his home at Sheffield, south of Stockbridge. Besides those whom I have named, there were numerous other distinguished people who were constantly coming and going. There is no more beautiful interior county in America than Berkshire, and there was none other in those days where refinement and culture were so universal. Every where the influence of the SEDGWICKS made itself felt, and affected the tone of society. This reminds me of a little story. About this time Mr. SIGOURNEY BARKER, son of the famous banker JACOB BARKER, of New York and New Orleans, came to Lenox to visit his sister, who had a beautiful estate there. Mr. BARKER was well known as a young gentleman of fashion, and a society man. Some three weeks after his arrival, a friend who had just come from New York called upon him and found him at home. "Well, BARKER," he asked, "what do you do with yourself here?" "Oh, nothing," was the listless answer. "Why, don't you shoot? I understand that there is capital woodcock-shooting in the neighborhood." "Oh, no; I never shoot." "And I am told that there is excellent trout-fishing in the mountain streams. You fish, of course?" "Never did such a thing in my life," BARKER indolently replied. "But the society here is charming, and that is exactly in your line. You surely enjoy that?" "I never go out any more." "Why, what in the world has happened to you, old fellow?" "Well," drawled SIGOURNEY, "I suppose that you won't let me off until I confess the whole truth, and here it is:

For the first ten days that I was here, I was out all the time at evening parties, picnics, expeditions to the ice-glen, and all sorts of things. I was charmed for a while; but at last, when I was driving home of an evening, it came to seem to me that the katydids and the frogs and the tree-toads had but one song, and that was 'Sedg-wick! Sedg-wick! Sedg-wick!' Since then I have kept to the house, and the most seductive invitations fail to lure me from it."

Every body there remembers Mrs. PIERCE BUTLER, who was always called by her maiden name of FANNY KEMBLE. She was certainly a lady of great genius, gifted with many masculine accomplishments. I distinctly remember a certain evening party at the Sedgwick Manor-house. When I arrived, I found Mrs. BUTLER at the piano in the front drawing-room, singing Spanish ballads, which she did very sweetly and effectively. After a time she ceased singing and entered into conversation with me. Her arms, which she called her "deformities," were bare, and they, as well as her face, were very much burned by the sun. She told me that she had been out all the day alone upon the lake, fishing; that she had had no dinner; that when she returned to the house, she for the first time heard of the party for that evening, and that she had not had the time to both eat and dress without detaining the rest of the family. The result was that she had not tasted food since breakfast, and felt very faint and exhausted. All this time she was carelessly drumming the keys of the piano. At length she arose from her seat and slowly sauntered into the back drawing-room, while I remained standing where I was. After a short interval, hearing very loud talking in the other room, I lounged into it to see what it meant. The rear of the house was very near the Housatonic, and it had a bay-window on that side. Seated in this window, with her back to the river, was Fanny Kemble, and sitting on either side of her were the Rev. Dr. Parker and the Rev. Justin Field, both clergymen of the Protestant Episcopal Church. Thereupon I drew up a chair, and, facing the lady, completed the *partie carrée.* She was doing the talking just then, and her subject was horses, for which animals she had a passionate fondness. From horses in general, she soon passed to war or cavalry horses. "By the bye," she went on to say, "this reminds me that the last time I was in England I met Sir Harry Smith. He told me that he was a captain of horse at Waterloo, but that his command was not called into action during the day. In the afternoon the Duke of Wellington, at the head of his staff, rode up to where he was, and called to him, 'Come, sir, get your troop in motion—get your troop in motion!' Now Sir Harry did not yet know any thing about the fortunes of the day; so, saluting his commander, he hesitatingly asked, 'Which way, sir?'" As she gave the Duke's reply, she rose to her feet like a tragedy queen, and, with clenched hand, shouted, "Forward, sir, by God!" At this her immediate auditors started as if electrified; but she calmly resumed her chair, and went on with the conversation as if unconscious that she had violated any of the proprieties. She soon fell a-talking about the transmigration of souls, Brahminism, and I can not recall what besides. When I withdrew from the party she was still engaged with some subject of mystical theology.

And this reminds me of a little excursion which Dar-

LEY, the artist, and myself once made together from Stockbridge. We started in a buggy to call upon MELVILLE, intending to go from there to Dr. HOLMES's, then to the hotel at Pittsfield to dine, and thence home. We found MELVILLE, whom I had always known as the most silent man of my acquaintance, sitting on the porch in front of his door. He took us to a particular spot on his place to show us some superb trees. He told me that he spent much time there *patting them upon the back.* When we were about to start for Dr. HOLMES's, we invited MELVILLE to accompany us, and he accepted. We found the poet-physician, to whom I was presented for the first time, at home, and he took us into a room at the back of his house, which overlooked the mountains. For some time the talk, in which all tried to participate, dragged, and I feared that our visit would only result in boring our host, if not ourselves. At length, somehow, the conversation drifted to East India religions and mythologies, and soon there arose a discussion between HOLMES and MELVILLE, which was conducted with the most amazing skill and brilliancy on both sides. It lasted for hours, and DARLEY and I had nothing to do but to listen. I never chanced to hear better talking in my life. It was so absorbing that we took no note of time, and the Doctor lost his dinner, as we lost ours. We took tea at Pittsfield, instead of dining there, and reached home late in the evening.

But I have very discourteously left Mr. JAMES all this time standing in his new house with his boxes unpacked. It took him a very short time to convert it into a home, and to fall into regular habits of living there. His nature was so genial, and his fund of recollections and anecdotes so inexhaustible, that he soon became the friend of every man, woman, and child who lived in his neighborhood. He bought property there; but I fear that, notwithstanding his long India-rubber boots and affectation of rustic attire, he was not a success as a farmer. In the mean time he was also industriously pegging away at book-making, although to the casual observer he appeared to be the least occupied man in the place. He never did any literary work after eleven o'clock A.M. until evening. He was not accustomed to put his own hand to paper, when composing, but always employed an amanuensis. At this time he had in his service in that capacity the brother of an Irish baronet, who spoke and wrote English, French, German, and Italian, and whom I had procured for him at the modest stipend of five dollars a week. When JAMES was dictating, he always kept a paper of snuff upon the table on which his secretary wrote, and he would stride up and down the room, stopping every few minutes for a fresh supply of the titillating powder. He never looked at the manuscript, or made any corrections except upon proof-sheets.

During the first few weeks that he and I were together at Stockbridge, I related to him several detached incidents in my own experience which I thought he might advantageously work up in his fictions. One day he told me that he was determined that we should write a novel together. The idea appeared to me an absurd one, and I discouraged it in every possible way, among other things telling him that I was sure that either of us could better write a book alone than we could write one together. But he would not be denied, and moreover he insisted that we should set to work at once. I continued to object, but saying I "would ne'er consent—consented."

It was a very few evenings after this conversation that we met at his house to construct our plot. After two hours' consideration, we completed it; but I may as well mention that, before we reached the middle of the book, we had deviated so far from it that we had to recast it. Our daily habit while engaged upon this work was as follows: At seven o'clock every evening we would retire into his library, and each read to the other what he had written on that day. Some filing and dovetailing was generally necessary to make the parts fit. Then we would determine what each was to do the next day—up to what point he was to carry the story. Now the hero was mine, and the heroine was Mr. JAMES's, and we were constantly and inevitably, in the progress of the tale, each distorting the ideal conception of the other. But we got over this the best way we could. After our evening's consultation, we retired to the dining-room, and usually supped upon a *finnie haddock*, prepared in national style by a Scotch cook. Mr. JAMES threw all his heart, which was as fresh as that of a boy, into a book. While he was writing a story, it was a reality to him. I remember that in our joint work, the wife at one time ran away from her husband, for we married our hero and heroine in the middle of the book, and left them, like young bears, to find all their troubles afterward. She left a letter behind her, explaining her reasons for going. It fell to Mr. JAMES's lot to write that letter, and when he read it to me his voice was choked, and he was overcome by emotion. JAMES's style was so well known to the public, and mine not at all, that I naturally endeavored to assimilate mine to his, and with good success, as the sequel proved. In five weeks after the book was commenced it was finished, and it was published under the title of "Adrian; or, The Clouds of the Mind." It was very kindly received by the critics, and attracted attention by the singularity of its dual authorship. I remember that my esteemed friend, Mr. RICHARD GRANT WHITE, reviewed it at length in the *New York Courier and Enquirer.* He undertook to assign particular passages to each of us, and in almost every instance he was mistaken. There was an old house described in the first chapter. Mr. WHITE said that if I had written that, I had better undertake to write "Rejected Addresses." Now, every word of it was mine. I had in my mind the old "Salstonstall" house, near New Haven.

One day JAMES and I started to call upon HAWTHORNE. As we approached his dwelling, we saw him in a vegetable garden at the side of it. As soon as he noticed our approach, he concealed himself, like a frightened school-boy, behind the house, and when we asked for him at the door, we were told that he was not at home. Tradition related that nobody had succeeded in interviewing him since he had first settled at Lenox.

Some time in the year 1852 Mr. JAMES was appointed Her Britannic Majesty's Consul at Norfolk, Virginia, and later at Richmond, in the same state. In 1858 he was made British Consul-General at Venice, and left this country forever. I was with him during the last evening that he spent in America, at the Union Place Hotel, in New York. WASHINGTON IRVING, between whom and himself there existed a sincere friendship, was also with us. James was telling us about all the kindness which he had received in Virginia. "They're a warm-hearted people—they're a warm-hearted people!" he said, while tears came into his eyes. The next morning I accompanied him to the steamer, and took my final leave of him. He died in Venice, after a comparatively short residence there.

If he was sometimes a tedious writer, he was always the best story-teller that I ever listened to. He had known almost every body in his own country, and he never forgot any thing. The literary anecdotes alone which I have heard him relate would suffice to fill an ordinary volume. He was a big-hearted man, too—tender, merciful, and full of religious sentiment; a good husband, a devoted father, and a fast friend. If I dwell longer upon him than upon some others who occupy a higher niche in the temple of fame, it is because I knew him so well, and there always existed so affectionate a regard between us.

I have already mentioned that in consequence of their alleged connivance in the enlistment of soldiers for the British Army upon American soil during the Crimean War, the Washington Government not only dismissed her Majesty's Minister at that capital, but also withdrew their exequaturs from her Consuls at New York, Philadelphia, and Cincinnati. When I was in England in the year 1856, I made some efforts to induce Mr. James's friends to secure for him the vacant Consulship at New York. But his own political party was not then in power, and whatever attempt, if any, was made by them, failed of success. Lord Derby's adherents did not like to ask favors of Lord Palmerston's administration.

Among others, I wrote in his behalf to the DUKES OF NORTHUMBERLAND and WELLINGTON and the MARQUIS OF DALHOUSIE, who had just returned home from the Governor-Generalship of India. I received the following replies to my letters:

"NORTHUMBERLAND HOUSE, June 20, 1856.

"SIR,—I entirely agree with you in the expressions contained in your letter of the 18th inst. in favor of Mr. JAMES. I have long had the pleasure of his acquaintance, and, therefore, have long esteemed and respected him. But I can not consent to take a part in the transaction you propose, as it would not produce the effect you anticipate. Yours faithfully, NORTHUMBERLAND.

"MAUNSELL B. FIELD, Esq."

"LONDON, June 19, 1856.

"SIR,—I am much obliged to you for your letter.

"A few days since I had an opportunity of talking to LORD CLARENDON respecting Mr. JAMES, and I have hopes that his position may be improved. I have the honor to be, sir, your obedient, humble servant, WELLINGTON.

"M. B. FIELD, Esq."

"EDINBURGH, June 30, 1856.

"SIR,—Your letter of the 18th inst. did not reach me until very lately, in consequence of my having left London before it was delivered at my address there.

"I can not pretend to the possession of any influence with her Majesty's Ministers; and I am, of course, ignorant of the course they intend to pursue with regard to the Consuls from whom the exequatur has been withdrawn.

"But you judge rightly in believing that I should be glad to serve Mr. JAMES if I could; and if a proper opportunity for doing so should present itself, I will not let it pass. I have the honor to be, sir, your obedient servant, DALHOUSIE.

"M. B. FIELD, Esq."

I have already devoted so much space to Mr. JAMES that it would be hardly fair to detain the reader to listen to many of the anecdotes which I heard from him. He had been personally acquainted with SCOTT, CAMPBELL, SOUTHEY, WORDSWORTH, DE QUINCEY, BYRON, and all the brilliant galaxy of poets and prose writers which illuminated the earlier part of the present century. He told me that the first time he met the author of the "Pleasures of Hope" he was taken to his residence, which was at Camden Town, or one of the other suburbs of London. It was a poor place; and he found the great lyric poet in a green-baize jacket, smoking a clay pipe! CAMPBELL sometimes showed at LONGMAN's literary dinners. Upon these occasions a screen was placed behind his chair, and behind that screen stood a table with a decanter of spirits upon it. To the latter he made such frequent application that he was usually under the dinner-table before the fish was removed.

JAMES intimately knew HOGG, "the Ettrick Shepherd." They were one day dining together at a table where HOGG happened to be seated next to a daughter of SIR WILLIAM DRYSDALE. She was a charming young lady —unaffected, affable, and clever. To some remark which he made, she replied, "You're a funny man, Mr. HOGG;" to which he instantly rejoined, "And ye're a nice lassie, Miss DRYSDALE. Nearly all girls are like a bundle of pens cut by the same machine — ye're not of the bundle." JAMES once arranged a party for an excursion to Lake St. Mary, and it was proposed to stop at HOGG's house on the way, and take him up. Before they reached it, however, they saw a man fishing in the Yarrow, not very far from the high-road. The fisherman, as soon as he noticed a carriageful of people, whose attention was apparently attracted to himself, gathered up his rod, and started to run in an opposite direction as fast as his legs could carry him. JAMES descended from the carriage, and shouted after him at the top of his voice. But it was of no use—the fugitive never stopped until he reached an elevated spot of ground, when he turned around to watch the movements of the intruders. Recognizing JAMES, he laughingly returned his greeting, and, approaching him, said—I translate his Scotch dialect into the vernacular—"Why, JAMES, my boy, how are you? I took you for some of those rascally tourists who come down upon me in swarms, and eat me out of house and home." His fears removed, he accompanied the party to the lake, and they had a merry day of it.

HOGG'S egotism was very amusing. Witness the following extract from his "Familiar Anecdotes of Sir Walter Scott:"

"One of SIR WALTER'S representatives has taken it upon him to assert that SIR WALTER held me in the lowest contempt! He never was further wrong in his life; but SIR WALTER would have been still further wrong if he had done so. Of that, posterity will judge."

JAMES was a mere youth at the time of his acquaintance with BYRON. The latter used to call him "little devil," and at one time proposed taking him abroad with him. He had frequent opportunities of noticing BYRON'S lameness; and upon a certain occasion, when they happened to meet at a fashionable hatter's on the Strand, his attention was particularly attracted to it. When he came in, the poet was seated before a table with his feet crossed under it. The boy (for boy he was) being somewhat piqued because BYRON had not interrupted the conversation in which he was engaged, to be civil to him, withdrew to the other side of the shop. Standing there, leaning against a counter, he satisfied his own mind that the lame foot was the *left* one. In this statement he disagreed with MOORE. The biographer says in a note: "In speaking of this lameness at the commencement of my work, I forbore, both from my own doubts upon the subject, and the great variance I found in the recollections of others, from stating in *which* of his feet the lameness existed. It will, indeed, with difficulty be believed what uncertainty I found upon this point, even among those most intimate with him. Mr. HUNT, in his book, states it to have been the left foot that was deformed; and this, though contrary to my own impression, and, as it appears, also to the fact, was the opinion I found also of others who had been much in the habit of living with him. On applying to his early friends at Southwell, and to the shoemaker of that town who worked for him, so little were they prepared to answer with any certainty on the subject, that it was only by recollecting that the lame foot 'was the off one in going up the street,' they at last came to the conclusion that his right limb was the one affected; and Mr. JACKSON, his preceptor in pugilism, was, in like manner, obliged to call to mind whether his noble pupil was a right or left hand hitter before he could arrive at the same decision." And yet, after all, I am inclined to think that JAMES was right and MOORE mistaken.

Many years ago I met at the "Sailor's Snug Harbor," near Port Richmond, Staten Island, a venerable old pensioner named WILLIAM GIRDHAM. He was the son of an English sailing-master who fell at Trafalgar, and had himself seen many years' service in the British Navy. In the year 1810 he was a seaman attached to the frigate *Salsette*, Captain Bathurst, on board of which Lord Byron embarked at Smyrna on the 11th of April in that year, and in which he remained as a guest, except when on shore at Constantinople, until he was landed at the Island of Zea, toward the end of the succeeding July. Girdham, being all this time cockswain of the Captain's gig, and always accompanying Lord Byron in his frequent excursions upon the water, had abundant opportunities of observing the peculiarities of the noble poet.

When Lord Byron and Lieutenant Ekenhead performed the feat of swimming from Sestos to Abydos, Girdham steered the boat that followed them. According to his statement, three or four times before they reached their destination, Byron swam up to the boat, and, holding on to the side for a minute or two, took some refreshment to strengthen him. Ekenhead, he asserted, was much the better swimmer of the two; that is, he swam faster and more gracefully. When they reached the opposite shore, neither of them appeared to be exhausted.

It was Byron's habit while at Constantinople to swim early every morning in the Bosphorus. Upon these occasions Girdham represented himself to have been his only companion. He rowed him out daily, he said, to a particular spot at six o'clock. His Lordship, who always provided himself with two eggs and a few biscuits, would, after undressing, toss one of the eggs into the air with all his strength. Then, noticing where it struck the water, he would swim after it. This proceeding he would repeat with the other egg, and afterward dress himself, eat his biscuits, and return to town.

I questioned GIRDHAM about BYRON's lameness. He said that he had a very distinct remembrance of it. The heel of one of the poet's boots was from three eighths to one half of an inch higher than the other, and the toes of the foot to which it belonged he turned in when walking. This inequality of gait was, however, so slight that a person might be some time in his company without perceiving it. GIRDHAM was sure that the *left* foot was the imperfect one. He noticed that when he was in the water he was almost powerless with the *left* leg. His attention was so frequently called to this circumstance, that he was certain that he could not be mistaken in his recollection of it.

At this period of his life BYRON appeared much older than he really was. He was born on the 22d of January, 1788, and consequently, in May, 1810, was a little more than two-and-twenty. And yet to the eyes of my informant he then looked at least thirty. He was already quite corpulent. His shoulders were broad and his waist slender. When undressed, however, his limbs appeared less muscular than one would expect to find them.

His manners were affable, communicative, and joyous. He was a great favorite with the sailors, both on account of his liberality and the frankness of his intercourse with them. HOBHOUSE, who was of the party, and whose bearing was more reserved and aristocratic, was less liked.

BYRON's dress upon ordinary occasions was exceedingly plain and unpretending. He had an English love for soap and water, and was always scrupulously neat about his person. When on board the frigate, he spent most of his mornings in the Captain's cabin, reading and writing.

Upon the plain of Troy, GIRDHAM remained three days

with the poet. On their return to the water's edge, there was some delay about the boat. LORD BYRON directed that his writing-desk be brought to him, which he placed upon his knees, and before they were ready to embark he had "covered a sheet of paper with verses."

Upon another occasion, GIRDHAM was sent with a boat from Scutari, where LORD BYRON happened to be with CAPTAIN BATHURST, to get some casks of wine. Upon its return, the boat was upset, and the casks floated off. BYRON's anxiety was all for the man, the Captain's for the wine—probably because he knew that the man was in no danger.

When BYRON was landed at the Island of Zea, he went ashore with a kid under each arm.

It is proper for me to add that, having myself visited that part of the world, and being tolerably familiar with its topography, I was able to confirm in my own mind the accuracy of GIRDHAM's descriptions. His recollections of the poet were given with but few leading questions from me, and there was an air of truth about him which satisfied me that he was drawing upon his memory, and not "spinning a yarn." I asked him, for my own information, the meaning of the word "Salsette," the name of CAPTAIN BATHURST's frigate. He replied that it is the name of an island near Bombay—that he was himself at Bombay with the frigate, and that he sailed in her in all ten years. In the year 1815, disgusted with the smallness of a pension which his sisters were receiving from the Government, he left the service. Since then he had been employed in merchant vessels belonging principally to Philadelphia and New York, until laid upon the shelf by age. When I saw him he was about seventy years old, and a fine specimen of an intelligent, veteran tar.

There are many engraved portraits of LORD BYRON, but it is said that none of them are very like him. Mr. JAMES assured me that the face of the Macedonian monarch in PAUL VERONESE's celebrated picture of "Alexander in the Tent of Darius," in Venice, is the exact image of his Lordship. Standing before it one day with a lady, he mentioned the extraordinary likeness to her, when the *cicerone* who accompanied them said, "Ah, sir! I see that you knew my old master well. Many a time since his death have I stood and gazed upon that face, which recalled his own so vividly!"

That picture has a curious history, and I may well deviate here a moment to relate it. The artist was invited by a hospitable family to spend some time with them at their villa upon the banks of the Brenta. While in the house, his habits were very peculiar. He remained in his room the greater part of the time, and refused to allow any one to enter it upon any pretext. The maid was not even permitted to make his bed, and every morning she found the sweepings of the room at the door, whence she was at liberty to remove them. One day the painter suddenly disappeared. The door of the room was found open. The sheets were gone from the bed. The frightened servant reported to the master that they had been stolen. A search was instituted. In one corner of the room was found a large roll. Upon opening it, it proved to be a magnificent picture—the famous "Alexander in the Tent of Darius." Upon close inspection it was discovered that it was painted upon the sheets of the bed! The artist had left it as a present to the family, and had taken this curious method to show his gratitude for their kindness.

CHAPTER IV.

I HAD a less intimate acquaintance with THACKERAY when in this country than with JAMES, but I also knew the former very well. We used constantly to meet on Saturday evenings at the Century Club, of New York, which then occupied a modest house on Clinton Place. Mr. THACKERAY very much enjoyed the company and the entertainment that he always found there, and sometimes protracted his visits late into the night. He usually unbent his bow to a very slack cord, and his propensity to ironical teasing he seldom laid aside. I happened to be there one evening after all had left except THACKERAY, GEORGE WILLIAM CURTIS, and LEUTZE, the painter. THACKERAY and CURTIS fell to talking about a most respectable young lady whom we all knew. THACKERAY was unlimited in his expressions of admiration for her, in some of which Mr. CURTIS, in the most gentleman-like manner, declined to concur.

We were all surprised, and, I confess, somewhat shocked to hear THACKERAY close the discussion by saying, "Well, CURTIS, you may say what you please about her, but she is a devilish good fellow!" He then took out his watch, said that it was late, and that he must go home. "To-morrow," he said, "I have to accompany a lady to church. In the afternoon I shall go to Philadelphia. When I arrive there, I mean to go directly to the Club, and forthwith begin to intoxicate myself." Of course, this was mere badinage, but it was THACKERAY all over.

JENNY LIND, the world-renowned singer, arrived at New York on a Sunday, in the month of September, in the year 1850. I had hardly reached my office on Monday morning before a messenger came there from her, bringing a letter of introduction in her favor, I think from the BARINGS, of London, to my law-partner, Mr. JOHN JAY, with the request that he would immediately call upon her at the Irving House, where she was then stopping. Mr. JAY happened to have recently gone abroad, and I sent Miss LIND word to that effect. The messenger soon returned with the request that I would come in his stead. As soon as I could dispose of some urgent business, I started for the hotel, which was in the building at the corner of Broadway and Chambers Street, now occupied by DELMONICO. Upon my arrival, I mentioned whom I desired to see, and was at once accosted by a stranger, who introduced himself to me as Mr. BARNUM. He offered to accompany me to Miss LIND's drawing-room, and I followed him up stairs. On the way, he turned to me and said, "I am going to introduce you to an angel, sir—to an angel!" We entered the drawing-room, but it was vacant, and Mr. BARNUM went to call the distinguished artist. He presently returned, saying that she would come directly, and while we were waiting he poured into my ear ceaseless praises of her. After a short delay, the object of his admiration entered the room, and Mr. BARNUM presented me to her. She wore a summer dress, cut low in the neck and with short sleeves, and she looked to me wonderfully substantial for an angel. We soon got to business. It appeared that she had come to America without any formal contract with Mr. BARNUM. There was nothing between them but a very vague memorandum which had been executed at Bremen, I believe, by herself and an agent of the great showman on his behalf. She desired me to prepare a proper agreement, and we three sat down together and settled its terms.

When, the next day, I had completed it, and had duplicate copies made of it, I returned to the hotel and submitted it to my client and to Mr. BARNUM, and it appeared to be perfectly satisfactory to both of them. Thereupon the two copies were duly signed, sealed, witnessed, and exchanged.

A day or two afterward the first rehearsal took place at Castle Garden, and I attended it. Never before and never since has New York witnessed such a furor as the advent of JENNY LIND produced. Mr. BARNUM, with unexampled skill and tact, fanned the public excitement, which he had largely created, to fever heat. Upon the occasion of this rehearsal, the entire Battery was covered with one dense mass of humanity. When the performance was over, Miss LIND took my arm to return to her carriage, which she had left standing opposite the Bowling Green. Immediately after we made our exit from the Garden, the crowd pressed upon us so wildly that the police had difficulty in forcing a passage for us. Some endeavored to thrust petitions for charity into her hand, and the only object of others was to gratify their curiosity by gazing into her face. The populace made up their minds that I must be BARNUM, and I was repeatedly addressed by that name. It was with no small difficulty, and after a great deal of embarrassment to me, that we finally reached the carriage and drove away.

After a time Miss Lind became dissatisfied with her contract, and I was sent for to revise it. Mr. Barnum made the required concessions. I prepared a substitute, and this also was duly executed.

Before the first concert came off, it was announced in the newspapers that Miss Lind intended to inaugurate her career in America by presenting her share of the proceeds to public charities in the city of New York. I believe that the suggestion came from Mr. Barnum, and it was a master-stroke of policy. The day after that concert I again saw Miss Lind, and received from her about eleven thousand dollars for distribution. I asked her to what institutions I was to present it, and she told me to select them myself. Accordingly I consulted with two or three gentlemen, and made out a list which I submitted to her for her approbation. She approved it, without hardly reading it, and I started upon my mission of mercy. Before I had got through it, I almost regretted that I had consented to be her almoner. Scarcely any body—there were a few praiseworthy exceptions—was satisfied. At almost every establishment at which I called, they tried to persuade me that a larger allotment should have been made to their particular institution, and that its needs and deservings were so much greater than those of such a sister one. Of course, we had been strictly impartial. We had no motive whatever to be otherwise.

Now the best of it is that, as I have since had reason to believe, the receipts of that first concert fell far short of Mr. Barnum's expectations, and that the public might not suspect the fact, he himself furnished a large portion of the money which figured as Miss LIND's share.

Again and again Miss LIND desired changes made in the contract to her own advantage, and every time Mr. BARNUM yielded. Whatever his motive, he was most obliging and complaisant, and although I have never since met him, I have always esteemed him for the good-nature and liberality which he exhibited at this time in his business relations with Miss LIND. I believe that she received every farthing that belonged to her, and that he treated her with the most scrupulous honor. Of what occurred afterward, I have not so much personal knowledge. Mr. JAY returned from Europe, and became the more immediate adviser of our fair client. In June, 1851, after singing at ninety-five concerts under Mr. BARNUM's management, the contract between them, which she had the privilege to extend to one hundred and fifty, was rescinded by mutual agreement, but at her request. The performances which she afterward gave in the States were on her own account.

I believe that the immediate cause of the rupture was that BARNUM desired her to sing in a building in Philadelphia which she denominated a circus. I heard that she told him that she was not a horse, and, therefore, would not appear there.

Miss LIND soon removed from the Irving House to the New York Hotel, and it was there that I saw her most frequently. The barytone of the troupe which accompanied her, who was in the same house, was madly in love with her, and he used to lie in bed all day, weeping and howling over his unrequited affection. The way in which she was hounded for charity all the time was disgraceful to the country. Besides receiving scores of letters, she was daily besieged by male and female beggars, who obtained access to her upon every pretext, and who tormented her for donations for themselves or others. The impudence of some of these people was almost incredible. I once saw her play the tragedy queen to perfection in her own drawing-room. One of her countrymen was an importunate petitioner for assistance, and not receiving at first a favorable reply, became insolent. The manner in which she ordered him from her presence would have done credit to Rachel or Ristori. I am ashamed to be compelled to say that many American ladies urged their pleas in behalf of objects, some of them undoubtedly meritorious, with an importunity which overstepped the bounds of propriety.

Miss LIND was a calm, sensible, conscientious woman of high principles, rather calculating than emotional. She detested *humbug*—a word which was constantly in her mouth. I was with her when a telegram was shown to her, mentioning the enormous sum that was paid in Boston for a choice of seats at her first concert. "What a fool!" she exclaimed, referring to the purchaser.

She had an abhorrence for negroes, which she could not overcome. "They are *so* ugly," she used to say.

CHAPTER V.

I FIRST became acquainted with GENERAL WINFIELD SCOTT in the spring of the year 1853, after his defeat for the Presidency by FRANKLIN PIERCE. He was undoubtedly very much chagrined that one of his least distinguished lieutenants in Mexico had been preferred by the American people to himself for the highest position within their gift; but he made no unseemly exhibition of his feelings. He was then living in his house in Twelfth Street, in New York; and I particularly remember one evening which I spent there, when one of the few persons in the world who could venture to take a liberty with him, galled him to the quick by lavish praises of FRANKLIN PIERCE. This person had just returned from Washington, and spoke of the President as the most polished gentleman in America, and as in all respects fitted for his exalted position. One could not help feeling that this was done with the intent to annoy the old soldier. But he gave no sign of impatience or vexation.

One afternoon, in the summer of the year 1863, I started for West Point by the steam-boat *Mary Powell.* A few minutes after myself, GENERAL SCOTT came on board, accompanied by his friend, Mr. VAIL, of the Bank of Commerce, who escorted him to the boat. The General took a seat in the cabin, and I took one at his side, and we did not remove from them during the entire passage. I had much agreeable talk with him. He told me that after he was taken prisoner at the battle of Queenstown Heights, in October, 1812, orders came in the evening to remove him to an interior place, distant some miles from the frontier. He was very indignant at what he considered an unnecessary and ungenerous proceeding. When he reached the end of his journey, he was informed that he was brought there only that he might participate in a ball which was about to take place. But here a difficulty arose. He had not a proper suit of clothes with him, and, as he was six feet four inches high, he could not reasonably expect to supply the deficiency by borrowing. But it so happened that Sir John Harvey, the Adjutant-General of the British Army, who was present, was precisely the same stature as himself, and from him he borrowed all that he needed for the occasion. He and Sir John grew to be fast friends. Sir John subsequently became Lieutenant-Governor of New Brunswick, and, later, Governor of Nova Scotia. During the boundary troubles between Maine and New Brunswick in the year 1839, when a recourse to arms seemed imminent on both sides, our Government sent General Scott to that province to co-operate with Sir John in keeping the peace, and allaying the disturbed feeling which existed. Their joint efforts were successful, and the matter was finally adjusted by the Ashburton Treaty concluded at Washington in the year 1842.

He told me that during the last war with Great Britain, before an action began between the two armies, it was customary for the respective commanders to ride forward, accompanied by their staffs, and formally salute each other. Each then returned to his own lines, and the battle opened.

General Scott expressed to me his great gratification that in the War of the Rebellion more than fifty per cent. of the officers of the regular army who were born in Virginia had remained loyal to the flag. The percentage of excess was not large, only four or five, I think he said. He had himself been at pains to make a careful estimate, and he was certain of its correctness.

I asked him his opinion of McClellan, Lee, and Grant. He told me that he had never been so disappointed in any one as he had been in George B. McClellan. Of Lee he remarked, in somewhat turgid language, that "Robert E. Lee had never but once in his life been guilty of an act unworthy a Christian, a soldier, and a gentleman!" He said that he only remembered Grant as a young lieutenant of average merit in Mexico. He little foresaw the eminence which that "young lieutenant" was to attain in both military and civil life! He has in his career presented the antithesis of what Washington Irving once said to my friend Charles Astor Bristed. Bristed was speaking to him of somebody as a "promising young man." "Ah! Charles," answered Irving, "most of us are promissory notes, only too liable to be protested at maturity!" Grant did not promise much in his youth, but his performances at maturity have excelled those of a generation of "promising young men."

I used very often to see the poet Fitz-Greene Halleck, but had not a personal acquaintance with him. He was stiff, angular, and clean-shaved; wore a high, standing shirt-collar, and in the finest weather carried a green cotton umbrella under his arm. He was for many years book-keeper to the late John Jacob Astor. He used to tell that gentleman that if he only had an independent income of two hundred dollars a year he could live contented. Mr. ASTOR, by his will, left to his old book-keeper just what he had professed would satisfy him. But his son, WILLIAM B. ASTOR, increased the annuity to an amount which enabled the aged poet to live comfortably in his native Connecticut until his death.

EDGAR A. POE I remember seeing on a single occasion. He announced a lecture to be delivered at the Society Library building on Broadway, under the title of the "Universe." It was a stormy night, and there were not more than sixty persons present in the lecture-room. I have seen no portrait of POE that does justice to his pale, delicate, intellectual face and magnificent eyes. His lecture was a rhapsody of the most intense brilliancy. He appeared inspired, and his inspiration affected the scant audience almost painfully. He wore his coat tightly buttoned across his slender chest; his eyes seemed to glow like those of his own raven, and he kept us entranced for two hours and a half. The late Mr. PUTNAM, the publisher, told me that the next day the wayward, luckless poet presented himself to him with the manuscript of the "Universe." He told PUTNAM that in it he solved the whole problem of life; that it would immortalize its publisher as well as its author; and, what was of less consequence, that it would bring to him the fortune which he had so long and so vainly been seeking. Mr. PUTNAM, while an admirer of genius, was also a cool, calculating man of business. As such, he could not see the matter in exactly the same light as the poet did, and the only result of the interview was that he lent POE a shilling to take him home to Fordham, where he then resided. After poor POE's death, the late RUFUS W. GRISWOLD, not altogether immaculate himself, treated his memory with undue severity. I had a correspondence upon the subject with his fellow-poet and old-time friend, N. P. WILLIS, who earnestly deprecated GRISWOLD's harshness. I knew Mr. WILLIS very well indeed, and have passed many delightful hours at his house, while he resided in New York. He had committed many errors in his life—as who has not? But, unlike some, age purified him. I recollect meeting him one day in Broadway, when his salutation to me was, "I am sixty years old to-day!" I first became acquainted with him in New Haven, when I was a mere boy, and he was at the zenith of his fame. He graduated at Yale College in the year 1827. He was always an immense dandy, and there was a college tradition that while there he dressed in white broadcloth, which he had imported expressly for himself from England.

EX-PRESIDENT JOHN QUINCY ADAMS I saw for the only time during the winter which preceded his death. The venerable statesman came to New York, on his way to Washington, to take his seat in the House of Representatives. On the evening of his arrival, the New York Historical Society, of which I was then one of the Secretaries, held its monthly meeting, and I was sent with one other member to Mr. ADAMS's hotel to invite him to attend it. He consented to do so, and on our way up town he asked me about its prominent members. Among others, I spoke in strong terms of Mr. GEORGE GIBBS, dwelling particularly upon the fact that he was a grandson of OLIVER WOLCOTT. I entirely forgot the quarrel that had occurred, and the bitter enmity which had grown out of it, between JOHN ADAMS and Mr. WOLCOTT. A descent from one whom his father had so disliked could hardly be a recommendation to the son. The even more venerable ALBERT GALLATIN was the President of the Society at that time, and the meeting between these two old public servants was interesting and affecting to those of younger generations who stood around them.

Mr. CHARLES FRANCIS ADAMS, himself an elderly man now, looks wonderfully like his father, and his intellectual and moral similarity to him are equally remarkable. Intelligent, learned, stubborn, and brave, tenacious in all things and compromisers in none, they stand out as the most distinguished representatives of the most remarkable family which this country has yet produced. Some two years ago Mr. CHARLES FRANCIS ADAMS read a very able paper before the same Historical Society upon the American doctrine of neutrality. He took occasion to treat the memory of EX-PRESIDENT MONROE with great severity, especially denouncing him for his "View of the Conduct of the Executive in the Foreign Affairs of the United States," commonly called the "Monroe Letter." Mr. MONROE was appointed in 1794 by PRESIDENT WASHINGTON Minister to France, to succeed GOUVERNEUR MORRIS. His first act upon his arrival in Paris was to fraternize with the President of the National Assembly by publicly presenting him with a United States flag, and receiving in turn from him one of the French Republic. His subsequent conduct was such as to seriously interfere with the successful negotiation of a treaty in England by Mr. JAY. For this violation of the neutral policy of our Government, GENERAL WASHINGTON recalled him in August, 1796. Upon his arrival at Norfolk, on his return, he received a public ovation. Stung by the unmerited disgrace, as he considered it, which had been inflicted upon him, he very soon afterward wrote the paper referred to, denouncing the President, and sent it to Philadelphia to be printed. Soon repenting his action, he wrote to the printer countermanding the order. Unfortunately, one hundred copies had already got out; and these he made every effort to buy up and suppress. A reconciliation took place between himself and WASHINGTON, and they continued on friendly terms ever afterward. These last-mentioned facts I learned from COLONEL JAMES MONROE, a nephew of the ex-President, in early life an officer upon GENERAL SCOTT's staff, and afterward a member of Congress from the city of New York. I mentioned them to Mr. ADAMS, who had never before heard of the attempt to suppress the "Monroe Letter" which was made by its author. It is supposed that there are very few copies of this letter in existence, and Mr. ADAMS informed me that he had two of them in his own library. COLONEL MONROE was a Virginia gentleman of the old school. He told me that he had been a "friend" in sixteen affairs of honor, and had in every instance arranged a satisfactory settlement without a fight. He was second to Mr. CUTTING, of New York, in his quarrel with Mr. BRECKENRIDGE, of Kentucky. This was a very difficult case to settle, but settled it was. He never went out but once himself, and then when very young. Although in the army, he served in some capacity in one of our frigates during the Algerine War. He quarreled upon some unimportant matter with a naval officer, and early one morning they took the field under the walls of a convent on the coast of Spain. After preliminaries were arranged, his adversary advanced to him and said, "LIEUTENANT MONROE, I have been in the wrong; I beg your pardon." "My dear fellow," answered MONROE, "if you had not been quite so quick, I should have anticipated you, and said exactly what you have said." He always declined to mention the name of his antagonist.

CHAPTER VI.

IN the year 1861, PRINCE NAPOLEON (JEROME), accompanied by his wife, the PRINCESS CLOTILDE, daughter of VICTOR EMANUEL, King of Italy, and a numerous suite, arrived in a steam yacht at the port of New York. Before landing, he invited me to dine with him on board his yacht, and I accepted the invitation. I found the Prince very much as he was, in appearance at least, when I had last seen him in Paris. There was a good deal of conversation at dinner about the Lake Superior copper mines—a subject upon which the Prince was minutely informed, and about which I knew little or nothing. He had numerous nuggets, or specimens, of this ore upon a table in his cabin, and to these he constantly referred for purposes of illustration. The dinner was not a very good one. I remember particularly that the bread was detestable.

A day or two afterward he came ashore with his immediate party, and took possession of the rooms at the New York Hotel which had previously been secured for their occupation. The Princess was not pretty, but she was a kind, unassuming, devotional little lady, who won the hearts of all who had occasion to pass much time in her company. She had but one lady of honor with her, a sprightly little Duchess, the widow of the oldest son of one of the first NAPOLEON's marshals, and together they made their drawing-room on Washington Place a delightful resort for those who had the advantage of their acquaintance. The CHEVALIER BERTINATTI, the Italian Minister in Washington, was a constant attendant upon the daughter of his king.

As the Prince's oldest acquaintance in this country, it devolved upon me to show him the sights of New York. Together we visited the Custom-House, the United States Treasury and Assay Office, the Astor Library, the New York Historical Society's collections, the Cooper Union, the Novelty Works, and numerous other places and institutions. But what I most desired him to see was a first-class New York private dwelling. Accordingly, with the permission of the owner, I accompanied him to the palatial residence at the corner of Fifth Avenue and Fifteenth Street, then belonging to and occupied by Mr. BENKARD, and now the house of the Manhattan Club. Nothing in New York interested the Prince so much. He was delighted with it. He went from cellar to garret, carefully examining the furnace, the boiler, the croton-water arrangements, the speaking-tubes, and all those appurtenances of a model American dwelling which we are accustomed to designate "modern improvements." This inspection occupied several hours, and when we left he expressed the opinion that in domestic architecture and appliances for comfort we were in advance of the rest of the world. "You know the state apartments in the Palais Impérial, and they are magnificent," he said; "but did you ever see the rooms in which we have to live there?" I told him that I had not. "Well," he resumed, "they are small, wretched holes, unprovided with any of the ingenious and labor-saving contrivances which I have just seen, and so uncomfortable that when I was first married I was ashamed to take my wife to them."

Afterward I escorted the Prince and Princess to the picture-galleries of Mr. BELMONT and Mr. ASPINWALL, who, being themselves absent from town, kindly permitted them to be thrown open for the purpose.

On the 19th of September, the CHEVALIER BERTINATTI gave a magnificent dinner to the Prince at the residence of the DUKE DI LICIGNANO, the Italian Consul-General at New York, in First Place, in Brooklyn. Sitting next to the Prince, all my talk with him on that occasion was upon the subject of the war, and I told him about the enormous price which our Government was compelled to pay for arms, and with what difficulty it procured them at all. I will here observe that his sympathies were thoroughly and warmly enlisted in favor of the Union, and against the supremacy of the slaveholding South. He professed great admiration for the American people. To what I told him about our condition in respect of arms, he at once replied that he could arrange the whole matter for us. He said that they had an excess beyond their requirements of altered muskets in the French arsenals, and that he could procure them for us at cost, which was about half the price that we were then paying. That, besides, the Swedish Government possessed a very large supply of muskets of the best quality, and that he had sufficient influence to secure some of them also for us; that from these two countries we could draw enough for our present needs; that Switzerland was also well provided with arms, but that the Government of that country would not part with any of them. If I could be made the agent in this transaction, he would guarantee the result. He told me that through him the Italians had received one hundred thousand stands of arms from the Imperial Government, and that they had not yet paid a single franc on account of the purchase. In conclusion, he advised me to immediately communicate with the authorities at Washington.

At this time I had no intimacy with any member of the Cabinet except SECRETARY CHASE, and to him I addressed a letter, giving an account of my conversation with the Prince. I received the following reply under date of October 3:

"MY DEAR SIR,—Accept my thanks for your very interesting letter and for the valuable information it contained. I fear negotiations in respect to arms through Mr. SCHUYLER are in such a condition that the Government will not be able to avail itself of your valuable services. Had I known some weeks since what I know now, important advantages might have been derived to the common cause.

"I shall always be glad to hear from you.

"Yours truly, S. P. CHASE.

"MAUNSELL B. FIELD, Esq."

So the matter fell through, and the occasion never arose to revive it.

The Prince carried out his purpose of going to Lake Superior, and also made a somewhat extensive tour through the West. During his absence from New York, the Princess passed nearly all her time with the ladies of the Sacred Heart at their convent at Manhattanville. After his return a magnificent dinner was given to him by the members of the Union Club, at their house at the corner of Fifth Avenue and Twenty-first Street. Ex-GOVERNOR JOHN A. KING, of New York, then President of the Club, received him, and EX-VICE-CHANCELLOR AND JUDGE ANTHONY L. ROBERTSON presided. The Prince found the dinner admirable, and was particularly pleased with the wines, which he pronounced equal to any that he had ever tasted at the Imperial table or elsewhere. The Prince's particular attention was attracted to Mr. LEONARD JEROME, and he said that, meeting him in any part of the world, he should take him for a French cavalry general. The following clipping from a newspaper of the next morning gives an accurate account of the affair:

"The dinner given to PRINCE NAPOLEON at the Union Club last evening was pronounced a capital success by the guests.

"At the door-way of the Club-house stood the inevitable BROWN, who acted as Master of Ceremonies. The interior of the building was profusely decorated with natural flowers, and DODWORTH'S Band discoursed music unseen behind a lattice-work erected in the hall, playing, among other things, '*Partant pour la Syrie*,' as the appropriate invitation music to the dinner.

JUDGE A. L. ROBERTSON, Secretary of the Club, occupied the chair. Mr. MAUNSELL B. FIELD, as an acquaintance of the Prince and Imperial family abroad, very properly held the place of a virtual Master of Ceremonies, having superintended all the preliminary arrangements of the banquet, and been appointed to the delicate office of placing the guests.

"In addition to the members of the Club, there were present at the dinner: His Imperial Highness PRINCE NAPOLEON (JEROME); COLONEL RAGON, the celebrated French officer who led the attack upon the Malakoff; CAPTAIN BONFILS, of the French Navy, and formerly Governor of Gaudeloupe; CAPTAIN DE BUISSON, Commander of the Imperial yacht; M. MAURICE SAND, son of the celebrated GEORGE SAND; M. MERCIER, French Minister to Washington; M. HOCMELLE; the MARQUIS DE MONTHOLON, French Consul-General at this port, accompanied by his Vice-Consul; Mr. BERTINATTI, Italian Minister to the United States, and the DUKE DI LICIGNANO,

Italian Consul-General at New York. The VICOMTE DE BEAUMONT, and COLONEL FERRI PISANI, though invited, were unavoidably absent, the latter being replaced by LIEUTENANT BECQUÉ, of the yacht.

"The restraint natural to Republicans who have to entertain representatives of a foreign nobility was removed as early as possible after the ceremonious placing of the guests, and a general conversation soon prevailed around the table.

* * * * * * * *

"After the removal of the cloth, the Chairman, JUDGE ROBERTSON, proposed the health of the French Emperor, which was replied to in a speech of great cordiality by the Prince. He expressed himself with an unexpected freedom from restraint, and was received with frequent applause. In return, he proposed the 'Welfare of the United States,' which, as need not be said, the party drank with great enthusiasm. After other toasts, and a free interchange of kindly sentiments, the Prince was escorted to his hotel by his friend, Mr. FIELD. By an unfortunate delay, GENERAL WOOL and his party came to the Club-house to pay their respects to the Prince and his entertainers just after his Highness had departed."

At a dinner given to the Prince at the Revere House, in Boston, Dr. OLIVER WENDELL HOLMES read the following spirited lines:

"VIVE LA FRANCE!

"The land of sunshine and of song!
  Her name your hearts divine;
To her the banquet's vows belong
  Whose breasts have poured its wine;
Our trusty friend, our true ally
  Through varied change and chance:
So fill your flashing goblets high—
  I give you VIVE LA FRANCE!

"Above our hosts in triple folds
The self-same colors spread,
Where Valor's truthful arm upholds
The blue, the white, the red;
Alike each nation's glittering crest
Reflects the morning's glance—
Twin eagles, soaring east and west:
Once more, then, VIVE LA FRANCE!

"Sister in trial! who shall count
Thy generous friendship's claim,
Whose blood ran mingling in the fount
That gave our land its name,
Till Yorktown saw in blended line
Our conquering arms advance,
And Victory's double garlands twine
Our banners? VIVE LA FRANCE!

"O land of heroes! in our need
One gift from heaven we crave—
To stanch those wounds that vainly bleed—
The wise to lead the brave!
Call back one Captain of thy past
From glory's marble trance,
Whose name shall be a bugle-blast
To rouse us! VIVE LA FRANCE!

"Pluck CONDÉ's baton from the trench,
Wake up stout CHARLES MARTEL,
Or find some woman's hand to clench
The sword of LA PUCELLE!
Give us one hour of old TURENNE,
One lift of BAYARD's lance—
Nay, call Marengo's chief again
To lead us! VIVE LA FRANCE!

"Ah, hush! our welcome Guest shall hear
But sounds of peace and joy;
No angry echo vex thine ear,
Fair daughter of Savoy!

Once more! the land of arms and arts,
 Of glory, grace, romance;
Her love lies warm in all our hearts!
 God bless her! VIVE LA FRANCE!"

I made the following translation of the above lines into very indifferent French verse, and read it at a dinner given at the same Club-house some time later to the Admiral commanding the French fleet on the North American station:

VIVE LA FRANCE!

Terre de la chanson, du soleil bien aimée,
 Qui nous verses le jus divin,
Terre des doux nectars, vos cœurs vous l'ont nommée,
 A toi les vœux de ce festin;
A l'allié fidèle, ami de notre enfance,
 Qui partagea notre destin!
 Debout! et que, le verre plein,
Chacun répète ce refrain: "Vive la France!"

Les trois mêmes couleurs de triples plis abritent
 De nos soldats les loyaux rangs;
Sur les champs de l'honneur quand vaillament s'agitent
 Les étendars rouges, bleus, blancs;
A l'aurore du jour le double aigle s'élance
 Embrassant de ses yeux ardents
 L'empire de deux continents!
Remplissons encore et buvons: "Vive la France!"

O! sœur qui partageas nos revers et nos peines!
 Pourrons nous oublier le don
Du sang de tes enfants répandu dans nos plaines
 Pour le salut de notre nom?
Jusqu'au jour où gaiement en double front s'avance
 La phalange de nos guerriers,
 Tressant ensemble les lauriers
Pour les drapeaux d'Yorktown, chantons: "Vive la France!"

Terre des chevaliers! en ce jour de misère,
  Découvrant notre flanc sanglant,
Nous demandons au ciel en notre humble prière
  Un sage, guide du vaillant!
Des guerriers dont tes fils gardent la souvenance
  Pour nous évoque les grands noms;
  Mêlés au bruit de nos clairons,
Qu'ils dispersent nos ennemis: "Vive la France!"

Le bâton que CONDÉ lança dans la tranchée,
  Ou le fer de CHARLES MARTEL,
Ou bien de JEANNE D'ARC la foudroyante épée,
  Pour nous attendent ton appel!
Prête nous de BAYARD l'incorruptible lance,
  Un jour de TURENNE, ou plutôt
  La grande ombre de Marengo!
Vainqueurs, nous les suivrons au cri: "Vive la France!"

Mais chut! qu'un chant de paix, que des accents de joie
  Charment l'hôte que nous fêtons;
Qu'aucun accent guerrier, fille de la Savoie,
  Jusqu'à toi ne porte ses sons!
A toi, terre des arts! à toi, douce espérance
  De la valeur, de la beauté!
  Par nous que ce cri repété
Arrive au Seigneur tout-puissant: "Vive la France!"

The evening before the Prince and Princess sailed on their return to France they gave a charming entertainment to a party of ladies and gentlemen on board the yacht, in return for some of the courtesies extended to themselves.

CHAPTER VII.

SOON after the Prince of Wales arrived in America in the year 1860, certain citizens of New York held a meeting at the Merchants' Bank for the purpose of inviting him to that city, and of tendering him some special civilities. A Committee was formed, and, after much consideration, it was decided to offer him a dinner. Many preferred a ball; but some of the most eminent members of the Committee had scruples upon the subject. Mr. PETER COOPER was appointed Chairman, and I Secretary, of the Committee. We had an invitation to a dinner, at such time as the Prince should designate, appropriately engrossed; and it was determined that a delegation from our number should proceed to Montreal, and there present it to him in person. Among those who went upon this mission were EX-GOVERNOR HAMILTON FISH, EX-GOVERNOR JOHN A. KING, Mr. JOHN JACOB ASTOR, Mr. ROBERT L. KENNEDY, and myself, as Secretary of the Committee. When we arrived at the railway station upon the St. Lawrence, opposite to Montreal, upon the 23d of August, we were met there by the American Consul-General in the British Provinces, who informed us that the Mayor of Montreal, Mr. RODIER, was awaiting us upon the other side, in order to receive us officially. This was very annoying intelligence to us. There were ladies in our party, and they, as well as ourselves, were covered with dust and begrimed by cinders. When we landed from the ferry-boat which transported us across, sure enough there was the Mayor in full regalia, chain and all. We had settled it that Mr. FISH must be the spokesman for us—very much to that gentleman's disgust. The Mayor made us a grandiloquent address in broken English, and Mr. FISH, his person ensconced in a linen duster, and with a traveling-bag in each hand, made a neat and even elegant reply. In the mean time the landing-place was covered by a miscellaneous crowd, principally composed of small boys, who shouted and cheered us. Then his Honor informed us that carriages were in waiting to conduct us to our hotel. They consisted of three or four of the ordinary Montreal street cabs, and we entered them, and were soon comfortably housed in Saint Lawrence Hall. I will here remark that a very extortionate bill for those cabs was sent to us in the course of a day or two, which we paid without demurrer.

On the afternoon of Friday, the 24th, the Prince arrived in town, and we were officially invited to be present upon the occasion. Saturday was distinguished by the formal opening of the Victoria Bridge. We were also provided with tickets to witness that ceremony, and we made the journey in the Prince's private car by his invitation. He received us with the greatest courtesy, shaking hands with us according to American usage, and treating us in every respect with marked attention.

That evening LORD LYONS and GENERAL BRUCE, the Prince's "Governor," called upon us at our hotel. They made merely a brief visit, in which the special business which had brought us to Montreal was only referred to in very general terms. But the next day they came again, and at that interview the conversation was very free. The Englishmen would have preferred any thing to a dinner. The Prince could not himself speak: he was to be in the States incognito, under the title of *Lord Renfrew.* Nor would it answer that any one should speak for him. Besides, at a large dinner it was to be apprehended that remarks might be made by some of the speakers which would become subjects for future regret. The Prince was very young. He was fond of amusement. A dinner, if there were no other objections to it, might be too heavy an affair to entertain him. In a word, they were sorry that we had decided for a dinner, although none the less mindful of the kindly feeling which had prompted the purpose, etc., etc., etc. And with this they left us, and we Americans remained for consultation. They had given us a cue, and we decided, in behalf of our constituents, to take the responsibility of following it. We unanimously determined to substitute a ball in place of the dinner, and, having done so, notified GENERAL BRUCE to that effect. He was delighted, and was sure that the Prince would be charmed to accept.

The next thing was to secure the services of a scrivener to re-engross the invitation which we had brought with us, so as to make it apply to a ball instead of a dinner. One was very soon found, who executed his commission with great celerity.

Thereupon we were asked to lunch with the Prince on Monday afternoon, at GENERAL SIR WILLIAM FENWICK WILLIAMS's house in the suburbs, where his Royal Highness was stopping. This was to be the occasion for presenting our invitation.

Our party included several persons besides those I have named. One of us had come in great haste, and had brought no dress coat with him; but he found a friend in town who supplied the deficiency. At the luncheon, the Prince and all his suite were in full uniform. All the Americans were suitably attired, and conformed to the usages of polite society, except one gentleman who sat opposite the Prince, and who ate with his knife, and wore a white waistcoat upon which the buttons were missing. He had, however, supplied their places with pins, and these pins were very provokingly visible. After dinner we retired to a reception-room, and there the invitation was read to the Prince by Mr. KING, and accepted by him in a few hesitating words.

We then returned to New York, reported our action to those who had sent us, and received their approval. The work of preparation commenced, and terribly laborious and trying work it was. The scheme adopted was to have a Committee of four hundred gentlemen, to be duly elected by the smaller Committee already formed. Each member of the Committee was to pay seventy dollars, and to be entitled to seven tickets; but he was required to submit a list of the persons for whom he intended them to an Executive Committee, who passed upon their eligibility. Of these seven tickets, at least four must be for ladies; but this was afterward reduced to three. Besides, every ticket had to be countersigned by a member of the sub-Committee on Tickets and Finance, and also by the member of the Committee at whose request it was issued. Seven sub-Committees were constituted—viz., one on *Invitations*, one on *Tickets and Finance*, one on *Reception*, one on *House and Music*, one on

Decorations, one on *Police and Carriages*, and one on *Supper and Floor*.

From the reports which we received from these sub-Committees, we were soon induced to believe that we should require more money than we had in hand. There was a supper-room to be built expressly for the occasion, and other expenses to be incurred which we had not at first thought of. Accordingly, we made an additional assessment of thirty dollars each upon the four hundred members of the General Committee, which was promptly paid into the treasury.

All New York soon became wild upon the subject of this ball. Venerable citizens who had never attended a place of public amusement in their lives humiliated themselves in every possible way in order to have their names placed upon the Committee. Ladies begged for tickets almost upon bended knees. Such importunities were never addressed to a Prime Minister as were beseechingly poured into the ears of those members of the Committee who had the misfortune to be prominent in the affair. The applications for complimentary invitations were also overwhelming. The Press, too, was very exacting.

Before coming to New York, the Prince made a journey to the West, to Virginia, to Washington, and to Philadelphia. At Washington he lodged in the Executive Mansion, and it is said that PRESIDENT BUCHANAN used to surreptitiously convey choice cigars into his room after his mentors had retired for the night. He left Philadelphia with his suite early on the morning of Thursday, the 11th of October. Mr. AUGUSTUS SCHELL, then Collector of the Port of New York, invited a distinguished party to embark on board the United States revenue cutter *Harriet Lane*, CAPTAIN FAUNCE, at half-past eight o'clock that morning, to proceed to Perth Amboy to meet and accompany the Prince and his suite to the city. The train from Philadelphia arrived on time, and a little after twelve his Royal Highness, followed by the DUKE OF NEWCASTLE, the EARL OF ST. GERMANS, and the other gentlemen who accompanied him, all in dusty garments, and wearing "shocking bad" white hats, stepped on board the cutter. It took some time to get their luggage on board, and then to the music of a royal salute the *Harriet Lane* started upon her return trip. The day was very lovely, and with a single exception every thing passed off very agreeably. One old and rather prosy gentleman deemed it especially incumbent upon him to entertain the Prince. For some time he monopolized his attention, and was evidently boring him to the very limit of his boyish patience. Seeing this, some of us held counsel together, and decided that GENERAL SCOTT must head a relief party. The old soldier carried out our suggestion with perfect success, and during the remainder of the passage the Prince was at liberty to converse with whom he pleased. After an elegant luncheon had been served, the Prince went upon the upper deck, and, with several of the juniors, smoked cigars of a very superior quality which he produced from his pocket—probably some of Mr. BUCHANAN'S. Afterward we went forward, and EX-JUDGE ROOSEVELT, then United States District Attorney, undertook to point out to the Prince the principal objects of interest in the harbor, and to explain the associations connected with some of them. While so doing, he had occasion to refer to a date in English history.

The Prince courteously corrected him. Mr. Roosevelt politely insisted that he was right. The Duke of Newcastle happened to be standing near, but out of ear-shot. His Royal Highness called him, and merely asked him what was the date in dispute. The Duke unhesitatingly confirmed the Prince's recollection of it.

We reached the pier at twenty minutes past two. On entering Castle Garden the Prince was received by the Mayor, Fernando Wood, and a delegation of both Boards of the Common Council. He immediately retired to the room of the Commissioners of Emigration, and exchanged his citizen's dress for the uniform of a Colonel in the British Army. He then mounted a horse expressly brought for his use from the Provinces, and reviewed upon the Battery the First Division of New York State Militia, under the command of Major-General Sanford. Afterward he entered an open carriage drawn by six horses, accompanied by the Mayor, the Duke of Newcastle, and the Earl of St. Germans, and drove to the City Hall, where he received the honor of a marching review. When he re-entered his carriage the day was already so far advanced that it was dark before he reached his quarters at the Fifth Avenue Hotel. All along the route he was vociferously cheered by the unprecedented multitude of people that filled Broadway; but the disappointment occasioned by the delay in carrying out the military programme, and the consequent inability of patient sight-seers to scan the Prince's features at so late an hour, called out many imprecations upon the devoted head of the commanding General.

It had been desired and intended that the Prince

should ride up Broadway on horseback. He himself preferred to do so, and the horse which he mounted on the Battery had been expressly brought on for the purpose. But some in authority thought that the street was too slippery, and therefore dangerous. Besides, there was a vague apprehension on the part of the English gentlemen that some of her Majesty's expatriated subjects, who constitute so large a proportion of the population of the metropolitan city, might attempt to harm and insult him, if too much exposed. There was not much foundation for their fears. Only once while in New York did he receive any discourtesy, and that was at the hands of an insane English mechanic, who was promptly arrested.

The question of how he should dress was also one that was much discussed. As he traveled through the States as *Lord Renfrew*, his own suite, as well as LORD LYONS, did not think that it comported with his incognito to appear otherwise than in ordinary citizen's costume. Our people thought differently. They desired to receive him as the Prince of Wales, the son of QUEEN VICTORIA. The matter was finally compromised by the arrangement that he should wear his military uniform at the review, and the ribbon of the Order of the Garter at the ball.

While the Prince remained in New York he was kept pretty constantly on the move. MAYOR WOOD gave a charming breakfast in his honor, at his residence, Wood Lawn, Bloomingdale. He called upon GENERAL SCOTT at his house on Twelfth Street. He lunched with the British Consul in New York, Mr. ARCHIBALD. He had several photographs taken by BRADY and GURNEY. He visited the Deaf and Dumb Asylum at Mount Washington, the University of the City of New York, the New York Free Academy (as then designated), the Cooper Institute, the Astor Library, etc. There was also a superb torchlight procession of the New York Fire Department in his honor. At that time the Department boasted of only one steamer, all the others being the old-fashioned engines worked by hand. Now there are none but steamers.

The ball took place on the evening of Friday, the 12th of October. A deputation of the reception Committee, of which I was one, went to the Fifth Avenue Hotel, at about nine o'clock, to escort the Prince and his immediate suite to the Academy of Music. All his party soon made their appearance in the drawing-room, but the Prince himself kept us waiting a long time. Finally he too came in, and, after shaking hands with us, retired to the entrance-door, and was for some time hopelessly engaged in an effort to force his not very small hands into a pair of gloves altogether too tight for them. After a moment I stepped up to him, and he said to me in an undertone, "These gloves were sent to me by a lady in this house, with the request that I should wear them to-night; I don't know who she is. They are much too small for me; but I intend to work my hands into them, if I can." He finally succeeded. He added, "I am a little late to-night, because I have been writing home to my mother." Although much older than himself, I was so much younger than the sexagenarians who chiefly had possession of him that he seemed to take very kindly to me.

I have no intention to particularly describe the ball. It was magnificent; but, in spite of all the efforts of the

Committee, there were too many elderly persons. Thirty-three exceptional tickets had been issued to young "dancing-men." The *contretemps* of the falling in of a portion of the floor was most unfortunate. The Committee had made very particular inquiries about its solidity, and had been assured that it was perfectly safe. The accident partly arose from the weight of an immense throng of people who collected around the Prince and concentrated upon one spot. The crowd was suffocating. The Committee had been misled as to the capacity of the house, and people deserted the upper boxes and swelled the tide below. At one time it was feared that some must have gained admission by presenting spurious tickets; but, upon a count, it was found that there were only three thousand and twenty-five tickets in the boxes, while three thousand one hundred and ninety-five paid and complimentary ones had been legitimately issued. Of those entitled to come, one hundred and seventy had stayed away.

The Committee had a great deal of trouble about the matter of partners for the Prince. Every woman in New York was dying to dance with him; and husbands, fathers, and brothers urgently pressed the claims of their fair relatives. Finally, the Committee referred the whole matter to Mr. William Butler Duncan, *with power*. This gentleman, as brave as he is courteous, undertook the obnoxious task of making selections, and performed it as judiciously and satisfactorily as it was possible to do. Still, of course, there were grumblers. Female ambition upon such a subject was insatiable.

The next Sunday the Prince attended divine service in Trinity Church. There were four bishops and thirty-five clergymen present. A full choral service was performed by nine men and fourteen boys. He was presented with a very handsome Bible, and almost equally handsome Prayer-book. The former was a royal octavo volume, bound in red morocco, with a large gold clasp, upon which was engraved a Prince of Wales plume, with the motto "*Ich Dien.*" On the cover was the following inscription in gold letters:

"To his Royal Highness, ALBERT EDWARD, Prince of Wales, from the Corporation of Trinity Church, New York, in memory of the munificence of the Crown of England. Nineteenth Sunday after Trinity, A.D. 1860."

The Prayer-book was bound in brown Russia leather, and had two silver clasps. On the inside was engraved the Garter, surmounted by a crown, with the motto, "*Honi soit qui mal y pense,*" and the royal standard of England in the centre. On the opposite page was inscribed:

"To his Royal Highness the Prince of Wales, from FRANCIS VINTON, D.D., and FREDERICK OGILBY, D.D., the clergymen in charge of Trinity Church, New York, as a memorial of the Nineteenth Sunday after Trinity."

The Rev. Dr. VINTON preached from the following text:

"Then the Presidents and Princes sought to find occasion against Daniel concerning the *kingdom;* but they could find none occasion nor fault; forasmuch as he was faithful, neither was there any error or fault found in him.

"Then said these men, We shall not find any occasion against this Daniel, except we find it against him concerning the law of his God" (Dan. vi., 4, 5).

The Prince and his party took their departure from

New York on the next, Monday, morning at ten o'clock. I called upon him at his hotel to take leave of him. He was very kind and cordial, and when informed that his carriage was waiting, he walked with me from his drawing-room to it, holding my hand boy-fashion all the way. He was at that time as amiable and good-natured a youth as I ever met.

When the ball Committee came to finally settle its accounts, the following was the result:

Total amount received . . .	$41,006 65
" " expended . . .	28,746 65
Balance on hand	$12,260 00

Or $30 65 for each of the four hundred subscribers, which was returned to them by checks of the Treasurer, Mr. ROYAL PHELPS.

I believe that there is no other instance on record of a Committee charged with the expenditure of money which did not spend the whole of it. In almost every other similar case that I have ever heard of there has been a deficiency. If for no other reason than the foregoing, the Prince of Wales ball in New York is entitled to be distinguished from every other public festival of which our metropolitan annals contain any mention.

CHAPTER VIII.

TOWARD the close of the year 1860, after the election of Mr. LINCOLN to the Presidency, but before the Legislatures of any of the states had passed ordinances of secession, it became necessary for the United States Government to negotiate a loan of ten millions of dollars. As the national credit up to this time continued unimpaired, the rate of interest was fixed at five per cent. But financiers were already beginning to be somewhat distrustful about the future of the country, and it was only through the unremitting exertions of the Hon. JOHN J. CISCO, the Assistant Treasurer at New York, that the whole amount was finally subscribed. In accordance with the terms of the loan, one per cent. of the amount taken by each subscriber was deposited by him at the time of making the subscription. A day or two after the transaction was thus far completed, the Hon. HOWELL COBB, of Georgia, the Secretary of the Treasury, arrived in New York. When he came to the Treasury, Mr. CISCO warmly congratulated him upon the success of the loan. His reply was, "CISCO, the people who have taken it are a pack of d—d fools. It will never be paid. The country is going to be broken to pieces. Georgia is going out of the Union; and when she goes, I shall go with her." "Why, Mr. Secretary," rejoined Mr. CISCO, "I am amazed to find *you* a secessionist."

The bonds were to be paid for by installments. Before

the time for the final payment arrived, several of the states had attempted to withdraw from the Union. Of the ten millions subscribed, only about seven millions in all was paid. Several prominent banking-houses in New York and Washington refused to fulfill their obligations, and allowed their deposits of one per cent. to be forfeited.

Mr. COBB withdrew from the Cabinet, as he had threatened to do, and was succeeded by Mr. THOMAS, of Maryland. In the mean time, nearly all the money in the Treasury had been used for ordinary disbursements. There was a large amount of interest upon the public debt due upon the first of January, 1861, and the means were unprovided to meet it. The Secretary wished Mr. CISCO to use for this purpose the moneys placed to the credit of the disbursing officers of the Government, but he peremptorily declined to do so. Mr. THOMAS was unable to command the confidence of the people of the North. At this juncture, a correspondence ensued between himself and Mr. CISCO, and he finally, with the approbation of the President, whom he consulted upon the subject, authorized that officer to obtain a Treasury-note loan, at the unprecedented rate of twelve per cent. per annum, in order to save the Government from going to protest upon its interest.

But even this was not an easy thing to do in the state of feeling which prevailed among capitalists. As a last resort, on the evening of the thirty-first of December, Mr. CISCO, accompanied by Mr. VAIL, Cashier of the Bank of Commerce, drove to the residences of the largest holders of the public debt in New York and Brooklyn. They represented to those gentlemen the fearful depreciation in the value of their property which must inevitably occur if the interest due on the morrow should not be promptly paid. The result was that they returned home at a very late hour, having contracted for a sufficient amount of notes to save the Government from the impending catastrophe.

Although Mr. Cisco was then and afterward satisfied that Secretary Thomas was a *loyal* man, so far as his purposes were concerned, still it is naturally presumable that in feeling he sympathized with the section of country to which he belonged. At all events, it was apparent that without another change in the Treasury Department there would be no more money forthcoming to the national coffers from New York. At this juncture Mr. Cisco wrote to President Buchanan, recommending the appointment of General John A. Dix as Secretary of the Treasury. A few days later a delegation of Bank Presidents and others proceeded to Washington for the purpose of urging the change. Shortly afterward the President telegraphed to General Dix that he desired him to come to Washington. The General complied with the request, and, upon his arrival at the capital, Mr. Buchanan insisted that he should be his guest at the Executive Mansion. They talked together that evening, and again the next morning at breakfast. The result was the immediate appointment of General Dix as Secretary of the Treasury. The advent as Financial Minister of this most respected, and most worthy to be respected, of all American statesmen, restored to the moneyed people of the North all that confidence in the Government which was possible in the unsettled condition of public affairs which then existed.

Mr. Dix continued a Cabinet officer only until the succeeding fourth of March, when Mr. LINCOLN coming in as President, Mr. S. P. CHASE, of Ohio, became his Secretary of the Treasury.

As soon as the new Administration was organized, Mr. CISCO sent to Mr. CHASE his resignation as Fiscal Agent of the Government in New York, with the request that he would immediately present it to the President, and secure the appointment of his successor at an early day. Some time passed and he heard nothing in reply. Having opposed Mr. LINCOLN's election, he was surprised at this delay. Besides, the condition of his health was such that he was anxious to be promptly relieved from the responsibilities of his office, which had been great in the past, and promised to become overwhelming in the future.

In the mean time no less than three gentlemen, eminent in the Republican party, and friends of Mr. CHASE, called upon Mr. CISCO at different times, for the purpose of obtaining detailed information upon the subject of the finances. They all admitted that they came in behalf of the Secretary. Mr. CISCO resented this action as a slight to himself, and informed them that, if the Secretary desired the information in question, the proper course would be for him to ask it directly from his own Fiscal Agent.

Then came a letter of apology from Mr. CHASE, whose only excuse was his want of personal acquaintance with him. At the same time he assured him that he had satisfied himself as to his thorough loyalty, his fidelity, and his eminent ability.

A short time afterward he again wrote to him, requesting him to remain in the Treasury, mentioning that such was also the desire of the President. This was followed by a letter from Mr. LINCOLN himself to the same effect. Under these circumstances, Mr. CISCO thought it his duty to yield to their wishes, and withdrew his resignation.

Shortly after it was settled that he should continue in office, I accepted an invitation from Mr. CISCO to come to him in a confidential capacity. As soon as Congress met they passed an Act authorizing the appointment of a Deputy Assistant Treasurer of the United States at New York, and the position was immediately tendered to me and accepted. I continued to hold it until I went to Washington in the year 1863, as Assistant Secretary of the Treasury.

The number of clerks employed in the New York Treasury office when I first entered it did not exceed twenty-five or thirty. The enormous volume of business which presently devolved upon it, as the medium through which the public loans were negotiated and collected, soon required the employment of a clerical force exceeding one hundred in number.

The new Administration had not been a very long time in office, when Mr. CHASE sent for Mr. CISCO, whom he had never met, to come to Washington. By his invitation he went as a guest to the Secretary's house, at the corner of E and Sixth Streets. In their first interview, which took place in the evening, Mr. CHASE told him that he desired his presence in order to consult with him in regard to a financial policy for the country. Upon this occasion they had a very protracted conversation, in which each was evidently endeavoring to take the measure of the other. "We are going to have a long, bloody, and costly war," said Mr. CISCO; "the only possible policy is that of long bonds and strong taxation." "How, sir?" replied the Secretary; "are you not aware that we shall soon have seventy-five thousand men in the field?" At this time some people high in place were talking about a sixty-days' war, and Mr. CHASE evidently shared this most mistaken impression. "As to strong taxation," he continued, "the people of this country will not bear it, and there is no need for it." Nevertheless, Mr. CISCO adhered to his expressed opinion, and assigned his reasons for it. Mr. CHASE eyed him curiously, as if he was meditating whether he, after all, could be a secessionist in disguise.

The next morning they had another long talk before breakfast. Mr. CHASE told Mr. CISCO that he had been very much impressed by his views, that he had been all night thinking over what he had said, but that he could not "go in" for strong taxation. "Without it," replied Mr. CISCO, "we shall inevitably drift into a suspension of specie payments." "Never," rejoined Mr. CHASE, "so long as I am Secretary of the Treasury!" Mr. CISCO also believed that taxation would hasten the termination of the war. In conclusion, he told Mr. CHASE that whatever policy he should decide upon, he might rely upon his earnest co-operation to aid him in carrying it out.

Thus commenced, from the very beginning, that series of successful expedients, that hand-to-mouth policy, which carried us along so far without a financial disaster.

Shortly after this, and when some grand negotiation had become necessary, Mr. CHASE visited New York, and met the leading bank-officers and capitalists of that city, and of Boston and Philadelphia, at Mr. CISCO's house, on the nineteenth of August, 1861. There was much desultory discussion at the begining; and then Mr. CHASE, after being pushed to the wall to say what he wanted, proposed a loan of fifty millions of dollars in Seven-thirty Treasury notes, with the privilege of converting them into Twenty-year bonds, with the option to the subscribers to take fifty millions more, and again the further sum of fifty millions—one hundred and fifty millions in all. Many regarded it as a most plausible suggestion, and a meeting of the officers of the Clearing-House banks was called for the next day at the American Exchange Banking-house. At this meeting both Mr. CHASE and Mr. CISCO were present. A protracted discussion took place, and there was some earnest opposition to the proposition. Mr. STEVENS, of the Bank of Commerce, and Mr. TAYLOR, of the City Bank, favored it, but Mr. GALLATIN, of the National Bank, vehemently opposed it. Mr. KNAPP, of the Mechanics' Bank, said that, if the obligations of the Government should become worthless, the property of the banks would become so too. Finally, after the meeting had lasted several hours, a resolution was adopted to accept substantially the terms proposed by the Secretary.

After the adjournment of the meeting, Mr. CHASE said to Mr. CISCO, "Well, we have fifty millions, but how about the next fifty?" "The banks will take them," answered Mr. CISCO; "do you not see that they have stepped into the same boat with you?" "And will they also take the last fifty?" asked the Secretary. "They will lend you another fifty millions; but then will come the suspension of specie payments," answered his subordinate. "Never, while I am Secretary of the Treasury!" was the confident reply.

The banks, after disposing of the first fifty millions

of Treasury notes, availed themselves of their privilege to take another like amount of them. They afterward refused to advance any more money against these notes, but agreed to take fifty millions in six per cent. bonds, redeemable after twenty years, at a rate that equalized them to similar seven per cent. bonds.

On Saturday, December the thirtieth, 1861, the banks decided to suspend specie payments on Monday, January the first, 1862. They carried their resolution into effect, and the Government simultaneously adopted the same course in respect to its ordinary disbursements.

The Government was again in straits to pay its interest on the public debt. There were demand notes out to the amount of sixty millions of dollars; and as these were receivable at the Custom-House the same as gold, and did not command so high a premium, duties on imports were almost exclusively paid in them, and little or no specie was received. About the same time, too, the principal of the "Texas Indemnity Bonds" fell due, and although the amount of them was small—say two or three millions—the embarrassment was by so much increased. "Pay both principal and interest in paper!" said the Secretary. It is easy to see what the effect of such a course would have been. It was of vital importance to continue to pay in coin both the interest and the principal of the public debt as they matured.

At this time the banks had large stores of gold in their vaults for which they had no use. Mr. CISCO proposed to borrow it from them. Mr. CHASE did not believe that they would lend it at all, or, if at all, only upon extortionate terms. Mr. CISCO succeeded in borrowing all that was wanted at the rate of *four per cent. per annum*, on notes payable on ten days' notice after thirty days. Mr. CHASE only consented to this arrangement on the Saturday preceding the Monday on which the bonds and the interest fell due. I remember that the Park Bank lent us a million. A few days afterward, and after the money had been used, the President of that institution became frightened, and, coming to the Treasury, asked to have his coin returned. Mr. CISCO told him to immediately send down his carts to receive it. This rather staggered him, for he had expected a flat refusal, and he then made up his mind to let the matter stand over till the morrow, when he could consult his directors. The next day he returned and said, "I shall leave it for the present." But he was told that he must choose between adhering to the terms of his agreement and removing his specie at once. He decided to do the former.

An enormous amount in paper on deposit as a temporary loan upon the foregoing conditions was afterward procured. The money accumulated as in a savings bank. This gave the Government the use of a hundred millions of dollars.

At one time the banks came very near failing on paper. The Treasury was then full of money. We gave them what they needed, and took their certified checks in return.

Nearly ninety per cent. of all the early loans negotiated were taken in New York. The Seven-thirty notes became very popular. The Treasury acted as the agent of the banks in disposing of them to the public. There were also private agents appointed for the same purpose. All classes of society, and persons of both sexes, came to subscribe for them. I remember that a hackney coachman left his carriage at the door, and came rushing in to us with a hundred dollars in his hand for a note of that denomination. A clergyman wrote from a Western city that he desired to do every thing within his power to support the Government, but that he had no money. He had, however, a very good horse, and he requested to be informed whether we could not give him a hundred-dollar Seven-thirty Treasury note for it.

As soon as specie payments were suspended, small silver change disappeared from circulation with marvelous rapidity. Postage-stamps came into use in its place. They were a most inconvenient and disgusting substitute for the metal which the public had been accustomed to, and as soon as possible they were replaced by what has ever since been known as "Fractional Currency." For a long time this currency could not be produced with sufficient rapidity to meet the popular demand. The importunities of the people for it were like petitions for charity.

During all the time that I was in the New York branch of the Treasury, in addition to the official correspondence, one or more letters, some semi-official and some altogether confidential, passed daily between the Secretary and the Assistant Treasurer. If those letters could be published, they would furnish the most interesting page in the financial history of the war. They contain a free discussion of every expedient presented, and the record of every purpose formed. I am proud to say that never upon a single occasion did a Government financial secret pass the four walls of the Treasury building until communicated to the entire community. That institution was the despair of the speculators. No pump applied there ever drew water.

The Government building on Wall Street hitherto employed as the Treasury soon ceased to furnish the necessary accommodations and security for the ever expanding business of the office. An arrangement was finally effected, involving some complicated negotiations, whereby the Treasury was transferred to the Custom-House, at the corner of Wall and Nassau Streets, and the Custom-House removed to the Merchants' Exchange building, where it still is. Mr. Barney, the Collector, was very unwilling to be disturbed. The Government hired the Exchange building for three years, at an annual rent of sixty or sixty-five thousand dollars, with the privilege of buying it for a million of dollars at any time during the term. When the time was about to expire, Mr. Fessenden was Secretary of the Treasury, and it was with some difficulty that he was induced to recommend the purchase to Congress. He did so, however; the necessary Act was passed, and the matter consummated. I presume that the ground alone is now worth three millions of dollars.

During the riots of July, 1863, very grave apprehensions were entertained lest an organized attempt should be made to sack the Treasury. Accordingly every thing was prepared to resist an attack. Arms were distributed to all the employés, and hand-grenades and carboys of vitriol were placed at every window. There was a military guard of raw troops about the building nearly all the time, but we apprehended more danger from it than from the rioters. We kept a loaded *mitrailleuse* facing the Pine Street entrance, and we had two field-pieces worked by gunners from the Brooklyn Navy Yard. A battery of artillery was kept upon Nassau Street, and there was a gun-boat lying at the foot of Wall Street with shotted guns commanding the street. All through the nights there were mounted pickets stationed at the doors, principally for communication with the Custom-House; and we had relays of confidential agents all over the city, watching the movements of the rioters. When one evening they surged down Greenwich Street, destroying every thing that came in their way, we thought that they were making for us. Had they come, they would have met with a warm reception. The chances are very great that they would never have succeeded in penetrating into the building, and, if they had done so, it is certain that they would have failed to get access to the treasure, then very large in amount, contained in the vaults. But they deemed it prudent, after learning the preparation made to receive them, to keep away; and we came off free of cost, except the expense of provisioning so large a number of men as we had there all the time.

In those trying times the civil servants of the Government suffered as well as the military, and the desk had its martyrs as well as the field. Incessant labors from early morning till late at night, and sometimes all night, with overwhelming responsibility and anxiety, were hardly less fatal than the enemy's guns.

In the summer of the year 1863, the Hon. GEORGE HARRINGTON, the Assistant Secretary of the Treasury, broke down completely in health, and by the advice of his physicians determined to seek repose and relaxation by withdrawing for a time from public affairs and visiting Europe. In this emergency, SECRETARY CHASE invited me to Washington.

CHAPTER IX.

I ENTERED upon my new duties as Assistant Secretary of the Treasury upon the first day of October, 1863, and continued in the discharge of them, under Secretaries CHASE, FESSENDEN, and McCULLOCH, until the first of July, 1865, when, with impaired strength and energy, I was transferred by PRESIDENT JOHNSON, at my own request, to a Federal office in the city of New York.

On the morning of the Sunday succeeding that of my arrival at Washington, I, in company with Mr. CHASE, attended service at the St. John's Episcopal Church. Mr. SEWARD occupied the pew directly in front of us. On our walk homeward, Mr. CHASE spoke to me in extremely kind terms of the Secretary of State, saying that, since they had been associated together as members of Mr. LINCOLN's Cabinet, he had learned to esteem and respect him much more than he had done in former years in the Senate. I soon after had an occasion to repeat these remarks to Mr. SEWARD, to whom the recital seemed to afford much gratification. He referred, in turn, to Mr. CHASE's handsome conduct in resigning his seat in the Cabinet immediately after he had himself temporarily withdrawn from it under pressure from the Senate, and the embarrassment from which this considerate action of his colleague had relieved both the President and himself. From that time forward my personal relations with Mr. SEWARD became quite intimate. I used frequently to meet him socially at the tables of the foreign Ministers, and I often visited him at his own house. The latter was particularly the case during the months of July and August in the year 1864. The intense heat had depleted Washington, driving from the city every body except those officials who found it impossible to get away. The great Bedouin camp had struck its tents for a season. One's evening visiting list thus became very much circumscribed, and SECRETARY SEWARD's house was one of the few where one could call with any probability of finding the master at home. At this time I often passed uninterrupted hours in his company. I frequently found him swinging in a hammock, which was slung upon the back porch, and smoking the inevitable cigar of portentous size and strength. As a smoker, Mr. SEWARD was in no way behind GENERAL GRANT. Sometimes, however, our interviews took place in the front parlor. The conversation was always of the most unreserved and familiar character. Upon one occasion, I remarked to the Secretary that I supposed he had kept a diary, or at least memoranda, of every thing that had occurred at Cabinet meetings since the incoming of the Administration. He told me, in reply, that during several months in the beginning he had very faithfully done so; but that very soon the personal relations between some of his colleagues became so inharmonious, and so much unworthy bickering, and even quarreling, was indulged in upon these occasions, that he discontinued making a record, and destroyed the notes which he had already taken. He said that a truthful statement of these occurrences, if ever published, would bring disgrace upon the country, and that they had better be buried in oblivion. Mr. SEWARD expressed the very highest opinion of Mr. LINCOLN as a *politician.* Indeed, I think it must be conceded by all who had intimate opportunities to study that remarkable man, that Mr. LINCOLN was the most consummate politician that this country has yet produced, except perhaps his great rival, STEPHEN A. DOUGLAS. He was in politics what the *London Times* is in journalism —never leading public opinion, but always following its wave so closely that, when it breaks, it is found swimming upon the crest. To the unobservant he appeared to lead, whereas he only followed. He had an unerring and rapid perception of the popular will, and the policy which he from time to time adopted was but the crystallization of that will.

Mr. SEWARD told me the story of the Emancipation Proclamation, and, as he related it, it was strikingly illustrative of this characteristic of Mr. LINCOLN. Months before it was issued, it was the subject of constant discussion at the meetings of the Cabinet. Day after day the most earnest and acrimonious debates took place in relation to the propriety or impropriety of the President issuing such a proclamation. Although an attentive listener to these discussions of his Secretaries, Mr. LINCOLN did not take an active part in them. So much was this the case that several, at least, of his advisers were very uncertain as to what his ultimate determination upon the subject would be. So bitter did the controversy grow, that it resulted, after a time, not only in a breach of personal, and to some extent even official relations between certain of the Cabinet officers, but eventually even in a prolonged discontinuance of Cabinet meetings. During the interregnum matters which had been usually discussed and disposed of at such meetings had to be settled by inter-departmental correspondence. One of the other Secretaries, with the obvious purpose of *annoying*—I use a mild word—Mr. CHASE, addressed several very important official communications directly to me, ignoring the head of the Department. This condition of things lasted until one day Mr. SEWARD received an autographic letter from the President requesting him to attend, without fail, a meeting of the Cabinet which he proposed to hold on the morrow. All the other Secretaries received similar letters, and not one of them knew or entertained any confident conjecture about the particular purpose for which they were called together. At the appointed time Mr. LINCOLN waited until they were all assembled, having been unusually reticent to the first comers. He then addressed them somewhat as follows: "Gentlemen, I have asked you to come here that I may have the opportunity of reading to you a proclamation which I am about to issue. Before proceeding to read it, however, I desire to say that not only do I not *invite* any discussion about the propriety or impropriety of its issue, but that I am *unwilling to listen* to any. My mind is made up. On the contrary, as to matters of form, I wish you all to make any suggestions that may occur to you." He then drew from his pocket a manuscript, and to the amazement of some, if not of all, there assembled, proceeded to read the *Emancipation Proclamation.* When he had finished, for a while nobody spoke. Mr. SEWARD was the first to break the silence, and to recommend a verbal alteration. Mr. LINCOLN adopted it without a word of objection. Other gentlemen suggested further changes. Mr. Lincoln accepted them all without discussion. When nobody had any more suggestions to make, the meeting broke up, and the Ministers soon dispersed. The next day the emancipation from slavery of four millions of human beings in the United States was published to the world. Mr. Lincoln had waited until the people were ripe for it; and what he had at first looked upon as inopportune, he had at last regarded as expedient and necessary.

Mr. Seward's version of how Mr. Stanton came into the Cabinet afforded another illustration in point. For a long time the maladministration and non-administration of the War Department had been a matter of the most serious concern to Mr. Seward and several of his colleagues. At one time, with the hope of relief, some of the duties of that Department were transferred to the State Department, and later others were turned over to the Treasury Department. But, notwithstanding this, the conduct of the War Department was constantly becoming worse and worse. The most serious apprehensions were entertained by those members of the Cabinet who conversed together upon the subject; but none of them ventured to call Mr. Lincoln's attention to so delicate a matter. They were, nevertheless, both surprised and distressed at his apparent blindness or indifference to so obvious and momentous an evil. "While things were in this condition," said Mr. Seward, "there was a ring at my door-bell one evening, and, as soon as the servant had answered it, the President walked into the room. He sat down by me on this sofa upon which we are now sitting, and abruptly commenced talking about the condition of the War Department. He soon made it apparent that he had all along observed and known as much about it as any of us, if not more, and that he had been up to that time restrained from taking decisive action, both because he hoped for an amendment in its administration, and because he had a natural reluctance to sever intimate official relations with a gentleman who had been one of his competitors for the Presidential nomination. However, his mind was now settled, and he had come to consult me about a successor to Mr. CAMERON." Mr. STANTON'S name was introduced. I can not now recollect whether Mr. SEWARD said that it was first mentioned by Mr. LINCOLN or by himself. At all events, it was very favorably considered by both, and, after some later negotiations, the War portfolio was tendered to and accepted by that gentleman. Mr. SEWARD told me that he believed that at the time of the conversation just referred to Mr. LINCOLN and Mr. STANTON had never met, except upon the occasion, years before, when they were together employed in a lawsuit in Cincinnati, and when Mr. STANTON so unmercifully snubbed his associate that the latter withdrew in disgust from the case.

I take the following extract from one of the little diaries in which Mr. CHASE was accustomed to jot down daily occurrences and transcribe some of his most secret thoughts. He wrote with a pencil, and, as he was in the habit of carrying these books loose in his pocket, much of the writing is wholly or partly obliterated. I have, however, been able to make out the following, but not without a great deal of difficulty:

"1862, *January* 12*th.*—At church in the morning. Good, plain sermon. Wished much to join in communion, but felt myself too subject to temptation to sin. After church went to see CAMERON by appointment; but being obliged to meet the President, etc., at one, could only excuse myself. At President's found Generals McDOWELL, FRANKLIN, and MEIGS, and SEWARD and BLAIR. MEIGS decided against dividing forces, and in favor of battle in front. President said McCLELLAN's health was much improved, and thought it best to adjourn till to-morrow, and have all then present attend with McC. at three. Home, and talk and reading. Dinner. CAMERON came in. Advised loan in Holland, and recommended BROOKS, LEWIS, and another whom I have forgotten. Then turned to Department matters, and we talked of his going to Russia and STANTON as successor, and he proposed I should again see the President. I first proposed seeing SEWARD, to which he assented. He declared himself determined to maintain himself at the head of his Department if he remained, and to resist hereafter all interference. I told him I would in that event stand by him faithfully. He and I drove to Willard's, where I left him, and went myself to SEWARD's. I told him at once what was in my mind—that I thought the President and CAMERON were both willing that C. should go to Russia. He seemed to receive the matter as new, except so far as suggested by me last night. Wanted to know who would succeed CAMERON. I said HOLT and STANTON had been named; that I feared HOLT might embarrass us on the slavery question, and might not prove quite equal to the emergency; that STANTON was a good lawyer and full of energy; but I could not, of course, judge him as an executive officer as well as he (S.) could, for he knew him when he was in BUCHANAN's Cabinet. SEWARD replied that he saw much of him then; that he was of great force—full of expedients, and thoroughly loyal. Finally he agreed to the whole thing, and promised to go with me to talk with the President about it to-morrow. Just at this point CAMERON came in with a letter from the President proposing his nomination to Russia in the morning! He was quite offended, supposing the letter intended as a dismissal, and, therefore, discourteous. We both assured him it could not be so. Finally he concluded to retain the letter till morning, and then go and see the President. SEWARD was expecting GENERAL BUTLER, and CAM-

ERON said he ought to be sent off immediately. I said, 'Well, let's leave SEWARD to order him off at once.' C. laughed, and we went off together, I taking him to his house. Before parting, I told him what had passed between me and SEWARD concerning STANTON, with which he was gratified. I advised him to go to the President in the morning, express his thanks for the consideration with which his wishes, made known through me as well as by himself orally, had been treated, and tell him frankly how desirable it was to him that his successor should be a Pennsylvanian, and should be STANTON. I said I thought that his wish, supported as it would be by SEWARD and myself, would certainly be gratified, and told him that the President had already mentioned STANTON in a way which indicated that no objection on his part would be made. I said also that, if he wished, I would see SEWARD, and would go to the President after he had left him, and urge the point. He asked why not come in when he should be there, and I assented to this. We parted, and I came home. A day which may have—and seemingly must have—great bearing on affairs. Oh, that my heart and life were so pure and right before God that I might not hurt our great cause! I fear Mr. SEWARD may think CAMERON's coming into his house pre-arranged, and that I was not dealing frankly. I feel satisfied, however, that I have acted right, and with just deference to all concerned, and have in no respect deviated from the truth."

There is more upon the same subject in the book, but, unfortunately, it can not be deciphered with any certainty.

Since copying the foregoing, I have been informed upon excellent authority that the President's letter to Mr. CAMERON was very brief, and that the following was the exact language that he used: "I have made up my mind to accept your resignation, and tender you the mission to St. Petersburg." That this was all. That Mr. CAMERON, though he had *talked* of resigning, had made neither a written nor verbal offer to do so. Now was

Mr. CAMERON justified or not in considering this a *dismissal?** My informant, whose communication is in writing, continues as follows:

"Four months before this,† Mr. LINCOLN expressed a probable intention to make changes in two Departments, but certainly in one—the War Department. Mr. STANTON, at that time a resident of Washington, contemplated removing to New York; but a communication having been made to him from an entirely trustworthy source that Mr. LINCOLN would regard his removal from Washington as inopportune, coupled with an intimation that he would probably soon be wanted in an important position under the Administration, he remained in the Federal city. The President's long delay in making sign in fulfillment of his expectations angered STANTON, and within a very few days before his appointment he said bitter things not only of the Republicans generally, but of Mr. LINCOLN personally. Mr. LINCOLN, in explaining the grounds of the intended change in the War Department, referred in severe terms to Mr. CAMERON'S bad management, saying, among other things, that when absent from Washington he had given telegraphic orders for the transfer of troops and munitions of war, of which no record had been made in the Department. Serious embarrassment and confusion had resulted. The President expressed disapprobation also of some of Mr. CAMERON'S personal affiliations."

It may not be generally known, but it is nevertheless true, that Mr. SEWARD entertained great admiration and a most sincere regard for GENERAL GEORGE B. MCCLELLAN, or "GEORGE," as Mr. LINCOLN used familiarly and affectionately to call him. Once, when speaking of the General, Mr. SEWARD told me that he considered him one

* It is well known that Mr. CAMERON took Mr. LINCOLN'S letter so much to heart that Mr. CHASE was induced to take it back to the President, whom he persuaded to substitute for it another letter containing expressions of regret and of compliment.

† This happened in September, 1861, in the early part of the month.

of the most forbearing, self-controlled, and patient men whom he had ever known. He only remembered a single occasion upon which he displayed an implacable feeling of resentment. This was after his rupture with Mr. Stanton, and his retirement from the command of the Army of the Potomac. The rebel invaders were pouring North, and the battle which is known to us by the name of "Antietam" was to be fought. There was a panic in Washington, and, after much consideration, it was determined to invite General McClellan to again head our forces. Mr. Seward was selected to convey the invitation to him and urge its acceptance. To his surprise and disappointment, he at first found "George" inexorable. He felt that Mr. Stanton had treated him with too much injustice to permit him to accept the offer consistently with his own self-respect. For a long time he would not recede from his refusal, and it was only after repeated urging by Mr. Seward that he was induced to undertake to fight the one battle, it being, however, distinctly understood that there should be no personal reconciliation between himself and the Secretary of War.

At the dinner-parties of the foreign Ministers, which Mr. Seward, being Secretary of State, frequently attended, he was looked upon as rather a tedious guest. Speaking no language but English, he compelled the conversation to be carried on in a tongue which was not familiar to many of those usually present.

Mr. Seward told me that soon after his first election as Governor of the State of New York, he had occasion to make a short journey from Albany by stage-coach. The day was fine, and he asked the driver's permission to mount the box and occupy a seat by his side. This favor was grumblingly granted by Jehu, who was entirely unacquainted with the Governor's person. Mr. SEWARD endeavored to propitiate him by presenting to him a choice cigar; the ice soon thawed, and they entered into an earnest conversation. After a while the coachman turned to him, and abruptly asked him who he was. Mr. SEWARD replied that people called him the Governor of New York. This was met by his companion with a laugh of incredulity. Mr. SEWARD then said that they could not proceed far without meeting somebody who knew him, who would confirm his statement. Presently they came up to a person on foot, with whom Mr. SEWARD was acquainted, and he requested the driver to stop the coach. Hailing the man at the side of the road, Mr. SEWARD told him that his identity had been questioned, and asked him if he was not, in fact, the Governor. "Certainly not," was the unexpected answer. "Pray, then, who is?" asked the astonished statesman. "Why, THURLOW WEED, of course," was the prompt reply. Mr. SEWARD laughed over the story as if the scene were still vividly before him.

I have mentioned that at one time there was an absolute discontinuance of Cabinet meetings, and that during that period very important matters, which were usually disposed of at such meetings, became the subject of correspondence between the several Departments. A very protracted and very able correspondence passed between the Treasury and the Navy Departments in relation to certain regulations issued by the former, affecting what was called "restricted trade." The Navy objected to these regulations, whose enforcement, it was claimed, would tend to interfere with an efficient blockade. On our side, Mr. Chase himself wrote every letter, and it is needless to say that they were very ably written. The letters from the Navy Department were, however, to say the least, equally able; and I could not help feeling that we were even a little overmatched in the controversy. Fox, the Assistant Secretary, we all said must have written those letters; they could have no other author. But it afterward turned out that they had been written by the Secretary, Mr. Welles, and that neither Mr. Fox nor any body else had even been consulted about them. This circumstance greatly raised my estimate of Mr. Welles; and from my subsequent intercourse with him I became convinced that he was one of the ablest, and in every respect one of the best of Mr. Lincoln's immediate advisers. The country has never done him any thing like justice. His patriarchal looks, his immense wig, his flowing beard, and his somewhat stolid manners, and the names of "Father Welles" and "Noah" applied to him by the slang talkers and writers of the day, created an altogether false impression of him in the public mind. Whenever I had occasion to call upon him officially, I always found him, perhaps to a greater degree than any of his associates, well up in all the details of the Department over which he presided. His personal management of its affairs was intelligent, thorough, and efficient. More, perhaps, than any other of his colleagues, he was given to minding his own business, and in the discharge of duty he was as inflexible as an old Roman.

It affords me pleasure to have here the opportunity to pay a brief tribute to a public officer who has, apparently, been so little appreciated by a country which he so intelligently and so faithfully served.

I think that, all things considered, Mr. CHASE should be rated first among the members of Mr. LINCOLN'S Cabinet. In intellectual greatness, he certainly was the foremost. I have so many reasons for affectionate regard for him and for devotion to his memory, that, however truthful a witness, I know that I am liable to be considered a partial one. That Mr. CHASE, as a financial minister, fell into occasional errors, I am the last person in the world to dispute. But who is there that in those terribly difficult times would not have fallen into them? He always had the good sense, which has not been common to all his successors, to constantly consult with those who had more practical experience than he himself possessed; and, except his great fundamental mistake at the commencement, he probably made as few as would have been made by any other person in his place.

CHAPTER X.

UNTIL the winter of 1861–2, Congress could not be induced to take up the subject of internal taxes. For the first year, the war was conducted without a revenue; for the import duties had fallen to a sum scarcely adequate to peace expenditures. When the committees of Congress went to work, Mr. CHASE determined to prepare also, on his part, a scheme of internal taxation. To assist him, at the suggestion of Mr. CISCO, he invited to Washington the Hon. JOHN D. VAN BUREN, a distinguished citizen of New York, of opposite politics to his own. Mr. VAN BUREN remained two months at the capital, as a volunteer unpaid attaché of the Treasury Department, in daily consultation with the Secretary. Some time before the Committee of Ways and Means had its Bill ready to report, Mr. VAN BUREN completed one for Mr. CHASE, levying taxes which, it was estimated, would yield over two hundred millions of dollars per annum. No income tax was included, Mr. VAN BUREN, after examining the decisions, coming to the conclusion that it was a direct tax, and therefore unconstitutional unless levied upon each state in proportion to population; in which view Mr. CHASE at that time acquiesced. This Bill was examined and, in some details, corrected by Mr. CHASE, and sent by him to the Committee of Ways and Means; but his note, accompanying it, was not so worded as to make it absolutely his own measure. The Committee had already made progress in, but had not completed, a scheme of its own. The advance sheets of its Bill, furnished to the Treasury Department, showed that it proceeded upon the theory of taxing every thing under the sun. The Bill submitted by Mr. CHASE had only ten or fifteen separate subjects of taxation. Under it the number of officials and the expense of collection would have been much less than under that of the Committee. One illustration will suffice on this point. The Bill submitted by the Secretary levied a tax of half a cent a mile on railroad passengers; which would have yielded a large revenue, the amount of which could be accurately estimated by the statistics given in the railroad report of the State Engineer of New York, and the reports of some other states; and all of which tax would have been collected by the railroads at the same time with their own fares. So a tax of one cent was proposed on every passenger by horse-railroads and ferries. This would have yielded a very considerable revenue—several millions of dollars. The Committee did levy a tax on horse-railroads and ferries, but put it down to about one third of a cent. The ferries and railroads charged an additional cent to their passengers, but two thirds of this went into their private treasuries. Another tax of the same nature, cheap of collection, served to illustrate a kind of patriotism that was very common in those days. All the moneyed interests were clamorous for taxation, but every body wanted the taxes laid on every body else than themselves. It was proposed to tax consumers of illuminating gas fifty cents a thousand cubic feet, to be collected with the monthly bills of the gas companies. This brought a swarm of presidents of gas companies from every quarter to Washington. They were loud and unanimous in their admissions that the Government must provide for itself an abundant revenue, but insisted that such a tax as this would bring absolute ruin on the gas companies. One of them from New York never forgave Mr. VAN BUREN for not being convinced by his arguments that, under such a tax, all the gas-consumers would go back at once to the use of tallow candles.

A very valuable suggestion was made by Mr. BIGELOW, of Boston, the well-known inventor of the carpet-loom. It was that all the internal taxes should be collected not in money, but in Government stamps; that the Treasury should issue stamps of various denominations up to a thousand dollars, good only in payment of taxes; and that the tax-payer should simply return his tax-bill to the Collector, with the necessary amount of canceled stamps affixed to it. This would have had many advantages. It would have reduced greatly the machinery and the number of officials to be engaged in collecting the taxes, and it would have secured the Treasury absolutely against losses by the dishonesty of its agents. There would have been no handling of money except at the sub-Treasuries, where, at wholesale, the stamps were to be sold, with an allowance to compensate the retail sellers. Moreover, the Treasury would thus have received its revenue always in advance. This proposal of Mr. BIGELOW was accepted by Mr. VAN BUREN, and urged by him upon Mr. CHASE. It may be doubted, however, whether there was any desire among members of Congress to keep down the number of officials to be created under the new tax system. The more offices, the more home patronage for each Representative.

The Committee of Congress had become attached to its own scheme, and adhered to it. It was manifestly anxious to make the taxes light, and hoped to do so by scattering them upon all things. Some of its members, in conversation, laughed at the tax of fifty cents a gallon on whisky, proposed in the Bill submitted by Mr. CHASE, as being absurdly heavy; their own Bill levying only about one fourth as much. Yet, in a year or two, Congress went to the other extreme, and put the tax at two dollars a gallon, giving rise, by excessive temptation, to an organized system of whisky frauds. The Committee expected that its Bill would yield a revenue of nearly two hundred millions of dollars; the most moderate estimate among the members was one hundred and sixty millions of dollars. Mr. VAN BUREN was urged by some of them to estimate its results, and he put them down as not exceeding sixty millions of dollars net. The returns for the year showed, I believe, about seventy millions of dollars gross.

The same mistake was made by Mr. CHASE and by Congress as that which Mr. PITT confessed he had made in the Napoleonic wars. Heavy taxes should have been imposed at the outset. The people were ready for taxation, but their agents were timid. We resorted to all sorts of expedients, bringing ruin upon our credit; and then had at last to come to the same amount of taxation which, if laid in the beginning, would have kept our credit always high. With the example and the confession of Mr. PITT before us, our public men were less excusable than he. A tax of two hundred millions of dollars, levied in the first year of the war, would, in Mr. VAN BUREN's opinion, have enabled us to borrow freely and to keep up specie payments; would have served, by the demonstration of our strength, as a warning to foreign powers disposed to meddle; would have discouraged the enemy, compelled themselves to resort at the outset to irredeemable paper money; and would have greatly shortened the contest. It would have avoided, probably, two thirds of our public debt. From how much demoralization and sin it would have saved us is beyond calculation.

It was, at the outbreak of the Rebellion, the opinion of the venerable AZARIAH C. FLAGG, formerly Comptroller of the State of New York, that the Government could afford to expend one thousand millions a year and yet maintain specie payments. Our annual expenditures, even when measured by depreciated paper money, did not come up to this.

The French proverb that "no man is a hero to his *valet de chambre*," has a wider significance than it expresses. It means that the great become little to those who are intimately associated with them. I have come into contact with many of those whom the world calls great, and, after a personal acquaintance with them, have found them very small. But, in the case of Mr. CHASE, I can honestly and sincerely say that, after the closest relations with him, both official and private, during a period of time which tried men's *brains* as well as their *souls*, I parted from him with a higher appreciation of his magnificent mind and character than I entertained when I only knew him as one of the leaders of the land. He had conspicuous weaknesses, but they only served to throw his great qualities into more prominent relief.

We all remember the movement that was made, previous to Mr. LINCOLN'S second nomination at Baltimore, to bring Mr. CHASE forward as a competing candidate. That Mr. CHASE was himself in nowise reluctant can not be denied, although I know that he all along doubted that such a movement had any chance of success. In those days he failed to appreciate Mr. LINCOLN at his true value, as, I think, Mr. LINCOLN failed to appreciate him. Indeed, it would be impossible to imagine two men more unlike, and having fewer points of contact. Mr. LINCOLN, at least, was entirely deficient in what the phrenologists call *reverence*. No man who ever lived could be in his presence and *dominate* him, as the French express it. There is a certain sort of intellectual atmosphere different from, if not higher than that in which he moved, and he troubled himself very little about it, or about those who dwelt in it. At any rate, he instinctively conceded nothing of superiority to any body, and often failed to comprehend those whose mental plane was different from his own. Mr. CHASE honestly felt his superiority to Mr. LINCOLN in some respects, and could not be reconciled to his undignified manners and strange ways. While the movement to bring Mr. CHASE forward as a Presidential candidate was in agitation, a United States Senator, who actively participated in it, one day came into my office in a towering rage. Striking his fist upon my desk, he said to me that he considered CHASE the —— (using a very strong expletive) fool in the world. He then went on to tell me that he and others had been unsuccessfully laboring with the Secretary to induce him to issue a "cotton permit" to somebody, precisely as he would issue one to any respectable person; only that the profits were to be applied in the interest of his nomination, instead of going into private pockets. There was an amount of principle and delicacy involved in Mr. CHASE's refusal which the Senatorial mind utterly failed to appreciate.

When speaking of Mr. CHASE's Presidential aspirations, I am reminded, as Mr. LINCOLN used to say, of a little story. When I first went to Washington, the Secretary occupied for his office a room on the south side of the Treasury building, with a beautiful outlook down the Potomac. Soon afterward it was proposed that he should remove to certain elaborately ornamented and elegantly furnished rooms on the west side of the building, which had been arranged for his occupation by Mr. MULLETT, the architect of the Department. Mr. CHASE had consented to make the change; but after the new rooms were ready he delayed removing. Several times he appointed a day to do so, but when the time came he had changed his mind. One afternoon, while he was still hesitating, I was standing with him at one of the windows of the largest of the new rooms which faced the Executive Mansion. Turning to me, he asked me to assign one sufficient reason why he should change his quarters. I told him that there was at least one obvious advantage in the exchange, and that was, if he should come to these offices, he would *always be able to keep his eye upon the White House!*

Mr. CHASE was a man of extremely nervous temperament, and he would sometimes be very violent, and occasionally even unjust, while swept by a gale of passion. On one occasion SENATOR FESSENDEN came into my room in a terrible rage, occasioned by a scolding which he had received from the Secretary. GOVERNOR BROUGH, of Ohio, visited Washington in the year 1864, and being an experienced railroad man and familiar with the cost of transportation, explained to Mr. Chase the fearful extravagance of the Quartermaster's Department in the West. Mr. Stanton, unfortunately for himself, happened to come into the Secretary's room shortly after the Governor had left it, when he received such a verbal castigation at the hands of Mr. Chase as few men would have ventured to inflict upon the great War Secretary. What was more remarkable, however, he bore it with great meekness.

But Mr. Chase was always just after the moment of anger had passed, and knew how to be magnanimous.

Among the innumerable duties of the Assistant Secretary of the Treasury, who was the executive officer of a Department employing at that time in Washington three thousand persons, was that of taking daily to the Secretary the warrants for his signature. Any body can readily imagine how numerous they always were, what a great scope of indebtedness they covered, and what large sums many of them represented. When they reached him they had already been through the auditing offices, the Register's office, and the Treasurer's office, and only awaited the Secretary's signature to be complete. Somehow, Mr. Chase did not seem to think that he was discharging a merely *ministerial* duty when he signed them. On the contrary, notwithstanding the valuable time that it occupied to do so, he always carefully scrutinized every one of them, and hardly a day passed that he did not lay aside a dozen or more unsigned for future explanations.

I happened once to be with the Secretary when the President, without knocking, and unannounced, as was his habit, entered the room. His rusty black hat was on the back of his head, and he wore, as was his custom, an old gray shawl across his shoulders. To the best of my recollection, this occurred in the spring of the year 1864. I said good-morning to Mr. LINCOLN, and then, as was the established etiquette when the President called, withdrew from the office. As Mr. LINCOLN, in his infrequent visits to the Secretary, usually remained a long time, I supposed that I had my freedom for at least half an hour, and proceeded to attend to the accumulation of business which awaited me in my own room. But I was mistaken. In less than five minutes I was summoned to return to the Secretary. Mr. SCHUCKERS, his private secretary, entered the room at the same time that I did. The President was gone, and there was lying upon one end of Mr. CHASE's desk a confused mass of Treasury notes, Demand notes, Seven-thirty notes, and other representatives of value. Mr. CHASE told us that this lot of money had just been brought by Mr. LINCOLN, who desired to have it converted into bonds. He informed us that the President said that it amounted to sixty-eight thousand dollars, but that he had not counted it. GENERAL SPINNER, the Treasurer, was then sent for. When the General came up from his office down stairs, he, Mr. SCHUCKERS, and myself, proceeded together to count the money. The amount proved to be, as represented, just sixty-eight thousand dollars, which was certainly a large sum for Mr. LINCOLN to have saved from his salary in three years. Possibly a good deal of this money may have been anonymous gifts. However, it may be said that there was very clever financiering done in the White House in those days, about which the President was supposed to have little or no knowledge. He only knew that the establishment was conducted in a marvelously economical manner. I had it from a Senator, who was appointed chairman of an investigating committee upon the subject at a secret session of the Senate, that a state dinner was paid for out of an appropriation for fertilizers for the grounds connected with the Executive Mansion. How far this "Heathen Chinee" business was carried, it would probably be difficult to ascertain at this distance of time. One thing only is certain, and that is that Mr. LINCOLN was personally thoroughly honest.

I remember a very absurd incident connected with Mr. CHASE. He and I happened to be going together one evening from New York to Washington. We engaged a coach at the Fifth Avenue Hotel to convey us to the Cortlandt Street Ferry. When we arrived there, alighting from the carriage, Mr. CHASE paid the driver, and we hastened toward the boat. We had not gone far, however, before the driver, who did not know his distinguished "fare," shouted to the Secretary to come back. We accordingly retraced our steps, and when we had again reached the carriage, the coachman exclaimed: "Halloo, old man, what do you mean by trying to pass bogus stamps on me? I have a great mind to have you arrested!" He then placed into Mr. CHASE's hand two fifty-cent fractional notes, which he asserted he had just received from him in part payment. The Secretary looked at them, and, saying that he could not see that they were bad, handed them to me for examination. I at once perceived that they were not only bad, but even *very* bad, being obviously impressions from a wooden block. I so informed Mr. CHASE, and he gave others for them. But it always struck me as a huge joke that he had been detected in the attempt, innocent though it was, to pass counterfeits of his own currency.

Very soon after he became Secretary of the Treasury, and before his person was known to many of the employés of the Department, he entered the Treasury building one Sunday, and, disregarding the protest of the watchman at the door, attempted to pass up stairs to his own room. There was a regulation prohibiting any one from coming in on that day except upon an order of the Secretary or of the Assistant Secretary. Finding his calls disregarded, the watchman started in pursuit of the intruder just as he reached the top step. Seizing Mr. CHASE by the collar, he was about to use violence, when the latter quietly asked him if it was his purpose to eject the Secretary from his own Department. The man, frightened at his act, attempted to excuse himself for his ignorance in assailing his chief, but Mr. CHASE cut him short by commending him for faithfully discharging his duty. Returning to his mate, he rubbed his hands and exclaimed to him, "That keeps me here at least four years longer!"

Mr. CHASE always entertained a very exalted opinion of GENERAL BUTLER's executive ability. I remember once, that as the General left the Secretary's room, the latter turned to me and said, "There is the fittest man in the United States to be Secretary of War!" During the winter of 1863–4, when the General was in command at Fortress Monroe, I took a revenue cutter and, accompanied by some friends, among whom were H. A. RISLEY, Esq., of the Treasury Department, the father of Mr. SEWARD's adopted daughter, and ARTHUR LEARY,

Esq., of New York, paid him a visit. Among other civilities, the General entertained us at dinner. The dinner was an excellent one, and was served upon old-fashioned blue china. The General remarked that he did not suppose it would injuriously affect our appetites to be informed that we were dining off a service which belonged to ex-Governor Henry A. Wise, of Virginia. There was a good deal of animated conversation at table, and one of those present expressed the opinion that when our civil war should be over, such a military spirit would have been engendered in the American people that we would become a nation of filibusters. "It is very likely," answered the General, "that we shall go about the world with a chip upon our shoulder!"

An excursion to Hampton, and a review of the first negro regiment ever raised, was proposed after dinner by the General. Accordingly, four saddle horses, one for him, two for his aids, and one for myself, besides two ambulances for the others of the party, were brought to the door with but little delay. As I was no equestrian, I declined the horse in favor of Mr. Risley, who is the most modest man in the world, and who deprecatingly accepted it; while I hastened to ensconce myself in the interior of an ambulance. It was a piercingly cold day, and Mr. Risley was as inexperienced a horseman as myself; but this I only learned afterward. The reins of the ambulance were reluctantly taken by Mr. Leary.

The General used very short stirrups, and sat on his horse like a monkey; but he went like the wind. Mr. Risley galloped at his side, looking like a centaur, and with a wonderfully complacent expression of countenance. And yet he was suffering martyrdom, and for ten days thereafter was unable to sit upright. Mr. LEARY endured agony—his hands were almost frozen. I was comparatively comfortable. I do not think that Mr. RISLEY quite forgave me for a long time, although he is the most amiable man of my acquaintance.

I went on to Washington once during the war in a private car placed at my disposal by the Baltimore and Ohio Railroad Company, and meeting GENERAL BUTLER at the station, invited him to share it with me. In order to give sleeping accommodations to the ladies who accompanied him, he and I had to sit up all night. I passed the time smoking, and listening to his delightful and instructive talk. I suppose that GENERAL BUTLER knows more about more subjects than any other man in this country, unless it be CALEB CUSHING. He is a kind, true, fast friend, and at the same time the most obliging, the bravest, and the most calumniated man living.

A reference just above to EX-GOVERNOR WISE reminds me of a little incident. I was traveling in the Southern States during the winter of 1859, and I happened to meet at Montgomery, Alabama, a Virginia gentleman who had formerly been in the Navy, and was afterward a member of the National Congress from his native state. He told me that during the Taylor campaign he stumped that state in favor of the hero of Buena Vista, while GOVERNOR WISE did the same thing on the other side. After the fashion that then prevailed in the South and the Southwest, the two speakers traveled together, and alternated in addressing their audiences. They arrived, in the course of their journey, at Lynchburg, where it was the Governor's turn to speak first. In his address he dwelt largely upon the incapacity and unfitness of GEN-

ERAL TAYLOR for the Presidency, said that he had been unable to write his own dispatches, and that they were all written by his son-in-law, COLONEL BLISS. He harped a long time upon his *ignorance*, even calling him "Old Ignorance." When my informant rose to reply, he made a short address upon the political issues involved in the election, and then closed with the remark that, in answer to what his friend had said about GENERAL TAYLOR's ignorance, his only reply was that, "Where *ignorance* is *Bliss*, 'tis folly to be *Wise!*" at the same time pointing his finger at the Governor.

Mr. COLFAX, late Vice-President, and Mr. WASHBURNE, now Minister to France, were competing candidates for the Speakership of the Thirty-eighth Congress. Some three weeks before the time for Congress to meet, Mr. COLFAX came to Washington, and immediately entered upon an active canvass for the post to which he aspired. Mr. WASHBURNE only made his appearance at a very late moment, and was surprised to find that the question of the Speakership was already virtually settled against him. He complained to Mr. CHASE that I was interfering in Mr. COLFAX's behalf; and the Secretary sent for me, and cautioned me against doing any thing in favor of or against either candidate, as they were both very good friends to our Department. Now what I had done, and all that I had done, in the premises was this: Before the organization of the House of Representatives, Mr. EDWIN CROSWELL, formerly of the *Albany Argus*, came to me in Washington in behalf of the Hon. HENRY G. STEBBINS, member of Congress elect from the first New York district. It is very likely that he came without Mr. STEBBINS's knowledge. He desired to have that gentleman made a member of the Committee of Ways and Means, and, at his instance, I not only gave him a letter to Mr. Colfax upon the subject, but also called several times upon that gentleman to urge him to appoint Mr. Stebbins upon that Committee, in case he should be the successful candidate for the Speakership. After Mr. Colfax's election, and before he had announced the committees, he told me that although he could not promise to comply with my wish, still, if Mr. Stebbins should, after all, find his name upon the list of committees where I desired to see it, I was at liberty to say to him that it was through my intervention that the matter was accomplished. Mr. Stebbins received the appointment, and by his course amply justified the Speaker's action. Although a Democrat, he ardently supported the Government, and during his brief term of service made two of the soundest and most eloquent financial speeches that were delivered during the war. His health soon failed, and he was compelled to withdraw for a time from all business. Mr. Chase told me that the Hon. Fernando Wood called upon him several times, with a view to a place upon the same committee. Mr. Chase was very much pleased with Mr. Wood at these interviews.

I could relate several anecdotes of General Spinner, the United States Treasurer, and the author of the amazing autograph which graces our national money, but I shall confine myself to a single one which he himself told me. The General is equally noted for his honesty and his profanity. Before he was made Treasurer of the United States by President Lincoln, he had been a member of Congress from the Herkimer District, New York. Senator Wade, of Ohio, was as conspicuous for the use of strong language as was Mr. Spinner. Shortly after the accession of the latter to office, he made an evening call upon Mrs. Wade. In course of conversation, it came out that he was no longer a member of the House of Representatives, as that lady supposed. "That explains," she said, "Mr. Wade's astonishingly increased profanity. Formerly he used to swear for the Senate and you for the House. Now he has to swear for both!"

At one time, when there was a constant apprehension that Washington would be attacked, we organized a regiment in the Treasury Department for home service. As I was anxious to do all in my power to encourage the enterprise, I enlisted as a raw recruit in the company of which Colonel Jones, of the Treasurer's office, was Captain. General Spinner, who was a veteran, joined the same company as a private. At the drills, I was always perpetrating the most awkward movements, and upon one occasion came very near putting out with my bayonet the eyes of a fellow-soldier who stood just behind me. He bore my homicidal attempt with all meekness, because I was Assistant Secretary of the Treasury. It used to be delightful to witness the fervor and energy with which General Spinner went through the manual. We had a very fine band of music, entirely composed of Department clerks, and the bray of their brazen instruments, as we marched through the echoing corridors of the Treasury building of an evening, still lingers in my ears.

Mr. Chase was induced, at a certain period, to adopt for the use of the Government, for its paper obligations, what was called a "membrane paper," which it was claimed rendered counterfeiting impossible. The printing was done in the Department, and the Secretary supposed that this paper was so carefully guarded and watched that it was impossible for the smallest piece of it to be abstracted or to get astray. He used to keep a little specimen of it, about four inches long by three wide, upon his desk, and to explain to those to whom he showed it that he had himself been compelled to give a receipt for it before he was allowed to take it, so scrupulous was the care with which it was guarded. It happened that I once had occasion to go down to the room where this paper was received, and where the sheets were counted before being stored in an apartment below. There were two doors to this room upon one of the corridors, and they were both open. The corridor was full of laborers, standing in a line, who had come to receive their pay from the disbursing agent. Upon a counter in the room were heaped sheets of the precious paper. A pile of mutilated sheets stood in one corner. Two women, upon their knees scrubbing the floor, were the only occupants of the room, the person in charge having temporarily gone elsewhere. I immediately ejected the women, locked both doors, and carried the keys to the Secretary. This little incident changed his views in relation to the Cerberus-like watchfulness with which his paper had been guarded.

We had at that time an elephant on our hands in the Department in the person of a brother of JOHN BROWN, "whose soul is marching on." FREDERICK BROWN had been successively detailed to almost every bureau, and after a few days dismissed from each as incompetent and insubordinate. He was a harmless, garrulous old man, who used to obstruct a corridor for hours, pouring out a ceaseless stream of talk upon whomsoever would stop to listen to him. Finally he became a nuisance that had to be in some way abated; but we were loth to abandon altogether a man so connected. So we had him appointed keeper of a light-house, situated upon a rock far off the coast of North Carolina! He was employed at one time in the office of the Light-House Board, of which the Secretary of the Treasury is, *ex-officio*, Chairman, and of which ADMIRAL SHUBRICK was then the acting chief. BROWN had the habit of sitting with his feet elevated upon a table even in the presence of his official superiors. He was remonstrated with, and told that he ought, at least, to resume a decent position when ADMIRAL SHUBRICK entered the room. "I don't see why I should," he answered; "the Admiral doesn't take down his feet when *I* come in!"

Upon another occasion ADMIRAL SHUBRICK, desiring to send him out with a communication, asked him—"Mr. BROWN, do you know where the Navy Department is?" "No," answered BROWN. "Do you know where the War Department is?" "No." "Do you know where Wilder's building is?" "No." "Well," emphatically demanded the old Admiral, "*what* do you know?" "I know," coolly replied BROWN, "that Admiral *Davis* is a gentleman."

One day the Superintendent of the printing of fractional currency came into my office accompanied by a beautiful but very pale girl of about sixteen. I was engaged, but I saw that he had something urgent to say, and so I immediately gave him my attention. He told me that for some time past there had been frequent thefts of entire sheets of fractional currency from his office, although he had supposed that he had adopted such checks as would render any abstraction impossible; that the amount taken at each successive time was larger than at the previous one; that the entire sum was altogether about twelve hundred dollars, whereof some four hundred had been stolen only two or three days before; that he had not dared to say any thing about it to the Secretary, and that he had just detected the little girl who was with him as the culprit. I turned to the girl, and asked her if the charge against her was true. With increasing pallor, but without shedding a tear, she admitted that it was. I directed the Superintendent to take her up stairs again, and await further orders, and I sent a messenger for POLICE DETECTIVE CLARVOE. Just then a middle-aged lady, who had been waiting my leisure, walked up to my desk and urged her claims to be appointed a clerk in the Department. I courteously made to her the stereotyped statement that we had thousands of applicants and no vacancies; and when I had finished, she turned upon me in a vixenish way and said: "If I were only young and pretty, like the young person who has just gone out, you would give me a place, as you have undoubtedly given her one." I made no reply, but I could not avoid thinking how differently she would have spoken had she known upon what business that poor child had been brought to me. Before CLARVOE came I had communicated with the Secretary upon the subject, and he very properly demanded the immediate arrest of the thief. So I was compelled to hand her over to the detective for incarceration, and I requested him to report to me as soon as possible all that he could ascertain about the case. The ensuing day he returned to me, and gave me her whole history. She was the daughter of an extensive importing merchant in one of our great cities, who had failed in business soon after the commencement of the war, and had then, regardless of his family, committed suicide. Some of the friends of the unfortunate man commanded influence sufficient to procure for the daughter the position which she held in the mechanical department of the Treasury. Soon afterward her mother went to the bad, and took up with a Portuguese blockade-runner. These two together corrupted the child. Every penny that she had abstracted had been taken at their instance, and for the benefit of one or the other of them. He had traced the money last stolen to one of the principal dry-goods shops in Washington, where she had purchased silk dresses and other articles for her mother, and paid for them with the uncut sheets, which the proprietor had very strangely accepted. Both the man and the woman had left Washington directly after the arrest. There was nothing to be recovered. I thought this a pretty hard case, and so said to the Secretary; but he insisted that it was his duty to criminally prosecute the girl for the sake of the example. Of course he was right in principle. But I then asked him where he supposed the public, if informed of the transaction, would attach most blame, to this tempted, unsophisticated girl, or to the Treasury Department, which surrounded its manufacture of paper money with such insufficient checks as to render the abstraction possible? He understood this as I intended it, and forthwith directed that the matter be dropped, upon the single condition that the girl should go away from the capital and not return there. I sent for CLARVOE, and communicated to him the Secretary's decision. I then ascertained that, instead of taking the child to jail, he had placed her in his own house in charge of his wife, who had kindly cared for her all the time. We discovered several other thefts in the Department during my time, but in every other instance we recovered the entire amount that had been taken.

I saw FREDERICK DOUGLASS several times in Washington, and he impressed me, as he did every one else, by his remarkable intelligence. I once heard him, born a slave, get decidedly the better of PRESIDENT JOHNSON in a political discussion; and I was present upon another occasion when he talked about banking to Mr. FREEMAN CLARKE, of the Committee of Ways and Means, with an astonishing ability and apparent familiarity with the subject.

CHAPTER XI.

A CORRECT version of the circumstances which induced and accompanied Mr. CHASE's withdrawal from Mr. LINCOLN's Cabinet has never, to my knowledge, been given to the public. About the first of June, 1864, Mr. CISCO tendered to the President, through the Secretary of the Treasury, his peremptory resignation of the office of Assistant Treasurer of the United States at New York, to take effect immediately after the close of the fiscal year, viz., on the first of July. Efforts were unsuccessfully made to induce him to withdraw it, and it then became necessary to find somebody to take his place. A furious competition for the office immediately sprang up. Mr. CHASE, after a few days, went to New York, where he remained some time. He offered the position to three leading bankers, but they declined it. He then returned to Washington, and remained inactive upon the subject until very late in the month. One morning he sent for me, and told me that he had some time before decided to nominate me to the President, but that, equally to his surprise and regret, a gentleman of high position and great influence had called upon him and objected to the nomination. However, he had ordered his carriage, and intended to go directly to the Senate, and canvass that body upon the subject; and if he found that I would be confirmed, he would send my name to the President that very afternoon. In conclusion, he desired me to call at his house at five o'clock.

Accordingly, at the appointed time I went there. Mr. CHASE told me that he had spent two hours upon the floor of the Senate, and that he thought I would be unanimously confirmed; that even the gentleman who opposed me would not, he believed, carry his opposition so far as to vote against my confirmation. I thus knew that the gentleman to whom he had referred in the morning was a Senator, and I fancied that he must be a Senator from New York. As I was acquainted with the favorable disposition of one of them toward me, I had no difficulty in concluding in my own mind who it was that was hostile to my nomination. Mr. CHASE had already sent my name to the President, and he desired me to leave for New York that very evening, so as to arrange for my official bonds, and be prepared to assume the duties of the office on the first of July. I objected to this, under the circumstances; but I promised the Secretary that I would take my departure immediately after Mr. LINCOLN should nominate me to the Senate.

The next day a recommendation that I be appointed, signed by every Union member of the Lower House from the State of New York, was transmitted to the President, and the friendly Senator called upon him to indorse it.

However, I was not nominated to the Senate on that day. The following morning Mr. CHASE again sent for me, and told me that he had received a letter from Mr. LINCOLN, in which he expressed a disinclination to nominate me on account of the opposition of one of the New York Senators, and invited him to a conference upon the subject. Mr. CHASE, instead of calling, replied by letter. For several days communications were passing between him and the President. This correspondence, however, I have never seen. Finally, one day as I was discharging my official duties as usual, with the room full of people, Mr. SCHUCKERS rushed in, and whispered into my ear, "We have no longer a Secretary; Mr. CHASE has resigned, and the President has accepted his resignation!" Thereupon I went directly to Mr. CHASE, and asked him if the news which I had just heard was true. He answered in the affirmative. I then requested his permission to tender my own resignation to the President. He told me that such action would look factious, and must not be thought of.

Then Mr. LINCOLN nominated to the Senate EX-GOVERNOR TOD, of Ohio, as Secretary of the Treasury. At this nomination the Senate and the country stood aghast. A Senatorial Committee called upon the President, and asked him to withdraw the nomination of Mr. TOD, but he refused to do so. Fortunately that gentleman, who knew that he had no chance to be confirmed, cut the knot by declining the appointment.

The afternoon of the day of the acceptance of Mr. CHASE's resignation, I was upon the floor of the House of Representatives. Members flocked around me, eager for information, and I was addressed by the facetious title of "Cabinet-smasher."

Then Congress and the country, with a united voice, demanded the appointment of Mr. FESSENDEN, at that time Chairman of the Committee on Finance in the Senate. Never did a man more reluctantly accept office. He knew better than any body else his want of fitness for an executive position. He said that his place, and his only place, was in a forensic assembly. During his administration of the affairs of the Treasury he confided much to his subordinates, who had more practical experience than himself; and I trust and believe that he was faithfully served.

Mr. Chase had been out of the Department nearly two months, when I happened to be spending an evening with Mr. Seward. In the course of the conversation, I referred to the transaction which had resulted in an exchange of the Treasury portfolio, and explained the reasons which had induced Mr. Lincoln to decline nominating me as Assistant Treasurer at New York, as I then understood them—viz., that he was unwilling to appoint to so important an office one of Democratic antecedents; that he had recognized the propriety of retaining Mr. Cisco, notwithstanding his politics, on account of his eminent services before and since the war; but that he thought that, if a change was to be made, the office should be treated as strictly party property. Mr. Seward assured me that I took an entirely erroneous view of the matter, and advised me to seek a personal explanation from the President. I asked Mr. Seward to have a preliminary talk with Mr. Lincoln upon the subject, which he kindly promised to do. I may here observe that Mr. Chase's feeling had been that the Assistant Treasurer at New York being his right arm, he ought not to be interfered with in making a selection.

A few days later I walked over to the Executive Mansion at about two o'clock in the afternoon. The President's ante-chamber was crowded with people awaiting an audience; but as soon as Mr. Lincoln received my card he gave orders to admit me. I expected to be with him ten minutes, at the utmost, but he detained me nearly two hours. The interview was, altogether, one of the most interesting and amusing I ever had in my life.

The President received me with great cordiality, and I began to repeat to him substantially what I had said to Mr. SEWARD. He listened to me laughingly, but impatiently, shaking his head all the time. When I had got through, he said: "You are altogether on the wrong track. Why, didn't I nominate, as CHASE's successor, DAVE TOD, who has been all his life a Democrat, and who worked and voted for DOUGLAS and against me? No, sir; I will tell you all about it. The Republican party in your state is divided into two factions, and I can't afford to quarrel with either of them. By accident, rather than by any design of mine, the radicals have got possession of the most important Federal offices in New York. I care nothing whatever about your personal politics. You were pressed by Mr. CHASE and opposed by SENATOR ———. Had I, under these circumstances, consented to your appointment, it would have been another radical triumph, and I couldn't afford one. That is all that there is about it, so far as you are concerned. But I'll tell you what happened at the time between myself and CHASE. One day, early in June, CHASE came to me and said, 'Mr. President, CISCO has resigned at New York, and I am going on there to see who is the best man to put into his place.'" Here Mr. LINCOLN's face assumed an indescribably droll expression, and, drawing his head toward mine, and placing his enormous hand upon my knee, he said, "That, you understand, was a *peg* that would fit any *hole!*" The President continued: "Well, CHASE went to New York, and in due time returned, I suppose, but he did not come near me. In the mean time there was the fiercest contest waging for the vacant office that I remember since I have been *in this place*." (This is the manner in which Mr. LINCOLN always referred to his position as President.) "I must confess that you were the most numerously indorsed, but ——— opposed you. The next time that I heard from CHASE upon the subject was when he wrote to me requesting me to nominate you. I answered his communication, and asked him to come and see me, and talk over the matter. Instead of doing so, he wrote me again, saying that he would have you and nobody else. And so we fired letters at each other for two or three days. I offered to nominate either of three gentlemen who happened to be acceptable to SENATOR ———; but CHASE objected to all of them. Finally, as I was sitting here at my desk one morning, with the room full of people, a letter from the Treasury Department was brought to me. I opened it, recognized CHASE's handwriting, read the first sentence, and inferred from its tenor that this matter was in the way of satisfactory adjustment. I was truly glad of this, and, laying the envelope with its inclosure down upon the desk, went on talking. People were coming and going all the time till three o'clock, and I forgot all about CHASE's letter. At that hour it occurred to me that I would go down stairs and get a bit of lunch. My wife happened to be away, and they had failed to call me at the usual time. While I was sitting alone at table my thoughts reverted to CHASE's letter, and I determined to answer it just as soon as I should go up stairs again. Well, as soon as I was back here, I took pen and paper and prepared to write; but then it occurred to me that I might as well read the letter before I answered it. I took it out of the envelope for that purpose, and, as I did so, another inclosure fell from it upon the floor. I picked it up, read it, and said to myself, '*Halloo, this is a horse of another color!*' It was his resignation. I put my pen into my mouth, and *grit my teeth* upon it. I did not long reflect. I very soon decided to accept it, and I nominated DAVE TOD to succeed him.

"But there is a history behind all this which I don't mind telling you. Are you aware that this was the *fourth* time that CHASE had tendered me his resignation? No? Well, it was. I will tell you how it all happened. The first occasion was when SEWARD tendered his, after the Republican Senators had passed resolutions hostile to him. CHASE soon followed suit, and by so doing rendered me a great favor, which I shall ever hold in grateful remembrance. Matters were *fixed up*, and neither of them left the Cabinet.

"Some time after this there was a Collector of Customs on the Pacific coast, one of CHASE's men, who was represented to me to be a worthless vagabond, and even a defaulter. I spoke to CHASE about him; but he had entire confidence in him, and refused to listen to any thing to his disadvantage. While matters stood thus, CHASE one day told me that he felt overworked, and proposed taking a little trip down the Potomac, but that he would not be gone longer than two days. I said, 'All right, Mr. Secretary,' and we shook hands and parted. As luck would have it, I was waited upon the very next day by a delegation of all the gentlemen from the Pacific coast, both official and unofficial, who then happened to be in Washington. They filed formal charges with me against the Collector to whom I have referred, and demanded his immediate removal. I told them that the Secretary of the Treasury was out of town, that it would be discourteous to him if I acted upon the matter in his absence, but that he would return in one or two days at the latest, and I invited them to call upon me again in about a week, when I promised, under all circumstances, a definite answer to their request. A week passed. No Chase. The delegation returned, and as I was thoroughly convinced of not only the propriety of, but even the necessity for the act, I removed the Collector, and appointed another in his stead. The first notice that I received of Chase's return was about three days afterward, when I found his resignation lying upon my table. I waited until evening, and then ordered my carriage and drove to his house. I found him in the office to the left as you enter the door. I went directly up to him with the resignation in my hand, and, putting my arm around his neck, said to him, 'Chase, here is a paper with which I wish to have nothing to do; take it back, and be reasonable.' I then explained to him what had occurred while he was away. I told him that the man whom I had appointed happened to have been dead several weeks; that I couldn't replace the person whom I had removed—that was impossible—but that I would appoint any one else whom he should select for the place. It was difficult to bring him to terms; I had to plead with him a long time, but I finally succeeded, and heard nothing more of *that* resignation.

"You remember," Mr. LINCOLN continued, "that when HIRAM BARNEY was appointed, at the beginning of this Administration, Collector of the Port of New York, every body supposed that he was CHASE's selection, and nobody else's. Now BARNEY was as much my choice as he was CHASE's; and when—CHASE, SEWARD, and myself standing round that table—BARNEY's appointment was decided upon, I believe that I was the most gratified person then present. Well, I have just as great confidence in Mr. BARNEY's integrity and patriotism now as I had then. But after a time things got *very mixed* in the New York Custom-House, and the establishment was being *run* almost exclusively in the interest of the radicals. I felt very great delicacy in doing any thing that might be offensive to my friend BARNEY. And yet something had to be done. There was no use in attempting to bring CHASE over to my views. But I tried it, and failed. Then I waited for a time. At last I made up my mind to take action, hoping to be able to afterward reconcile CHASE to it. So I sent for SEWARD, and told him that he must find a diplomatic position in Europe for BARNEY. SEWARD said that it was not an easy thing to do; but I was peremptory, and told him it *must* be done. After two or three days SEWARD came back, and reported to me that he had found the place. Just then CHASE became aware of my little conspiracy. He was very angry; and he told me that the day that Mr. BARNEY left the New York Custom-House, with or without his own consent, he, CHASE, would withdraw from the Secretaryship of the Treasury. Well, I *backed down* again. Now I ask you, as a reasonable man, whether, when the resignation with which you are concerned came, I *could*, with any self-respect, hesitate to accept it?"

This is the substance of what Mr. LINCOLN told me that afternoon. When I got home in the evening, I took notes of the conversation, and I have here endeavored to reproduce his part of it as faithfully as possible. It was Mr. CHASE's nature to command, not to obey. He would have made an admirable President, but he could not subordinate himself to any superior authority. I have in my possession a copy of a letter addressed by Mr. CHASE to the President, under date of January 13, 1864. It is, apparently, in reply to two received from him, one upon the subject of Mr. BARNEY's removal, and the other complaining about a biographical sketch of himself which Mr. CHASE had permitted to be written for a magazine published in the city of Philadelphia. It is as follows:

"MY DEAR SIR,—I am to-day fifty-six years old. I have never, consciously and deliberately, injured a fellow-man. It is too late for me to begin by sacrificing to clamor the reputation of a man whom I have known for more than twenty years, and whose repute for honesty has been all that time unsullied. I shall not recommend the removal of Mr. BARNEY except upon such show of his misconduct or incapacity as makes it my duty to do so. In such a case I shall not shrink from my duty.

"I pretend no indifference to the consequences, personal to myself, which you refer to as likely to follow this avowal on my part. But the approval of my own conscience is dearer to me than political position, and I shall cheerfully sacrifice the latter to preserve the former.

"I received some days ago your note in relation to a biographical sketch to be printed in a Philadelphia periodical. It was a matter in which I had no concern. If any body wants my autograph, and I have time, I give it; if any body wants to take my daguerreotype or photograph, and I have time, I sit for it; if any body wants to *take my life*, in the way of a biographical sketch, *I let him take it*, and, if I have time, give such information as is wanted, that he may take it the more easily. Some friends wanted such a sketch prepared, and engaged a gentleman to prepare it. The publisher of the *American Exchange and Review*—a respectable periodical, by the way, I am told—was about to print a series of such sketches, and proposed to begin with that of me. How could I object? He asked for subscriptions, and obtained them. How could I control or supervise that? I was very busy with the affairs of my Department, and had no time to look after such matters, even had I been aware of what was being done. If I had been consulted, I should certainly have objected to any subscription by Mr. Jay Cooke or his brother; except such a moderate one as any friend might have made. Not that any wrong was intended or done, but because the act was subject to misconstruction, and there are so many to misconstrue. Mr. Jay Cooke is a friend; and though he did not subscribe to the sketch, he doubtless sanctioned the subscription of his brother Henry, who is also a friend (and the son of a friend), whose friendship was formed when I was powerless to bestow favors. Neither of the brothers, nor the father, have ever received at my hands, since I have had some power, any favor which they have not earned by strenuous and untiring labors for the public interest; nor any which my worst enemy would not have received as freely had he rendered the same services. What Mr. H. D. Cooke did about the unfortunate biography was done of his own accord, without prompting from me, and his brother's approval was given in the same way.

"You will pardon me if I write as one somewhat moved. It makes me hate public life when I realize how powerless are the most faithful labors and the most upright conduct to protect any man from carping envy or malignant denunciations; and how little he can expect even from the best and most intelligent when such noises prevail. It is almost equally painful to think how little friends are disposed to bear with the mistakes and inadvertencies of other friends, and how ready to make me responsible for them as well as my own. Very sincerely yours,

"S. P. Chase.

"To the President."

CHAPTER XII.

MR. FESSENDEN, while he was Secretary of the Treasury, was a martyr to dyspepsia. He was much more familiar in his manners than Mr. CHASE, and failed to inspire his subordinates with that awe which his predecessor had always done. He came to be very much liked. I do not remember any of the moderns who could stand up successfully against him in an impromptu discussion in the Senate. It is said that, before the war, JEFFERSON DAVIS feared to cross swords with him more than he did with any other member of that body. Mr. FESSENDEN *hated* Mr. SUMNER, and Mr. SUMNER very much disliked Mr. FESSENDEN. Upon one and the same day, Mr. FESSENDEN spoke to me of Mr. SUMNER as "no gentleman," and Mr. SUMNER designated Mr. FESSENDEN as "a mere Senatorial gladiator." I believe that their relations improved, if they did not become actual friends, before Mr. FESSENDEN'S death.

I remember that one day, immediately after a Cabinet meeting, Mr. FESSENDEN, entering his room in the Department where I was awaiting his return, advanced toward me with glowing countenance, and said, "I tell you, Mr. FIELD, Mr. LINCOLN is more of a politician than all his Cabinet put together!" Before he had the opportunity to explain what had so excited his enthusiasm, somebody came in upon business, and the matter was dropped.

Mr. FESSENDEN told me what an unruly lad he had

been when a student at Bowdoin College. I think he said that he was finally dismissed without receiving a degree. At any rate, he mentioned that when he left there, in more or less disgrace, he told the President or the Faculty that he would return in less than five years as a Trustee of the institution—and he did it.

During my time, the present Assistant Secretary of the Treasury, the Hon. JOHN F. HARTLEY, was Chief Clerk. This excellent and modest gentleman was a college contemporary of Mr. FESSENDEN. He has now been connected with the Department nearly forty years; and is, unquestionably, the best revenue lawyer in the country. Ex-SENATOR JOHN P. HALE, of New Hampshire, told me that FRANKLIN PIERCE, WILLIAM PITT FESSENDEN, NATHANIEL HAWTHORNE, HUGH MCCULLOCH, JOHN F. HARTLEY, and himself, were all at Bowdoin College, Maine, at the same time, although not all in the same class; and that, had they then been told that among their number there was one who was destined to achieve great future distinction, all would have agreed that HARTLEY must be the man. Going to Washington for his health more than a generation ago, he accepted a clerkship in the Treasury Department, and there he has ever since remained. In every Department of the Government there are to be found a few of these old officials, whose services have become almost indispensable, and who have grown so accustomed to a life of routine that they can not emancipate themselves from it. Such were my old friends Mr. WEST, Mr. WOOD, and Mr. HANDY, all since deceased; and my college class-mate, Mr. GAINES, and others, who still remain.

There used to be a clerk in the Register's office who

belonged to one of those Washington families which ever since the foundation of the Government have considered themselves, by prescriptive right, entitled to be provided for by it. At the same time, his father was chief of one of the bureaus in the War Department, and he had a brother who was employed in the Interior Department. He had also another brother who had been in the Army, but, becoming disabled by illness, had been honorably discharged. For *this* brother, too, he was determined to secure a place in the civil service. With this object he went from Department to Department, but always without success. Finally he determined to go directly to the President himself, and to appeal to him to intervene in behalf of the discharged soldier. Mr. LINCOLN, it would seem, had heard of the case before the Treasury clerk secured the audience with him which he sought. When the interview had terminated, the disappointed clerk rushed back to our Department and into my office, and commenced, in the most indiscreet and intemperate manner, to express his disgust with the President. "It is a disgrace to the country," he said, "that such a boor should be President of the United States!" I drew from him the story of what had occurred between the President and himself, and it was something like this: Mr. LINCOLN received him kindly, and listened to his request. "Why don't you go directly to the Secretaries?" he asked. "I have been to them all, and failed with all," was the answer. "Hasn't your brother sufficiently recovered his health to enable him to return to the Army?" inquired the President. "No, sir, he has not," was the reply. "Let me see," continued Mr. LINCOLN, "I believe that you yourself are a clerk in one of the Departments—which one is it?" "The Treasury Department, sir." "I thought so. Has your brother as good clerical capacity as you possess?" "Yes, sir." "I think that I have somewhere met your father. Doesn't *he* hold an office in Washington?" "Yes, sir; he is chief of the ——— bureau in the War Department." "Oh, yes; I now recollect him perfectly well. Has your brother good references as to character?" "Yes, sir; the very best." "Is there *any other* of your family holding office under the Government?" "Yes, sir; I have a younger brother in the Interior Department." "Well, then, all I have to say to you, Mr. ———, is *that there are too many hogs and too little fodder!*"

I was once in Mr. LINCOLN's company when a sectarian discussion arose. He himself looked very grave, and made no observation until all the others had finished what they had to say. Then, with a twinkle of the eye, he remarked that he preferred the Episcopalians to every other sect, because they are equally indifferent to a man's religion and his politics.

This is not quite so bad as the remark attributed to the revivalist preacher, ELDER KNAPP, that "it is easier for a codfish to climb a tree, tail foremost, with a loaf of bread in his mouth, than for an Episcopalian to go to heaven."

It happened that at one time a blockade-runner going out of Charleston harbor was captured, and on board of her were found certain dispatches from the Spanish Consul in that city for his own Government. These dispatches were very improperly opened by the captor, and then forwarded to the State Department at Washington. Mr.

SEWARD, immediately after they reached his hands, sent for the Spanish Minister, Mr. TASSARA, and, with expressions of great regret that the envelopes had been tampered with, offered him the dispatches. The Minister, highly indignant, declined to receive them. Then Mr. SEWARD proposed to forward them to their destination through the medium of our own agents. This proposition was equally unacceptable, and the Secretary of State was at a loss what to do. He shortly afterward explained the difficulty to the President, whom it reminded of "a little story." "When I lived in Indiana," he said, "there resided very near us an old negro, known as *Uncle Josh.* He was a very pious darkey, but was so infirm that it was impossible for him to go to the neighboring schoolhouse to listen to any itinerant preacher who might happen to discourse there on a Sunday. However, in order to make up as far as possible for his own inability to attend, he always compelled his grandchildren to go; and they were required, not only to recollect the text, but also to be able to give the old man some account of the sermon. On one occasion a Methodist came and preached. He told the congregation that there were two kinds of people in this world, Methodists and Baptists; that the Methodists followed a road that led to heaven, and the Baptists one that led to hell. The next Sunday there presented himself a hard-shell Baptist, who had heard about the sermon of his Methodist brother. He told his auditors that it was true that there were two kinds of people in the world, Methodists and Baptists, and that they followed different roads; but that it was the *Baptist* road that led to heaven, and the *Methodist* road that led to hell. When old Uncle Josh heard this, he scratched his wool, and said: 'Each one says that there are only two roads, and that his own leads to heaven, and the other to hell. Well, this old nigger will go across lots!' SEWARD, you will have to go across lots!"

Story-telling was often with Mr. LINCOLN a defensive weapon, which he employed with great skill. Frequently, when he was unwilling to grant a request, he would tell a story. It was so much easier to do this than to refuse outright. Many a petitioner was dismissed by him, overcome with laughter, and forgetting, perhaps, until he was outside the house, that his visit had been a failure. With civility the President was not overburdened, and his manners were any thing but acceptable to the fair sex. I used constantly to observe in Washington during the war, that, whereas all men appeared more or less abashed on approaching, at least for the first time, the nation's leaders, the ladies shared in none of this diffidence. On one occasion a lady was talking to Mr. LINCOLN, asking a favor at that, and he remained sitting while she stood. After a while he arose and drew up another chair, as she supposed with the intention of offering it to her. Nothing of the sort. He stretched out his own long legs upon it. This was more than female patience could endure. "Mr. LINCOLN," exclaimed the lady, "I think you are the worst-bred man in the world." "Halloo," asked the President, "what have I done now?" The lady explained, and Mr. LINCOLN, in the best temper, admitted that he believed she was right.

But Mr. LINCOLN did not always deal exclusively in burlesque. He received once a call from a delegation of bank Presidents, at one of the gloomiest periods of the war, when depression and even discouragement prevailed in many places. One of the financial gentlemen asked the President if his confidence in the future was not beginning to be shaken. "Not in the least," he answered. "When I was a young man in Illinois," he continued, "I boarded for a time with a deacon of the Presbyterian Church. One night I was aroused from my sleep by a rap at my door, and I heard the deacon's voice exclaiming, 'Arise, Abraham, the day of judgment has come!' I sprang from my bed, and rushed to the window; and there I saw the stars falling in a shower. But I looked beyond those falling stars, and far back in the heavens I saw—fixed, apparently, and immovable—the grand old constellations with which I was so well acquainted. No, gentlemen; the world did not come to an end then, nor will the Union now!"

Mr. Lincoln possessed extraordinary kindness of heart when his feelings could be reached. He was fond of dumb animals, especially cats. I have seen him fondle one for an hour. Helplessness and suffering touched him when they appealed directly to his senses, or when you could penetrate through his intelligence to them. His imagination was not vivid. He might know as a fact that whole hecatombs were lying upon a battle-field in the agonies of death without being very deeply affected. One afternoon I happened to be in Baltimore, and met there one of the most eminent physicians of the city, who told me a pitiful story. A gentleman of large wealth and of the highest social position was lying in his own house in the last stages of consumption. He sympathized with the rebel cause, but had never aided it by deed or money. He had an only daughter and child, who had been educated in Paris, and who had been a recognized belle at home. She married there her cousin, and went to reside with him in Virginia. When the war broke out, her husband was appointed a General in the Confederate service, and was killed in one of the first engagements. He left his widow with an infant. For a long time she made vain efforts to go to her father. Finally, accompanied by her child and a negro nurse, she followed in the wake of EARLY'S raid into Pennsylvania. Sometimes she walked, and sometimes she was permitted to ride upon a baggage-wagon, until she finally reached the Pennsylvania mountains—poor, exhausted, and ill. But even here her troubles were not at an end, for our authorities refused to allow her to go to Baltimore to join her dying father. It so happened that, visiting Baltimore when a very young man, I received many courtesies at the hands of this gentleman. I expressed a desire to call upon him, and, jumping into the doctor's gig, I accompanied him to the house. I found my old friend in a very shocking condition. I expressed to him my sympathy and my desire to do any thing within my power to bring father and daughter once again together. He thanked me, but assured me that my efforts would prove vain. GENERAL DIX, while in command there, and others, had done all that they could, but Mr. STANTON was inexorable. I parted from him, and returned to Washington. The next day I went to Mr. LINCOLN and told him the story, much better, I hope, than I have told it here. I succeeded in moving him, and in obtaining directly from him a telegraphic order permitting the lady to come to Baltimore, and to reside there under surveillance. I never heard any thing more about it, but presume that the order was carried out, unless the brutal

STANTON overruled it, which he was quite capable of doing.

Probably next to Mr. LINCOLN, the best story-teller in Washington was SENATOR NYE, of Nevada, commonly known as "JIM NYE." Unfortunately, however, like some of Mr. LINCOLN'S, many of his stories will not bear repetition. I remember a dinner that was given at Washington in the club-room at Willard's, by the representatives of the leading express companies, upon the occasion of the conclusion of a contract with the Treasury Department for the transportation of national bank-notes, and which was attended by a very distinguished company. If my memory does not fail me upon that point, among others present was GENERAL GRANT. At all events, NYE was there in the happiest possible mood. After the cloth was removed, he kept the table in a continuous roar of laughter, as he has done before and since "many a time and oft." Among the best of his stories was the following, which he related with a gravity and an unction that it would be impossible to imitate upon paper. In brief, and divested of NYE'S solemn details and rich verbiage, it ran somewhat as follows: While NYE was Governor of Nevada, there came to Carson City an old man who had been, with varying luck, wandering among the mines of California since the first discovery of gold there in 1849. At last he had succeeded in accumulating a snug fortune, and he had come to Carson to visit an old companion in those early days, who was then residing there. The visitor very soon after his arrival fell ill. His host, who was a pious man, begged to be permitted to call a clergyman, but the guest obstinately refused to allow it. He rapidly grew worse, and his condition soon became critical. But all his friend's importunities that he should see a clergyman proved unavailing. Finally the physician in attendance declared that the sick man had but a few hours to live; and the host's conscience impelled him to renew the attack, and to tell his friend that, if he adhered to his determination, and continued to refuse to indicate a preference for a clergyman of any particular denomination, *he himself* was determined to send for his own pastor. The moribund, who was rapidly sinking, turned his head upon his pillow, and, articulating with difficulty, replied: "I can't see—what occasion—I have—for the services—of a clergyman. I never—voted—the Democratic—ticket—in my life."

While I was in Washington, HORACE GREELEY used occasionally to visit us there. I remember that he once breakfasted with me, if I recollect aright, *tête-à-tête*. Mr. GREELEY had long before this discarded Graham bread and a vegetable diet, and had grown to be a very hearty devourer of animal food. After breakfast I lighted a cigar, and offered one to him, although I knew that he did not smoke. Of course, he declined it. He was in capital humor, and, turning to me, he asked me if I knew that he claimed to be the most polite man in the country. I told him that I recognized his many excellent qualities, but was not aware that he was especially remarkable for the graces of politeness. He assured me that he *was*, and told me that he had never been beaten in politeness but once in his life. That happened, he said, many years ago, before the days of railroads. Early one morning he left Baggs's Hotel, at Utica, in the stagecoach, westward bound. There was but one passenger besides himself—a gentleman of very prepossessing appearance, with whom he soon fell into conversation. After a while the stranger slowly and, as it were, mechanically drew a cigar-case from his pocket, and, opening it, tendered it to Mr. GREELEY, who declined the proffered offer. The conversation was resumed; and presently the stranger, extracting a cigar from the case, placed it in his mouth, and returned the case to his pocket. Another interval of talk ensued, when the stranger abruptly but deferentially remarked to Mr. GREELEY, "I hope, sir, you have no objection to a cigar?" "None in the world, sir," replied Mr. GREELEY, "when it is not alight." "Oh," replied his companion, "I had not the most remote thought of lighting it!" Thereupon Mr. GREELEY felt that he had been conquered in politeness; and he afterward ascertained that the victor was the famous CAPTAIN SHERMAN, of Lake Champlain.

He also told me that when he was residing in one of the up-town streets of New York, and before the dissolution of the political firm of "Seward, Weed, and Greeley," Mr. SEWARD came to breakfast with him one day, just as he had then been breakfasting with me. The breakfast finished, SEWARD lighted a cigar, just as I had done. Now Mrs. GREELEY happened to be ill in a room just over that in which the gentlemen were, and her husband knew that just so soon as the cigar-smoke should make its way to her nostrils through the flue of the chimney, she would descend upon them like an avalanche in whatever costume she happened just then to be. "I was fearfully terrified," said Mr. GREELEY; "and, starting up, I said to SEWARD, 'SEWARD, it's a fine day; let's take a little walk.' In less time than I can tell it I had him out of the house, and we walked round and round the block more than an hour. And the best of it is that SEWARD doesn't know to this day what my motive was in so unceremoniously dragging him away from the house that morning." He told the story so earnestly and so quaintly that I hardly knew while he was relating it whether I was laughing with him or at him.

It was by means of a letter of introduction from Mr. GREELEY that I made the acquaintance in Washington of the late MAJOR CHARLES G. HALPINE, better known to the literary public by his *nom de plume* of *Miles O'Reilly*. Mr. GREELEY thought that the Major, who was a *War Democrat*, could furnish us important information about the condition of the New York Custom-House. It turned out, however, that all that he could tell us of a reliable character we already knew. The Major possessed much talent as a song and squib writer, but he was only an indifferent politician. The confidence with which he used to stammer out his reading of the political horoscope was very amusing to those who knew him.

With a single exception, the foreign Ministers accredited to our Government during the war of the Rebellion had very little faith in the ultimate success of the Union cause. That exception was BERTINATTI, the Italian. I met him the day after that on which we received authentic intelligence of the Bull Run disaster. He declared to me his conviction that it was the most fortunate thing that could have happened to us; that it would serve to unite and arouse the people of the loyal states; and that the end would be the abolition of slavery, and the re-establishment of a Union free in fact as well as in name. Who of us then made a more promising and more intelligent forecast of our national future?

LORD LYONS, whatever his opinions, which he was too trained a diplomatist to express, did excellent service to our country as well as to his own. He and Mr. SEWARD acted as two policemen to keep the peace between Great Britain and the States. LORD LYONS was a most intelligent, cultivated, and laborious man. He had extraordinary flashes of wit, and, like WASHINGTON IRVING in his later years, the habit of suddenly falling asleep, any where and at the most inopportune moments. He treated the juniors of his legation with great kindness, but he compelled them to work. Some of these young gentlemen, who had been in the habit of kicking their heels in Paris and Vienna, rather chafed under the restraint of compulsory business hours. Of all houses, LORD LYONS preferred the Russian Minister's, because there he felt perfectly at home. He and a lot more of us used to congregate upon the steps of that hospitable mansion, and on the sidewalk in front of it, during the intolerably hot summer nights, when sleep was an impossibility, and sip tea *à la Russe* until almost daylight. In this connection, were there occasion to do so, I might speak more of the friendly BERTINATTI, who just before the end of his mission here married a beautiful widow, the possessor of large estates in Mississippi, which she secured from confiscation by her diplomatic alliance; and say something of that exaggerated cherub, the amiable PIPER; the jovial, card-loving STOECKL; the dissatisfied MERCIER; the crafty BLONDEEL; the kind but timid VON GEROLT; SCHLEIDEN, the giver of Gothic dinners, at which always figured that famous "Heidelberg wine;" the good-humored and hospitable LISBOA; the somewhat saturnine TASSARA; the courtly and elegant BARREDA; and that eccentric invalid, GEORGI. And I might talk about the scenes of horror after the battles of the Wilderness, when for days long files of ambulances filled with the wounded and dying passed through the unpaved streets of Washington, on their way to the hospitals on the outskirts of the city; of the admirable administration of those hospitals; of touching incidents which I witnessed in their wards; and of a thousand other things of daily or occasional occurrence. But let it all pass—at least for the nonce.

CHAPTER XIII.

IT was an April afternoon in the year 1865. I was driving alone on the Fourteenth Street road in the direction of the Soldiers' Home. Presently I heard a clatter behind me, and, looking out of the carriage-window, I saw Mr. LINCOLN approaching on horseback, followed by the usual cavalry escort. He soon came up to me, and, while he rode for some time at my side, we conversed together upon indifferent subjects. I noticed that he was in one of those moods when "melancholy seemed to be dripping from him," and his eye had that expression of profound weariness and sadness which I never saw in other human eye. After a while he put spurs to his horse and hurried on, and he and his followers were soon lost to view.

The next evening I was sitting alone in the reading-room of Willard's Hotel, where I resided during the absence of my family from Washington. Presently I was joined by Mr. MELLEN, Special Agent of the Treasury Department. I never saw the hotel so apparently deserted as it was that evening. The usually crowded corridors were empty. Ten o'clock came, and Mr. MELLEN left me to retire to his room. I then picked up the evening newspaper, intending, after I had read it, to follow his example. Scarcely had I commenced reading, when two men rushed headlong into the hotel, shouting that the President had been shot at Ford's Theatre! I sprang from my seat to follow them to the office, but before I could reach it a third person entered, more calm than the two who had preceded him, and confirmed their statement.

I immediately dashed up stairs and called Mr. MELLEN. He was already partly undressed, but he got ready as soon as possible, and together we rushed down E Street to the theatre. We found assembled in front of it about a hundred persons, many of whom knew us. They crowded around us, and each of them had a different story to tell about what had occurred. We learned that five minutes before our arrival Mr. LINCOLN had been carried over to the house of PETERSEN, a German tailor, in Tenth Street, and directly opposite the theatre. I do not remember what became of Mr. MELLEN, but I at once entered the house, the street door of which was standing open. In the hall I met Miss HARRIS, the daughter of SENATOR HARRIS, of New York, who had been one of the Presidential party at the theatre. As soon as she saw me, she exclaimed, "Oh, Mr. FIELD, the President is dying! but for heaven's sake do not tell Mrs. LINCOLN!" I inquired where Mrs. LINCOLN was, and was informed that she was in the front parlor. I entered the parlor, and found her there entirely alone. She was standing by a marble-topped table in the centre of the room, with her bonnet on and gloved, just as she had come from the theatre. As I came in she exclaimed, "Why didn't he shoot me? Why didn't he shoot me? Why didn't he shoot me?" I asked her if there was any thing that I could do, and she begged me to run for Dr. STONE, the President's family physician. I started to do so, but met in the hall MAJOR ECKERT, of the War Department, who told me that the doctor had already been sent for, and, not having yet arrived, he was himself going to bring him. I returned to the parlor, made this explanation to Mrs. LINCOLN, and inquired if there was any thing else that she desired me to do. She requested me to try to find Dr. HALL, a retired physician of the highest reputation. It took me a long time to reach him, for he lived at a distance, but I finally succeeded, and started with him to walk back to PETERSEN'S house. As we approached it, we found a military cordon drawn around the door, and, although the doctor was permitted to pass, the same privilege was refused to me.

I returned to Willard's Hotel, and went up to the room of Mr. RUFUS ANDREWS, then recently Surveyor of the Port of New York, where I met the late CITY JUDGE RUSSELL. I remained there perhaps two hours, and then again started for PETERSEN'S house, accompanied by Mr. ANDREWS. When we arrived there we found the guard withdrawn, and had no difficulty in getting in. We proceeded directly to the room in which Mr. LINCOLN was lying, a small extension room at the end of the hall, from which you descended to it by two steps. The room was plainly furnished, and there were some prints hanging upon the walls. The President was lying transversely across the cottage bedstead, as he was too tall to be placed in any other position. His head was supported upon two pillows on the side nearest the windows, and his feet rested against the opposite end of the foot-board. Dr. STONE was sitting upon the bed. SECRETARY WELLES occupied a rocking-chair, which he did not vacate, I believe, during the entire night. SURGEON-GENERAL BARNES was sitting in an ordinary chair by the bedside, holding Mr. LINCOLN's left hand. All the other persons in the room were standing. SENATOR SUMNER and ROBERT LINCOLN were, the greater part of the time, leaning over the head-board. The others who were in the room during the whole or a part of the night, were SECRETARY McCULLOCH, SECRETARY STANTON, SECRETARY USHER, ATTORNEY-GENERAL SPEED, CHIEF JUSTICE CHASE, GOVERNOR FARWELL, of Wisconsin, GOVERNOR OGLESBY, of Illinois, SPEAKER COLFAX, GENERALS HALLECK, MEIGS, and AUGUR, ASSISTANT SECRETARY OF THE INTERIOR OTTO, CONGRESSMAN FARNSWORTH, of Illinois, ASSISTANT SURGEON-GENERAL CRANE, COLONEL JOHN HAY, the President's Assistant Private Secretary, COLONEL TODD, the Rev. Dr. GURLEY, CHARLIE, Mr. LINCOLN's body servant, and perhaps a few others whom I do not at present recall. From time to time Mrs. LINCOLN was brought into the room, but she never remained there long. The President's eyes were closed and ecchymose. Below the lids and around the cheek-bones the flesh was black. Blood and brains were oozing from the wound in his head upon the uppermost of the pillows which supported it. He had been stripped of all clothing, and whenever one of the physicians turned down the sheet which covered his person, in order to feel the beatings of his heart, his brawny chest and immensely muscular arms revealed the hero of many a successful wrestling-match in his youthful days at New Salem.

His breathing was for a long time loud and stertorous, ending in deep-drawn sighs. He was totally unconscious from the moment that he was struck by the assassin's bullet. Except his breathing, and the sobbing of his wife, son, and devoted servant, not a sound was to be heard in that chamber for hours. The dropping of a pin would have been audible.

What a tragic episode in life's history was this to all there assembled! And not only to us, but to the nation and to the world!

His pulse was vacillating all through the night—at times strong and rapid, and at others feeble and slow. His vital power was prodigious, or he would have died within ten minutes after he was shot.

The night wore on, long and anxious, and finally the gray dawn of a dull and rainy morning began to creep slowly into the room. And still the martyr lived—if living it could be called.

The town clocks struck seven. Almost immediately afterward the character of the President's breathing changed. It became faint and low. At intervals it altogether ceased, until we thought him dead. And then it would be again resumed. I was standing directly opposite his face, with my watch in my hand.

At last, at just twenty-two minutes past seven, he ceased to breathe.

When it became certain to all that his soul had taken its flight, Dr. Gurley dropped upon his knees by the bedside and uttered a fervent prayer. Never was a supplication wafted to the Creator under more solemn circumstances.

When it was finished, most of the persons assembled began slowly to withdraw from the chamber of death. I, however, with a few others, remained. We closed the eyes completely, and placed silver coins upon them, and with a pocket-handkerchief we tied up the jaw, which had already begun to fall. Mr. Stanton threw open the two windows of the room. Just then PETERSEN entered, and rudely drawing the upper pillow from under the head of the dead, tossed it into the yard. Shortly afterward we retired from the room. Mr. STANTON locked the door, and stationed a sentry in front of it. I then went into the front parlor, where I found Dr. GURLEY again praying. Mrs. LINCOLN was lying upon a sofa, moaning, and her son ROBERT was standing at her head. When Dr. GURLEY had finished his prayer, ROBERT LINCOLN assisted his mother to rise, and together we walked to the front door. The President's carriage was standing before the house in the dripping rain, as it had stood there all through that terrible night. As Mrs. LINCOLN reached the door-steps, she cast a hurried glance at the theatre opposite, and three times repeated, "Oh, that *dreadful* house !" She was then helped into the carriage, which drove away.

Perhaps the most affecting incident connected with this drama occurred an hour later. Mr. LINCOLN'S body, inclosed in a plain wooden box, around which was wrapped the American flag, was borne from the house by six private soldiers; then placed in an ordinary hearse, behind which the soldiers marched like mourners; and so carried to the Executive Mansion. As the *cortége* passed along, it attracted but little attention, for but few persons knew what burden was being carried past their doors. It was fitting that this great man of the people —plain UNCLE ABE then, as in years gone by in his Western home—should pass through the silent streets of the capital under the escort of common men. The rude backwoodsman, who had become a MOSES to lead a people to deliverance from servitude, when dead, first fell into the arms of men humble as he himself had been. But none the less was the pageantry which followed appropriate for that President of the United States whose name is destined to stand upon the roll of our nation's history only second to that of the immortal WASHINGTON.

I walked back to Willard's alone that morning. Just as I turned from Tenth into E Street, I met the Chief Justice hurrying in the opposite direction. His eyes were bloodshot, and his entire face was distorted as I had never before seen it. "Is he dead?" he asked. I answered, "Yes," and gave him a very brief account of Mr. LINCOLN'S last moments. He passed on, and half an hour later he proceeded to the Kirkwood House, accompanied by some of the members of Mr. LINCOLN'S Cabinet, and administered there the oath of office to ANDREW JOHNSON, as President of the United States.

When I reached my hotel, I went directly to my room, and after washing and arranging my disordered dress, I came down to breakfast. The tables were crowded with ladies and gentlemen, the greater number of whom had only that morning heard of the tragedy, and they were eating as quietly, and apparently as unconcernedly, as if nothing unusual had occurred. I distinctly remember how this jarred upon my overwrought feelings. The contrast between the two scenes was too violent to be endured long. I could not eat, so I lighted a cigar, and walked up to the Treasury building. I went directly to my own office, and threw myself upon a lounge. Presently Mr. HARTLEY and one or two of the bureau officers came in to me. There were but very few of the persons employed in the Department who came there at all that day. No interruption of business was formally announced, but there was nobody there to transact any. Gloom, despondency, and even alarm pervaded all Government circles. It was known that Mr. SEWARD and his son FREDERICK had been stricken down. It was reported that Mr. STANTON had been laid in wait for. The wildest rumors about the extent of the conspiracy were circulated. Nothing was positively known, not even that it was WILKES BOOTH who had murdered Mr. LINCOLN. I remember that somebody brought me a revolver, and insisted that I should carry it for my own protection. Presently a reporter from the *New York Times* obtained access to me, and insisted that I should write for his paper an account of the President's death. I excused myself upon the plea of weariness; but he would not let me off until I had dictated to him a statement, which he took down in short-hand. Then followed a reporter of the *Philadelphia Inquirer*, and I had to do the same thing for him. I believe that these were the only circumstantial accounts of the last scenes which were published at the time, perhaps at any time. My head felt dazed, and I took a street car and went to Georgetown. I called upon FATHER EARLY, the principal of the College there, and he told me about a mysterious person who had been lurking around their grounds the previous night. Then I came home, and being by this time completely exhausted, went directly to bed, and soon fell into a profound sleep.

Three days afterward followed Mr. LINCOLN's funeral, of which my colleague, Mr. HARRINGTON, had the principal charge. The various official bodies who were to attend it met before proceeding to the Executive Mansion in separate rooms assigned to each of them in the Treasury building. They were to go thence to the White House in the reverse order of dignity, and it was my duty to so marshal them that there should be no break in the procession. And here occurred one of those little conflicts of etiquette which will sometimes obtrude themselves upon the most solemn occasions. The Chief Justice insisted that the diplomatic body precede himself and his associates, while the foreign representatives demanded that the Supreme Court precede them. The rooms occupied by the disputants were distant from each other. I had to run from one to the other. Finally BARON VON GEROLT, the dean of the diplomatic corps, gave way *for the occasion*, without prejudice, however, to any claims, etc.

As I saw Mr. LINCOLN lying in state in the East Room of the Executive Mansion, his appearance was quite unlike what it had been immediately after his death. The black had gone from his eyes and his face, which had resumed a natural color. This, I was informed, was the *work of an artist.* The pencil had been employed to produce the change. While his corpse was being carried in procession through the cities of the land, before it was exposed to public gaze, the coffin was opened, the dust was brushed from the face, and the discolored parts were retouched. And so he went to his rest!

INDEX.

THE END.

VALUABLE & INTERESTING WORKS

FOR PUBLIC AND PRIVATE LIBRARIES,

PUBLISHED BY HARPER & BROTHERS, NEW YORK.

☞ *For a full List of Books suitable for Libraries, see* HARPER & BROTHERS' TRADE-LIST *and* CATALOGUE, *which may be had gratuitously on application to the Publishers personally, or by letter enclosing Six Cents.*

☞ HARPER & BROTHERS *will send any of the following works by mail, postage prepaid, to any part of the United States, on receipt of the price.*

FLAMMARION'S ATMOSPHERE. The Atmosphere. Translated from the French of CAMILLE FLAMMARION. Edited by JAMES GLAISHER, F.R.S., Superintendent of the Magnetical and Meteorological Department of the Royal Observatory at Greenwich. With 10 Chromo-Lithographs and 86 Woodcuts. 8vo, Cloth, $6 00.

HUDSON'S HISTORY OF JOURNALISM. Journalism in the United States, from 1690 to 1872. By FREDERICK HUDSON. Crown 8vo, Cloth, $5 00.

PIKE'S SUB-TROPICAL RAMBLES. Sub-Tropical Rambles in the Land of the Aphanapteryx. By NICHOLAS PIKE, U. S. Consul, Port Louis, Mauritius. Profusely Illustrated from the Author's own Sketches; containing also Maps and Valuable Meteorological Charts. 8vo, Cloth, $3 50.

TYERMAN'S OXFORD METHODISTS. The Oxford Methodists: Memoirs of the Rev. Messrs. Clayton, Ingham, Gambold, Hervey, and Broughton, with Biographical Notices of others. By the Rev. L. TYERMAN, Author of "Life and Times of the Rev. John Wesley," &c. Crown 8vo, Cloth, $2 50.

TRISTRAM'S THE LAND OF MOAB. The Result of Travels and Discoveries on the East Side of the Dead Sea and the Jordan. By H. B. TRISTRAM, M.A., LL.D., F.R.S., Master of the Greatham Hospital, and Honorary Canon of Durham. With New Map and Illustrations. Crown 8vo, Cloth, $2 50.

SANTO DOMINGO, Past and Present; with a Glance at Hayti. By SAMUEL HAZARD. Maps and Illustrations. Crown 8vo, Cloth, $3 50.

LIFE OF ALFRED COOKMAN. The Life of the Rev. Alfred Cookman; with some Account of his Father, the Rev. George Grimston Cookman. By HENRY B. RIDGAWAY, D.D. With an Introduction by Bishop FOSTER, LL.D. Portrait on Steel. 12mo, Cloth, $2 00.

HERVEY'S CHRISTIAN RHETORIC. A System of Christian Rhetoric, for the Use of Preachers and Other Speakers. By GEORGE WINFRED HERVEY, M.A., Author of "Rhetoric of Conversation," &c. 8vo, Cloth, $3 50.

CASTELAR'S OLD ROME AND NEW ITALY. Old Rome and New Italy. By EMILIO CASTELAR. Translated by Mrs. ARTHUR ARNOLD. 12mo, Cloth, $1 75.

THE TREATY OF WASHINGTON: Its Negotiation, Execution, and the Discussions Relating Thereto. By CALEB CUSHING. Crown 8vo, Cloth, $2 00.

PRIME'S I GO A-FISHING. I Go a-Fishing. By W. C. PRIME. Crown 8vo, Cloth, $2 50.

HALLOCK'S FISHING TOURIST. The Fishing Tourist: Angler's Guide and Reference Book. By CHARLES HALLOCK, Secretary of the "Blooming-Grove Park Association." Illustrations. Crown 8vo, Cloth, $2 00.

SCOTT'S AMERICAN FISHING. Fishing in American Waters. By GENIO C. SCOTT. With 170 Illustrations. Crown 8vo, Cloth, $3 50.

ANNUAL RECORD OF SCIENCE AND INDUSTRY FOR 1872. Edited by Prof. SPENCER F. BAIRD, of the Smithsonian Institution, with the Assistance of Eminent Men of Science. 12mo, over 700 pp., Cloth, $2 00. (Uniform with the *Annual Record of Science and Industry for* 1871. 12mo, Cloth, $2 00.)

COL. FORNEY'S ANECDOTES OF PUBLIC MEN. Anecdotes of Public Men. By JOHN W. FORNEY. 12mo, Cloth, $2 00.

MISS BEECHER'S HOUSEKEEPER AND HEALTHKEEPER: Containing Five Hundred Recipes for Economical and Healthful Cooking; also, many Directions for securing Health and Happiness. Approved by Physicians of all Classes. Illustrations. 12mo, Cloth, $1 50.

FARM BALLADS. By WILL CARLETON. Handsomely Illustrated. Square 8vo, Ornamental Cloth, $2 00; Gilt Edges, $2 50.

POETS OF THE NINETEENTH CENTURY. The Poets of the Nineteenth Century. Selected and Edited by the Rev. ROBERT ARIS WILLMOTT. With English and American Additions, arranged by EVERT A. DUYCKINCK, Editor of "Cyclopædia of American Literature." Comprising Selections from the Greatest Authors of the Age. Superbly Illustrated with 141 Engravings from Designs by the most Eminent Artists. In elegant small 4to form, printed on Superfine Tinted Paper, richly bound in extra Cloth, Beveled, Gilt Edges, $5 00; Half Calf, $5 50; Full Turkey Morocco, $9 00.

THE REVISION OF THE ENGLISH VERSION OF THE NEW TESTAMENT. With an Introduction by the Rev. P. SCHAFF, D.D. 618 pp., Crown 8vo, Cloth, $3 00.

This work embraces in one volume:

I. ON A FRESH REVISION OF THE ENGLISH NEW TESTAMENT. By J. B. LIGHTFOOT, D.D., Canon of St. Paul's, and Hulsean Professor of Divinity, Cambridge. Second Edition, Revised. 196 pp.

II. ON THE AUTHORIZED VERSION OF THE NEW TESTAMENT in Connection with some Recent Proposals for its Revision. By RICHARD CHENEVIX TRENCH, D.D., Archbishop of Dublin. 194 pp.

III. CONSIDERATIONS ON THE REVISION OF THE ENGLISH VERSION OF THE NEW TESTAMENT. By J. C. ELLICOTT, D.D., Bishop of Gloucester and Bristol. 178 pp.

NORDHOFF'S CALIFORNIA. California: For Health, Pleasure, and Residence. A Book for Travelers and Settlers. Illustrated. 8vo, Paper, $2 00; Cloth, $2 50.

MOTLEY'S DUTCH REPUBLIC. The Rise of the Dutch Republic. By JOHN LOTHROP MOTLEY, LL.D., D.C.L. With a Portrait of William of Orange. 3 vols., 8vo, Cloth, $10 50.

MOTLEY'S UNITED NETHERLAND'S. History of the United Netherlands: from the Death of William the Silent to the Twelve Years' Truce—1609. With a full View of the English-Dutch Struggle against Spain, and of the Origin and Destruction of the Spanish Armada. By JOHN LOTHROP MOTLEY, LL.D., D.C.L. Portraits. 4 vols., 8vo, Cloth, $14 00.

NAPOLEON'S LIFE OF CÆSAR. The History of Julius Cæsar. By His late Imperial Majesty NAPOLEON III. Two Volumes ready. Library Edition, 8vo, Cloth, $3 50 per vol.

Maps to Vols. I. and II. sold separately. Price $1 50 *each*, NET.

HAYDN'S DICTIONARY OF DATES, relating to all Ages and Nations. For Universal Reference. Edited by BENJAMIN VINCENT, Assistant Secretary and Keeper of the Library of the Royal Institution of Great Britain; and Revised for the Use of American Readers. 8vo, Cloth, $5 00; Sheep, $6 00.

MACGREGOR'S ROB ROY ON THE JORDAN. The Rob Roy on the Jordan, Nile, Red Sea, and Gennesareth, &c. A Canoe Cruise in Palestine and Egypt, and the Waters of Damascus. By J. MACGREGOR, M.A. With Maps and Illustrations. Crown 8vo, Cloth, $2 50.

WALLACE'S MALAY ARCHIPELAGO. The Malay Archipelago: the Land of the Orang-Utan and the Bird of Paradise. A Narrative of Travel, 1854–1862. With Studies of Man and Nature. By ALFRED RUSSEL WALLACE. With Ten Maps and Fifty-one Elegant Illustrations. Crown 8vo, Cloth, $2 50.

WHYMPER'S ALASKA. Travel and Adventure in the Territory of Alaska, formerly Russian America—now Ceded to the United States—and in various other parts of the North Pacific. By FREDERICK WHYMPER. With Map and Illustrations. Crown 8vo, Cloth, $2 50.

ORTON'S ANDES AND THE AMAZON. The Andes and the Amazon; or, Across the Continent of South America. By JAMES ORTON, M.A., Professor of Natural History in Vassar College, Poughkeepsie, N. Y., and Corresponding Member of the Academy of Natural Sciences, Philadelphia. With a New Map of Equatorial America and numerous Illustrations. Crown 8vo, Cloth, $2 00.

WINCHELL'S SKETCHES OF CREATION. Sketches of Creation: a Popular View of some of the Grand Conclusions of the Sciences in reference to the History of Matter and of Life. Together with a Statement of the Intimations of Science respecting the Primordial Condition and the Ultimate Destiny of the Earth and the Solar System. By ALEXANDER WINCHELL, LL.D., Professor of Geology, Zoology, and Botany in the University of Michigan, and Director of the State Geological Survey. With Illustrations. 12mo, Cloth, $2 00.

WHITE'S MASSACRE OF ST. BARTHOLOMEW. The Massacre of St. Bartholomew: Preceded by a History of the Religious Wars in the Reign of Charles IX. By HENRY WHITE, M.A. With Illustrations. 8vo, Cloth, $1 75.

LOSSING'S FIELD-BOOK OF THE REVOLUTION. Pictorial Field-Book of the Revolution; or, Illustrations, by Pen and Pencil, of the History, Biography, Scenery, Relics, and Traditions of the War for Independence. By BENSON J. LOSSING. 2 vols., 8vo, Cloth, $14 00; Sheep, $15 00; Half Calf, $18 00; Full Turkey Morocco, $22 00.

LOSSING'S FIELD-BOOK OF THE WAR OF 1812. Pictorial Field-Book of the War of 1812; or, Illustrations, by Pen and Pencil, of the History, Biography, Scenery, Relics, and Traditions of the Last War for American Independence. By BENSON J. LOSSING. With several hundred Engravings on Wood, by Lossing and Barritt, chiefly from Original Sketches by the Author. 1088 pages, 8vo, Cloth, $7 00; Sheep, $8 50; Half Calf, $10 00.

ALFORD'S GREEK TESTAMENT. The Greek Testament: with a critically revised Text; a Digest of Various Readings; Marginal References to Verbal and Idiomatic Usage; Prolegomena; and a Critical and Exegetical Commentary. For the Use of Theological Students and Ministers. By HENRY ALFORD, D.D., Dean of Canterbury. Vol. I., containing the Four Gospels. 944 pages, 8vo, Cloth, $6 00; Sheep, $6 50.

ABBOTT'S FREDERICK THE GREAT. The History of Frederick the Second, called Frederick the Great. By JOHN S. C. ABBOTT. Elegantly Illustrated. 8vo, Cloth, $5 00.

ABBOTT'S HISTORY OF THE FRENCH REVOLUTION. The French Revolution of 1789, as viewed in the Light of Republican Institutions. By JOHN S. C. ABBOTT. With 100 Engravings. 8vo, Cloth, $5 00.

ABBOTT'S NAPOLEON BONAPARTE. The History of Napoleon Bonaparte. By JOHN S. C. ABBOTT. With Maps, Woodcuts, and Portraits on Steel. 2 vols., 8vo, Cloth, $10 00.

ABBOTT'S NAPOLEON AT ST. HELENA; or, Interesting Anecdotes and Remarkable Conversations of the Emperor during the Five and a Half Years of his Captivity. Collected from the Memorials of Las Casas, O'Meara, Montholon, Antommarchi, and others. By JOHN S. C. ABBOTT. With Illustrations. 8vo, Cloth, $5 00.

ADDISON'S COMPLETE WORKS. The Works of Joseph Addison, embracing the whole of the "Spectator." Complete in 3 vols., 8vo, Cloth, $6 00.

ALCOCK'S JAPAN. The Capital of the Tycoon: a Narrative of a Three Years' Residence in Japan. By Sir RUTHERFORD ALCOCK, K.C.B., Her Majesty's Envoy Extraordinary and Minister Plenipotentiary in Japan. With Maps and Engravings. 2 vols., 12mo, Cloth, $3 50.

ALISON'S HISTORY OF EUROPE. FIRST SERIES: From the Commencement of the French Revolution, in 1789, to the Restoration of the Bourbons, in 1815. [In addition to the Notes on Chapter LXXVI., which correct the errors of the original work concerning the United States, a copious Analytical Index has been appended to this American edition.] SECOND SERIES: From the Fall of Napoleon, in 1815, to the Accession of Louis Napoleon, in 1852. 8 vols., 8vo, Cloth, $16 00.

BALDWIN'S PRE-HISTORIC NATIONS. Pre-Historic Nations; or, Inquiries concerning some of the Great Peoples and Civilizations of Antiquity, and their Probable Relation to a still Older Civilization of the Ethiopians or Cushites of Arabia. By JOHN D. BALDWIN, Member of the American Oriental Society. 12mo, Cloth, $1 75.

BARTH'S NORTH AND CENTRAL AFRICA. Travels and Discoveries in North and Central Africa: being a Journal of an Expedition undertaken under the Auspices of H. B. M.'s Government, in the Years 1849-1855. By HENRY BARTH, Ph.D., D.C.L. Illustrated. 3 vols., 8vo, Cloth, $12 00.

HENRY WARD BEECHER'S SERMONS. Sermons by HENRY WARD BEECHER, Plymouth Church, Brooklyn. Selected from Published and Unpublished Discourses, and Revised by their Author. With Steel Portrait. Complete in 2 vols., 8vo, Cloth, $5 00.

LYMAN BEECHER'S AUTOBIOGRAPHY, &c. Autobiography, Correspondence, &c., of Lyman Beecher, D.D. Edited by his Son, CHARLES BEECHER. With Three Steel Portraits, and Engravings on Wood. In 2 vols., 12mo, Cloth, $5 00.

BOSWELL'S JOHNSON. The Life of Samuel Johnson, LL.D. Including a Journey to the Hebrides. By JAMES BOSWELL, Esq. A New Edition, with numerous Additions and Notes. By JOHN WILSON CROKER, LL.D., F.R.S. Portrait of Boswell. 2 vols., 8vo, Cloth, $4 00.

DRAPER'S CIVIL WAR. History of the American Civil War. By JOHN W. DRAPER, M.D., LL.D., Professor of Chemistry and Physiology in the University of New York. In Three Vols. 8vo, Cloth, $3 50 per vol.

DRAPER'S INTELLECTUAL DEVELOPMENT OF EUROPE. A History of the Intellectual Development of Europe. By JOHN W. DRAPER, M.D., LL.D., Professor of Chemistry and Physiology in the University of New York. 8vo, Cloth, $5 00.

DRAPER'S AMERICAN CIVIL POLICY. Thoughts on the Future Civil Policy of America. By JOHN W. DRAPER, M.D., LL.D., Professor of Chemistry and Physiology in the University of New York. Crown 8vo, Cloth, $2 50.

DU CHAILLU'S AFRICA. Explorations and Adventures in Equatorial Africa: with Accounts of the Manners and Customs of the People, and of the Chase of the Gorilla, the Crocodile, Leopard, Elephant, Hippopotamus, and other Animals. By PAUL B. DU CHAILLU. Numerous Illustrations. 8vo, Cloth, $5 00.

BELLOWS'S OLD WORLD. The Old World in its New Face: Impressions of Europe in 1867–1868. By HENRY W. BELLOWS. 2 vols., 12mo, Cloth, $3 50.

BRODHEAD'S HISTORY OF NEW YORK. History of the State of New York. By JOHN ROMEYN BRODHEAD. 1609–1691. 2 vols. 8vo, Cloth, $3 00 per vol.

BROUGHAM'S AUTOBIOGRAPHY. Life and Times of HENRY, LORD BROUGHAM. Written by Himself. In Three Volumes. 12mo, Cloth, $2 00 per vol.

BULWER'S PROSE WORKS. Miscellaneous Prose Works of Edward Bulwer, Lord Lytton. 2 vols., 12mo, Cloth, $3 50.

BULWER'S HORACE. The Odes and Epodes of Horace. A Metrical Translation into English. With Introduction and Commentaries. By LORD LYTTON. With Latin Text from the Editions of Orelli, Macleane, and Yonge. 12mo, Cloth, $1 75.

BULWER'S KING ARTHUR. A Poem. By EARL LYTTON. New Edition. 12mo, Cloth, $1 75.

BURNS'S LIFE AND WORKS. The Life and Works of Robert Burns. Edited by ROBERT CHAMBERS. 4 vols., 12mo, Cloth, $6 00.

REINDEER, DOGS, AND SNOW-SHOES. A Journal of Siberian Travel and Explorations made in the Years 1865–'67. By RICHARD J. BUSH, late of the Russo-American Telegraph Expedition. Illustrated. Crown 8vo, Cloth, $3 00.

CARLYLE'S FREDERICK THE GREAT. History of Friedrich II., called Frederick the Great. By THOMAS CARLYLE. Portraits, Maps, Plans, &c. 6 vols., 12mo, Cloth, $12 00.

CARLYLE'S FRENCH REVOLUTION. History of the French Revolution. Newly Revised by the Author, with Index, &c. 2 vols., 12mo, Cloth, $3 50.

CARLYLE'S OLIVER CROMWELL. Letters and Speeches of Oliver Cromwell. With Elucidations and Connecting Narrative. 2 vols., 12mo, Cloth, $3 50.

CHALMERS'S POSTHUMOUS WORKS. The Posthumous Works of Dr. Chalmers. Edited by his Son-in-Law, Rev. WILLIAM HANNA, LL.D. Complete in 9 vols., 12mo, Cloth, $13 50.

COLERIDGE'S COMPLETE WORKS. The Complete Works of Samuel Taylor Coleridge. With an Introductory Essay upon his Philosophical and Theological Opinions. Edited by Professor SHEDD. Complete in Seven Vols. With a fine Portrait. Small 8vo, Cloth, $10 50.

DOOLITTLE'S CHINA. Social Life of the Chinese: with some Account of their Religious, Governmental, Educational, and Business Customs and Opinions. With special but not exclusive Reference to Fuhchau. By Rev. JUSTUS DOOLITTLE, Fourteen Years Member of the Fuhchau Mission of the American Board. Illustrated with more than 150 characteristic Engravings on Wood. 2 vols., 12mo, Cloth, $5 00.

GIBBON'S ROME. History of the Decline and Fall of the Roman Empire. By EDWARD GIBBON. With Notes by Rev. H. H. MILMAN and M. GUIZOT. A new cheap Edition. To which is added a complete Index of the whole Work, and a Portrait of the Author. 6 vols., 12mo, Cloth, $9 00.

HAZEN'S SCHOOL AND ARMY IN GERMANY AND FRANCE. The School and the Army in Germany and France, with a Diary of Siege Life at Versailles. By Brevet Major-General W. B. HAZEN, U.S.A., Colonel Sixth Infantry. Crown 8vo, Cloth, $2 50.

www.ingramcontent.com/pod-product-compliance
Lightning Source LLC
LaVergne TN
LVHW010203110826
845151LV00002B/589

* 9 7 8 1 4 2 5 5 3 5 7 9 7 *